THE MIGHTY THOR

WRITER
MATT FRACTION

PENCILER
OLIVIER COIPEL
WITH KHOI PHAM (ISSUE #5)

INKER
MARK MORALES
WITH DEXTER VINES (ISSUES #5-6) & CAM SMITH (ISSUE #6)

COLORIST
LAURA MARTIN
WITH JUSTIN PONSOR & PETER STEIGERWALD (ISSUE #1)

LETTERER
VC'S JOE SABINO

COVER ART
OLIVIER COIPEL, MARK MORALES
& LAURA MARTIN

ASSISTANT EDITORS
CHARLIE BECKERMAN & JOHN DENNING

EDITORS
RALPH MACCHIO & LAUREN SANKOVITCH

COLLECTION EDITOR: JENNIFER GRÜNWALD · EDITORIAL ASSISTANTS: JAMES EMMETT & JOE HOCHSTEIN
ASSISTANT EDITORS: ALEX STARBUCK & NELSON RIBEIRO · EDITOR, SPECIAL PROJECTS: MARK D. BEAZLEY
SENIOR EDITOR, SPECIAL PROJECTS: JEFF YOUNGQUIST · SENIOR VICE PRESIDENT OF SALES: DAVID GABRIEL
SVP OF BRAND PLANNING & COMMUNICATIONS: MICHAEL PASCIULLO

EDITOR IN CHIEF: AXEL ALONSO · CHIEF CREATIVE OFFICER: JOE QUESADA
PUBLISHER: DAN BUCKLEY · EXECUTIVE PRODUCER: ALAN FINE

THE MIGHTY THOR BY MATT FRACTION VOL. 1. Contains material originally published in magazine form as THE MIGHTY THOR #1-6. First printing 2011. Hardcover ISBN# 978-0-7851-5691-8. Softcover ISBN# 978-0-7851-5624-6. Published by MARVEL WORLDWIDE, INC., a subsidiary of MARVEL ENTERTAINMENT, LLC. OFFICE OF PUBLICATION: 135 West 50th Street, New York, NY 10020. Copyright © 2011 and 2012 Marvel Characters, Inc. All rights reserved. Hardcover: $24.99 per copy in the U.S. and $27.99 in Canada (GST #R127032852). Softcover: $19.99 per copy in the U.S. and $21.99 in Canada (GST #R127032852). Canadian Agreement #40668537. All characters featured in this issue and the distinctive names and likenesses thereof, and all related indicia are trademarks of Marvel Characters, Inc. No similarity between any of the names, characters, persons, and/or institutions in this magazine with those of any living or dead person or institution is intended, and any such similarity which may exist is purely coincidental. **Printed in the U.S.A.** ALAN FINE, EVP - Office of the President, Marvel Worldwide, Inc. and EVP & CMO Marvel Characters B.V.; DAN BUCKLEY, Publisher & President - Print, Animation & Digital Divisions; JOE QUESADA, Chief Creative Officer; JIM SOKOLOWSKI, Chief Operating Officer; DAVID BOGART, SVP of Business Affairs & Talent Management; TOM BREVOORT, SVP of Publishing; C.B. CEBULSKI, SVP of Creator & Content Development; DAVID GABRIEL, SVP of Publishing Sales & Circulation; MICHAEL PASCIULLO, SVP of Brand Planning & Communications; JIM O'KEEFE, VP of Operations & Logistics; DAN CARR, Executive Director of Publishing Technology; SUSAN CRESPI, Editorial Operations Manager; ALEX MORALES, Publishing Operations Manager; STAN LEE, Chairman Emeritus. For information regarding advertising in Marvel Comics or on Marvel.com, please contact John Dokes, SVP Integrated Sales and Marketing, at jdokes@marvel.com. For Marvel subscription inquiries, please call 800-217-9158. **Manufactured between 10/10/2011 and 11/7/2011 (hardcover), and 10/10/2011 and 5/7/2012 (softcover), by R.R. DONNELLEY, INC., SALEM, VA, USA.**

10 9 8 7 6 5 4 3 2 1

ASGARD CAME TO EARTH. ASGARD FELL.

FROM ITS RUINS, THE ASGARDIANS RISE.

ODIN, AWAKENED FROM UNEASY SLEEP,
STANDS ABOVE ALL, THE FIRST KING OF
ASGARD. THE ALL-FATHER.

LOKI, WHOSE BETRAYAL CAST THE SHINING
CITY INTO DESTRUCTION AND DEVASTATION,
HAS BEEN RESURRECTED AS THE YOUNG GOD
HE ONCE WAS. ALL THE SAME, THERE ARE
SOME WHO WILL NEVER FORGIVE HIM.

THOR AND SIF STAND AT THE READY FOR
WHATEVER MAY COME NEXT.

DURING BATTLE WITH TREMENDOUS FOES
FROM BEYOND THE WORLD TREE, THE
MIGHTY THOR DREW THE POWERFUL
ODINSWORD FROM ITS ETERNAL SCABBARD
AND SPLIT YGGDRASIL IN TWAIN--THE
BRIDGE OF WORLDS WAS THUS RENDERED
PERMANENT AND FIXED, A SPEWING GEYSER
OF STRANGE LIGHT SHOOTING UPWARDS
FOREVER FROM THE AMERICAN--AND
ASGARDIAN--HEARTLAND...

SOME SEE IT AS A SHINING BEACON.

SOME SEE IT AS A WARNING.

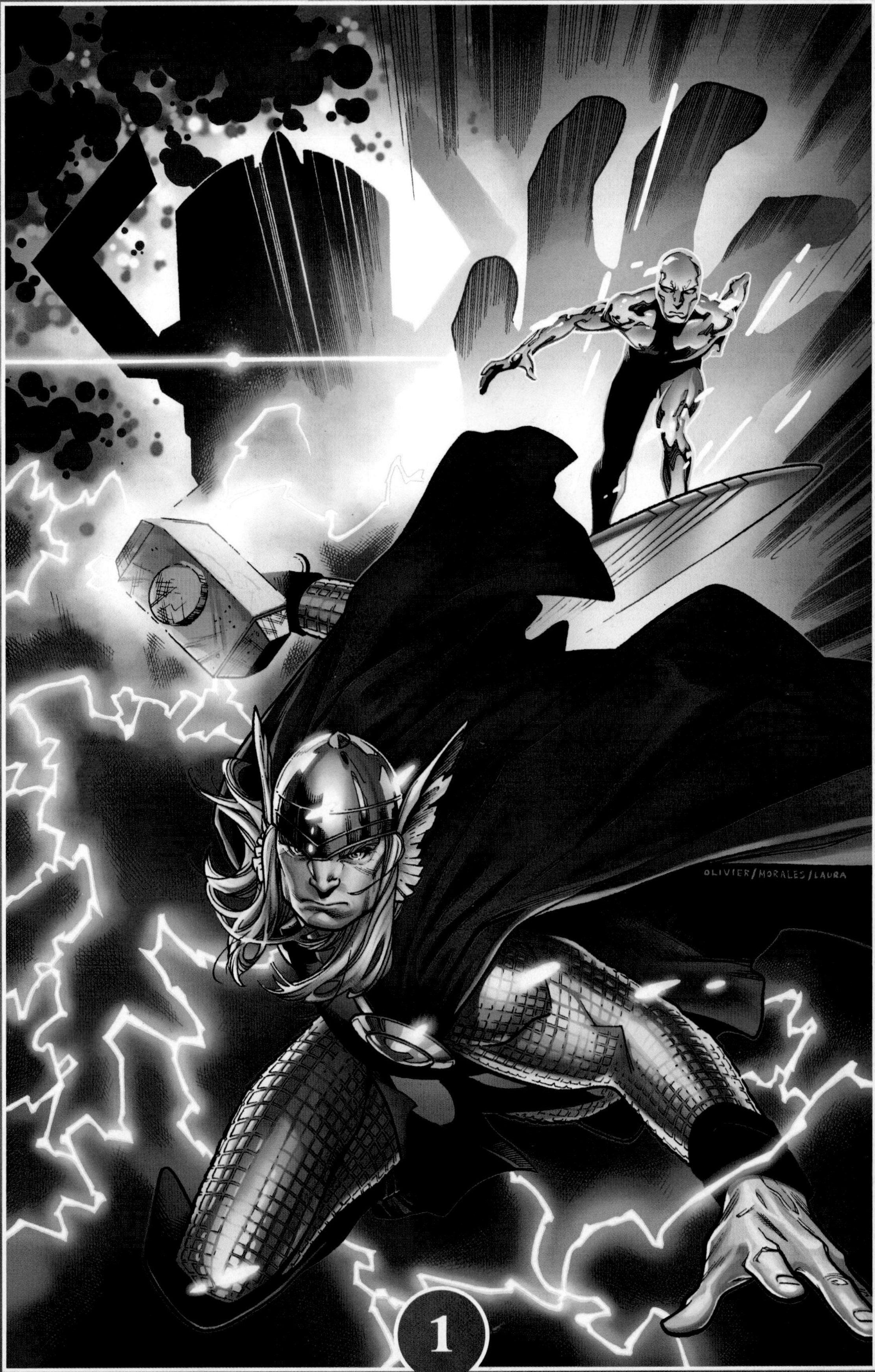
OLIVIER/MORALES/LAURA

1

THE GALACTUS SEED 1: THE SILENCE

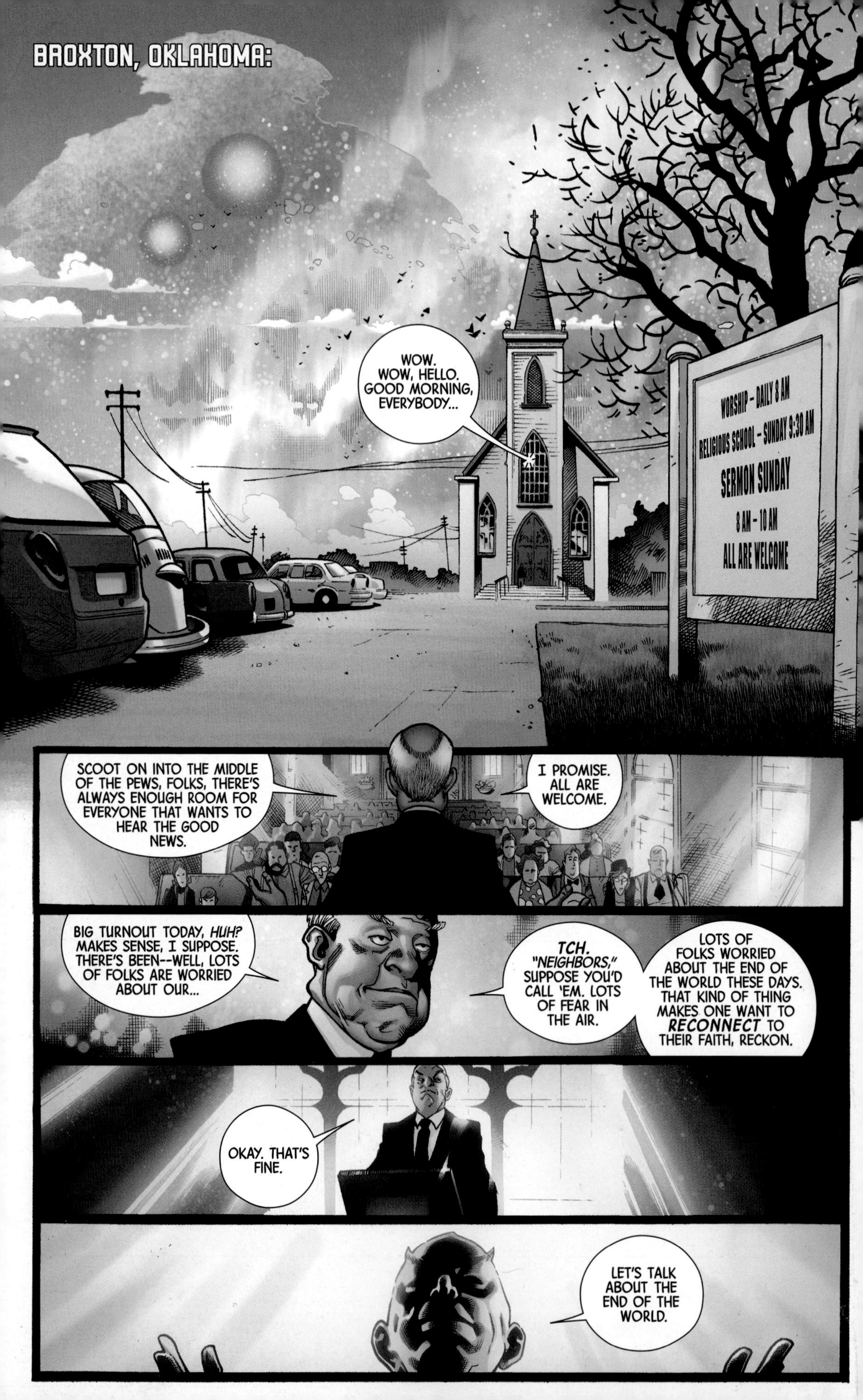
BROXTON, OKLAHOMA:
WOW. WOW, HELLO. GOOD MORNING, EVERYBODY...
WORSHIP - DAILY 8 AM
RELIGIOUS SCHOOL - SUNDAY 9:30 AM
SERMON SUNDAY
8 AM - 10 AM
ALL ARE WELCOME
SCOOT ON INTO THE MIDDLE OF THE PEWS, FOLKS, THERE'S ALWAYS ENOUGH ROOM FOR EVERYONE THAT WANTS TO HEAR THE GOOD NEWS.
I PROMISE. ALL ARE WELCOME.
BIG TURNOUT TODAY, *HUH?* MAKES SENSE, I SUPPOSE. THERE'S BEEN--WELL, LOTS OF FOLKS ARE WORRIED ABOUT OUR...
TCH. *"NEIGHBORS,"* SUPPOSE YOU'D CALL 'EM. LOTS OF FEAR IN THE AIR.
LOTS OF FOLKS WORRIED ABOUT THE END OF THE WORLD THESE DAYS. THAT KIND OF THING MAKES ONE WANT TO *RECONNECT* TO THEIR FAITH, RECKON.
OKAY. THAT'S FINE.
LET'S TALK ABOUT THE END OF THE WORLD.

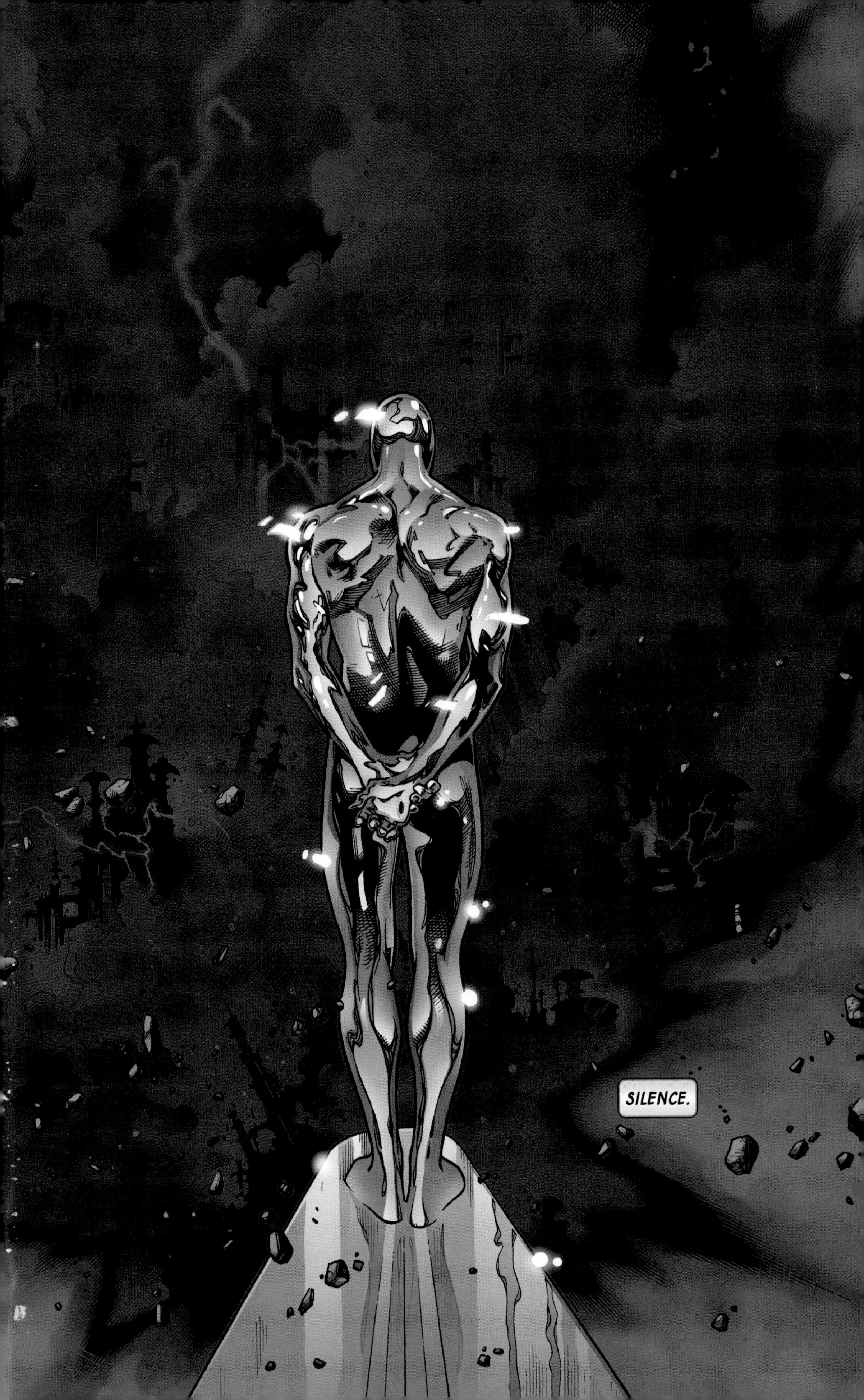
SILENCE.

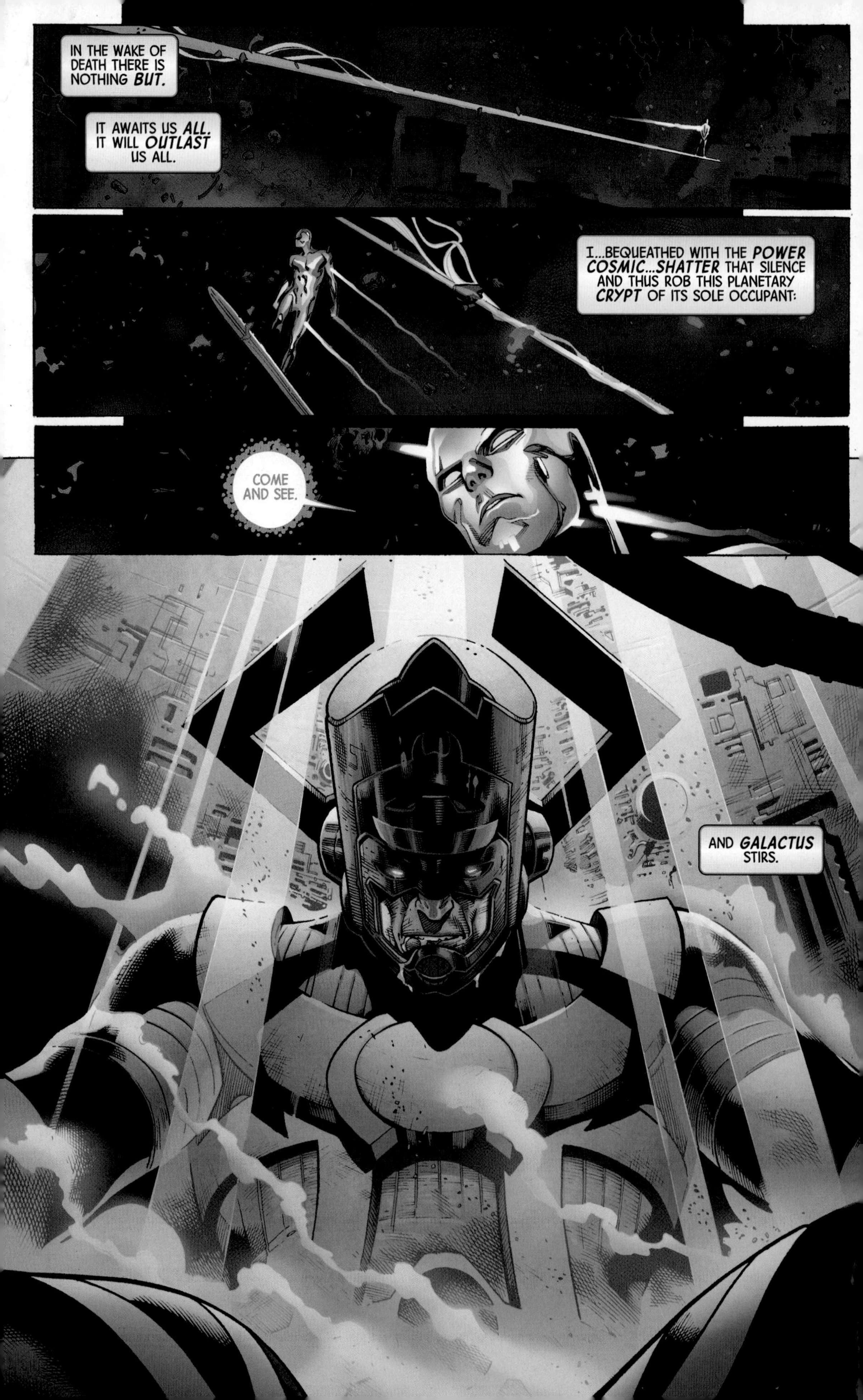
IN THE WAKE OF DEATH THERE IS NOTHING BUT.
IT AWAITS US ALL. IT WILL OUTLAST US ALL.
I...BEQUEATHED WITH THE POWER COSMIC...SHATTER THAT SILENCE AND THUS ROB THIS PLANETARY CRYPT OF ITS SOLE OCCUPANT:
COME AND SEE.
AND GALACTUS STIRS.

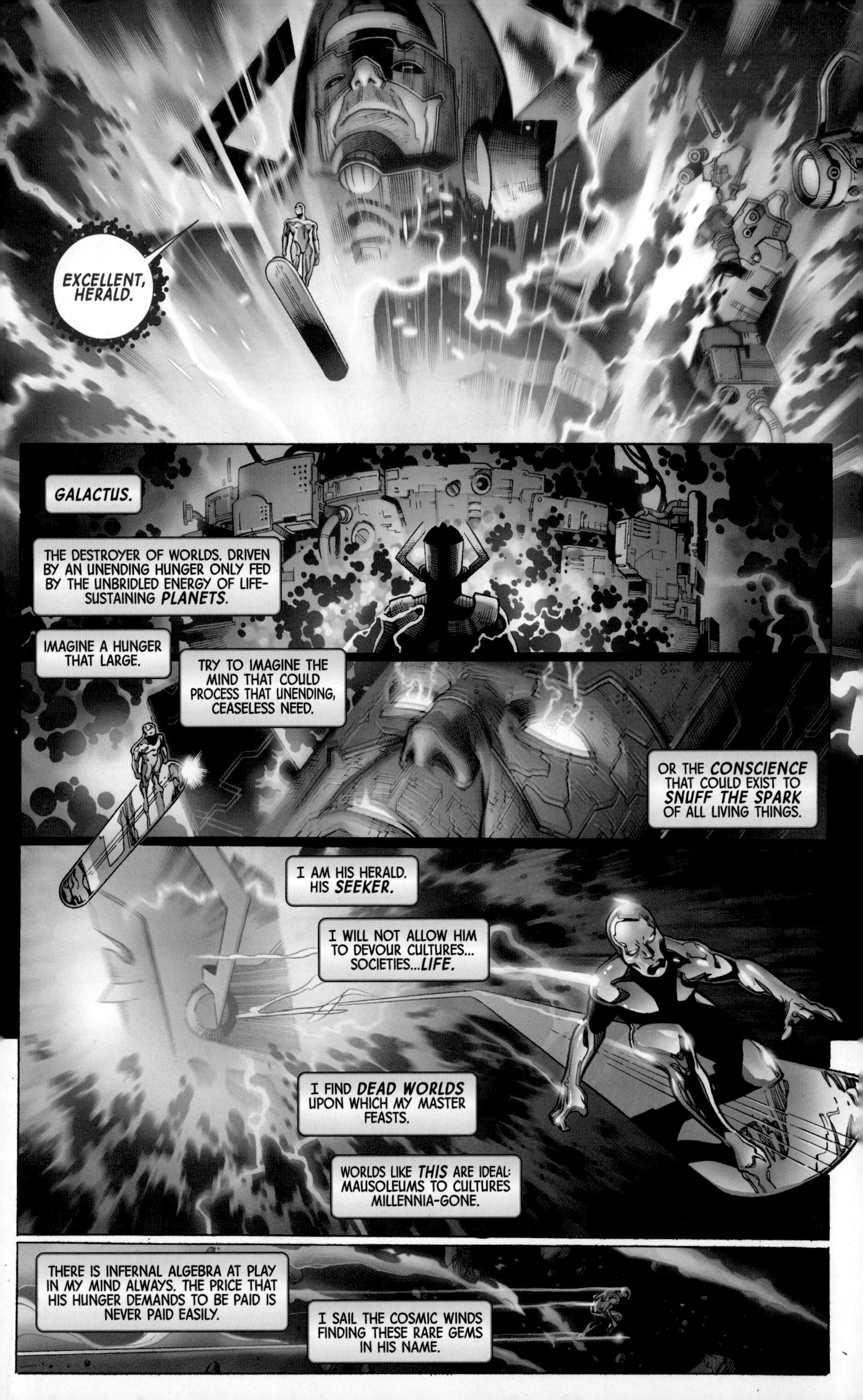
EXCELLENT, HERALD.
GALACTUS.
THE DESTROYER OF WORLDS. DRIVEN BY AN UNENDING HUNGER ONLY FED BY THE UNBRIDLED ENERGY OF LIFE-SUSTAINING PLANETS.
IMAGINE A HUNGER THAT LARGE.
TRY TO IMAGINE THE MIND THAT COULD PROCESS THAT UNENDING, CEASELESS NEED.
OR THE CONSCIENCE THAT COULD EXIST TO SNUFF THE SPARK OF ALL LIVING THINGS.
I AM HIS HERALD. HIS SEEKER.
I WILL NOT ALLOW HIM TO DEVOUR CULTURES... SOCIETIES...LIFE.
I FIND DEAD WORLDS UPON WHICH MY MASTER FEASTS.
WORLDS LIKE THIS ARE IDEAL: MAUSOLEUMS TO CULTURES MILLENNIA-GONE.
THERE IS INFERNAL ALGEBRA AT PLAY IN MY MIND ALWAYS. THE PRICE THAT HIS HUNGER DEMANDS TO BE PAID IS NEVER PAID EASILY.
I SAIL THE COSMIC WINDS FINDING THESE RARE GEMS IN HIS NAME.

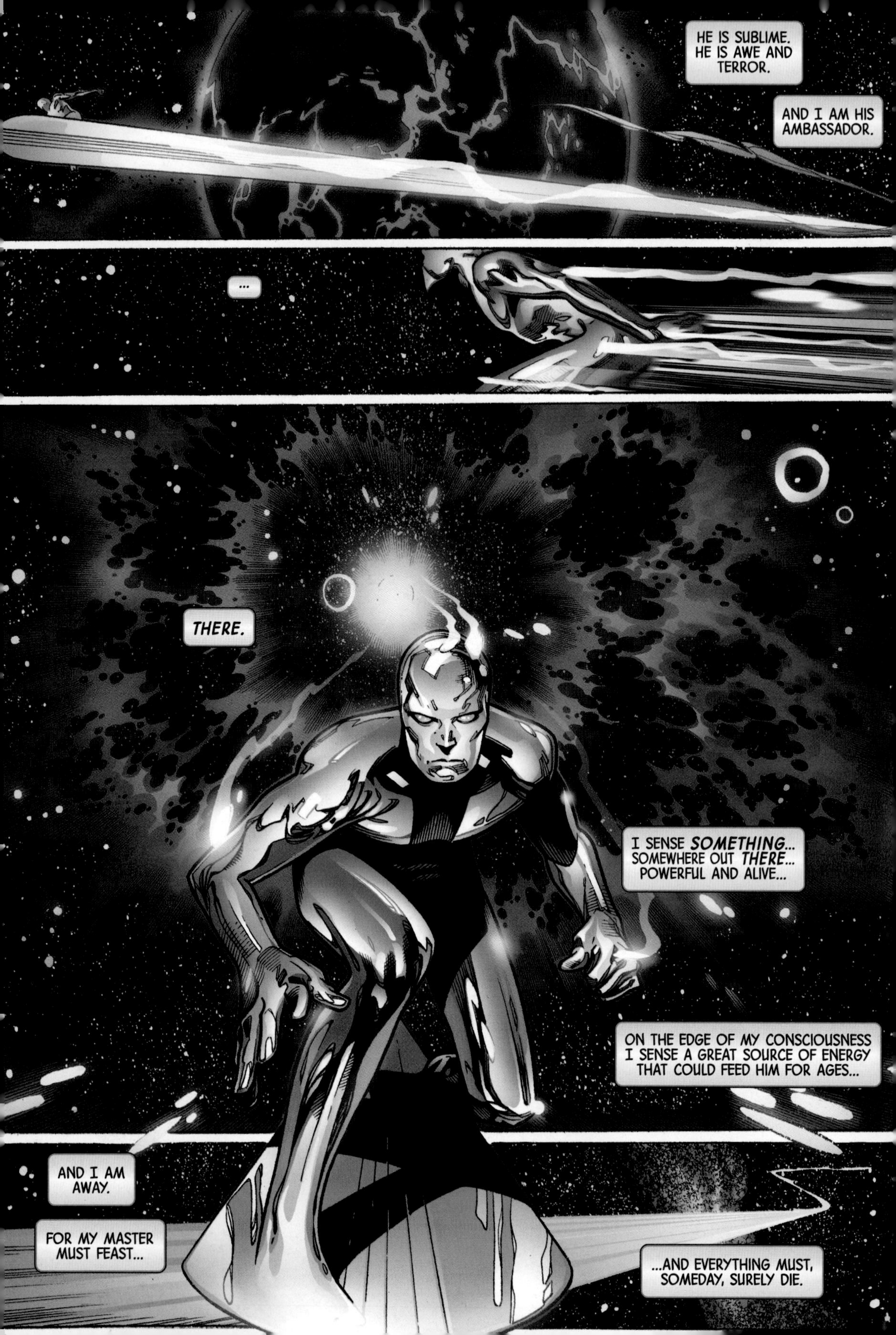
HE IS SUBLIME. HE IS AWE AND TERROR.
AND I AM HIS AMBASSADOR.
...
THERE.
I SENSE SOMETHING... SOMEWHERE OUT THERE... POWERFUL AND ALIVE...
ON THE EDGE OF MY CONSCIOUSNESS I SENSE A GREAT SOURCE OF ENERGY THAT COULD FEED HIM FOR AGES...
AND I AM AWAY.
FOR MY MASTER MUST FEAST...
...AND EVERYTHING MUST, SOMEDAY, SURELY DIE.

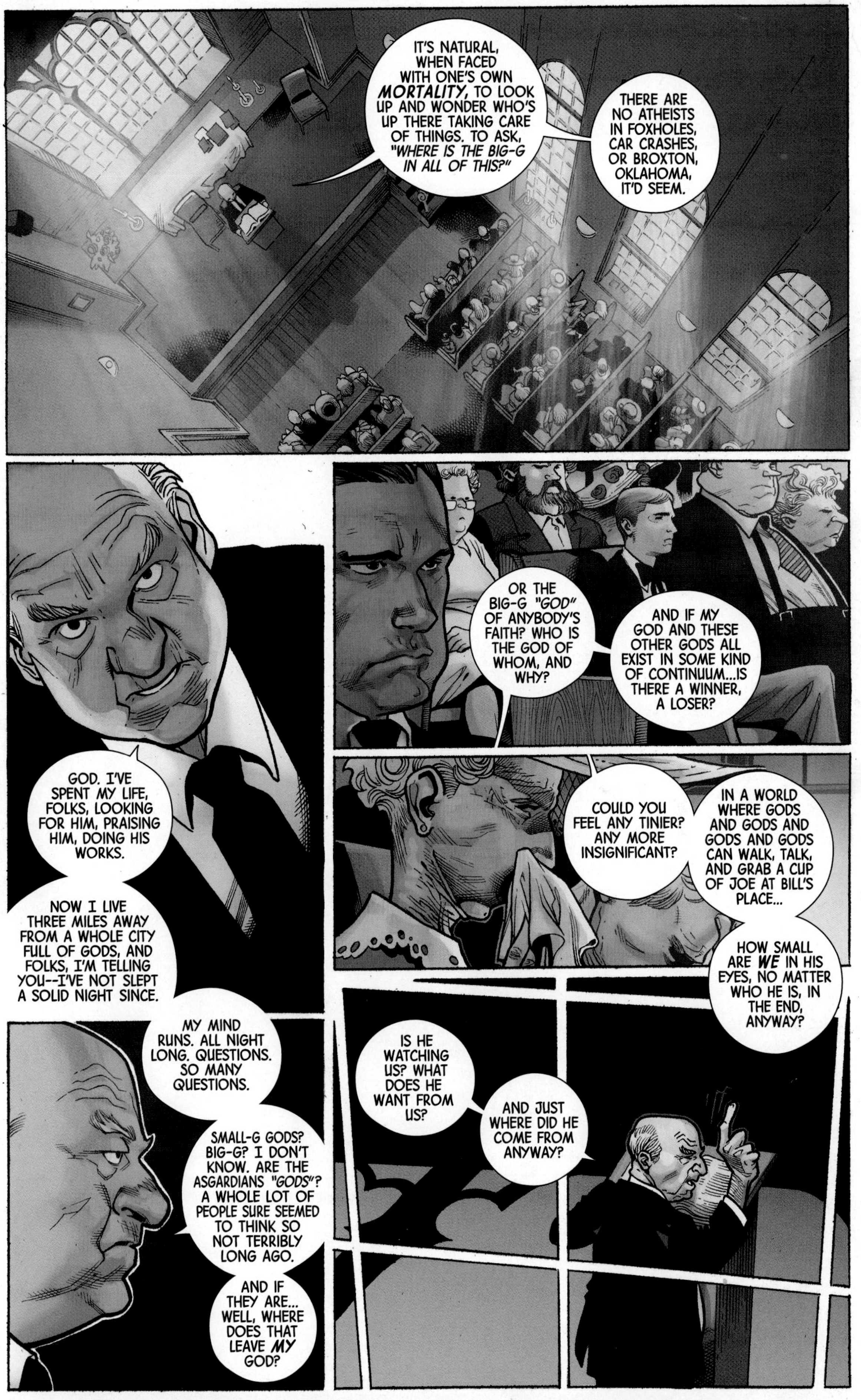
IT'S NATURAL, WHEN FACED WITH ONE'S OWN MORTALITY, TO LOOK UP AND WONDER WHO'S UP THERE TAKING CARE OF THINGS. TO ASK, "WHERE IS THE BIG-G IN ALL OF THIS?"
THERE ARE NO ATHEISTS IN FOXHOLES, CAR CRASHES, OR BROXTON, OKLAHOMA, IT'D SEEM.
GOD. I'VE SPENT MY LIFE, FOLKS, LOOKING FOR HIM, PRAISING HIM, DOING HIS WORKS.
NOW I LIVE THREE MILES AWAY FROM A WHOLE CITY FULL OF GODS, AND FOLKS, I'M TELLING YOU--I'VE NOT SLEPT A SOLID NIGHT SINCE.
OR THE BIG-G "GOD" OF ANYBODY'S FAITH? WHO IS THE GOD OF WHOM, AND WHY?
AND IF MY GOD AND THESE OTHER GODS ALL EXIST IN SOME KIND OF CONTINUUM...IS THERE A WINNER, A LOSER?
COULD YOU FEEL ANY TINIER? ANY MORE INSIGNIFICANT?
IN A WORLD WHERE GODS AND GODS AND GODS AND GODS CAN WALK, TALK, AND GRAB A CUP OF JOE AT BILL'S PLACE...
HOW SMALL ARE WE IN HIS EYES, NO MATTER WHO HE IS, IN THE END, ANYWAY?
MY MIND RUNS. ALL NIGHT LONG. QUESTIONS. SO MANY QUESTIONS.
SMALL-G GODS? BIG-G? I DON'T KNOW. ARE THE ASGARDIANS "GODS"? A WHOLE LOT OF PEOPLE SURE SEEMED TO THINK SO NOT TERRIBLY LONG AGO.
AND IF THEY ARE... WELL, WHERE DOES THAT LEAVE MY GOD?
IS HE WATCHING US? WHAT DOES HE WANT FROM US?
AND JUST WHERE DID HE COME FROM ANYWAY?

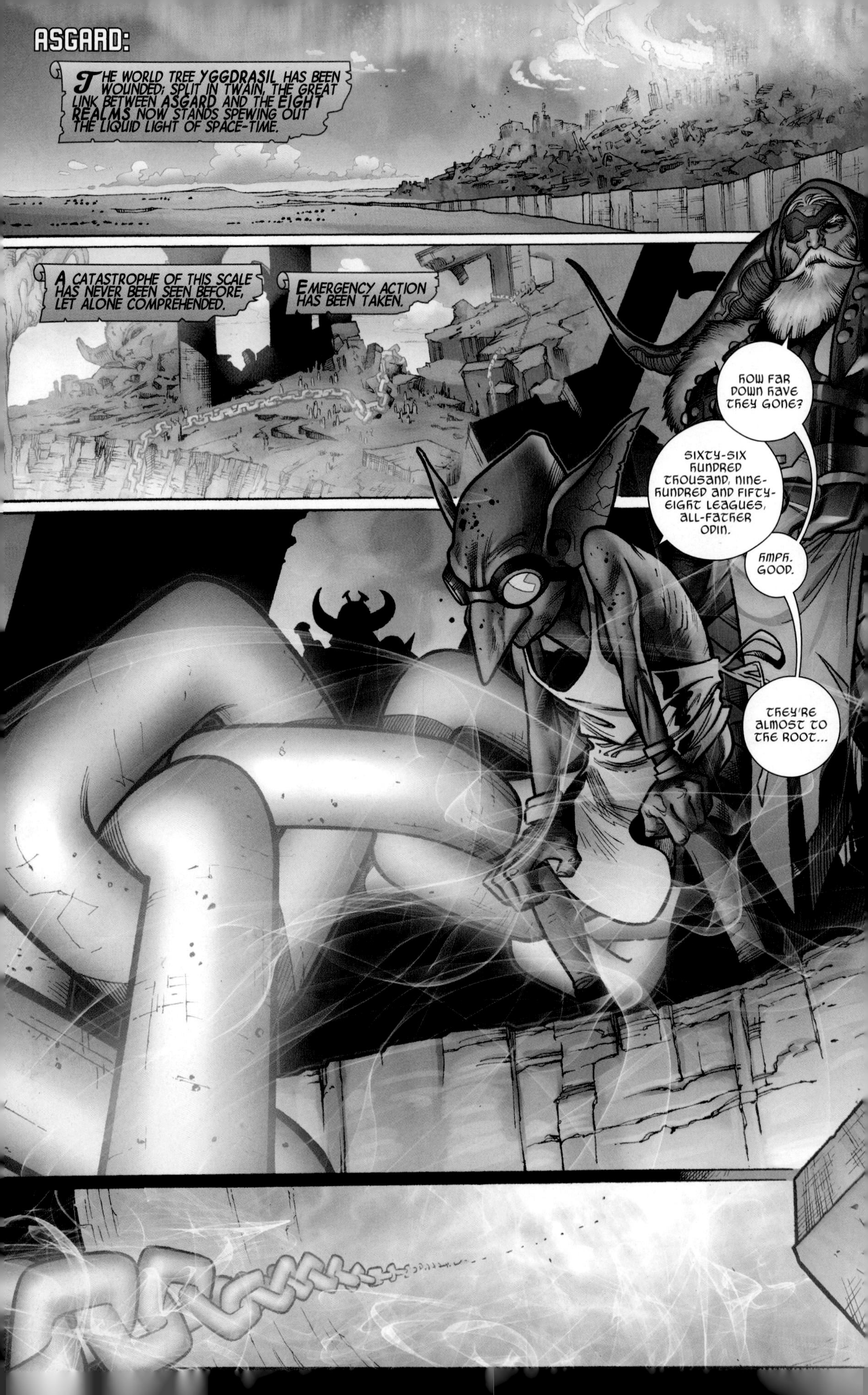
ASGARD:
THE WORLD TREE YGGDRASIL HAS BEEN WOUNDED; SPLIT IN TWAIN, THE GREAT LINK BETWEEN ASGARD AND THE EIGHT REALMS NOW STANDS SPEWING OUT THE LIQUID LIGHT OF SPACE-TIME.
A CATASTROPHE OF THIS SCALE HAS NEVER BEEN SEEN BEFORE, LET ALONE COMPREHENDED.
EMERGENCY ACTION HAS BEEN TAKEN.
HOW FAR DOWN HAVE THEY GONE?
SIXTY-SIX HUNDRED THOUSAND, NINE-HUNDRED AND FIFTY-EIGHT LEAGUES, ALL-FATHER ODIN.
HMPH. GOOD.
THEY'RE ALMOST TO THE ROOT...

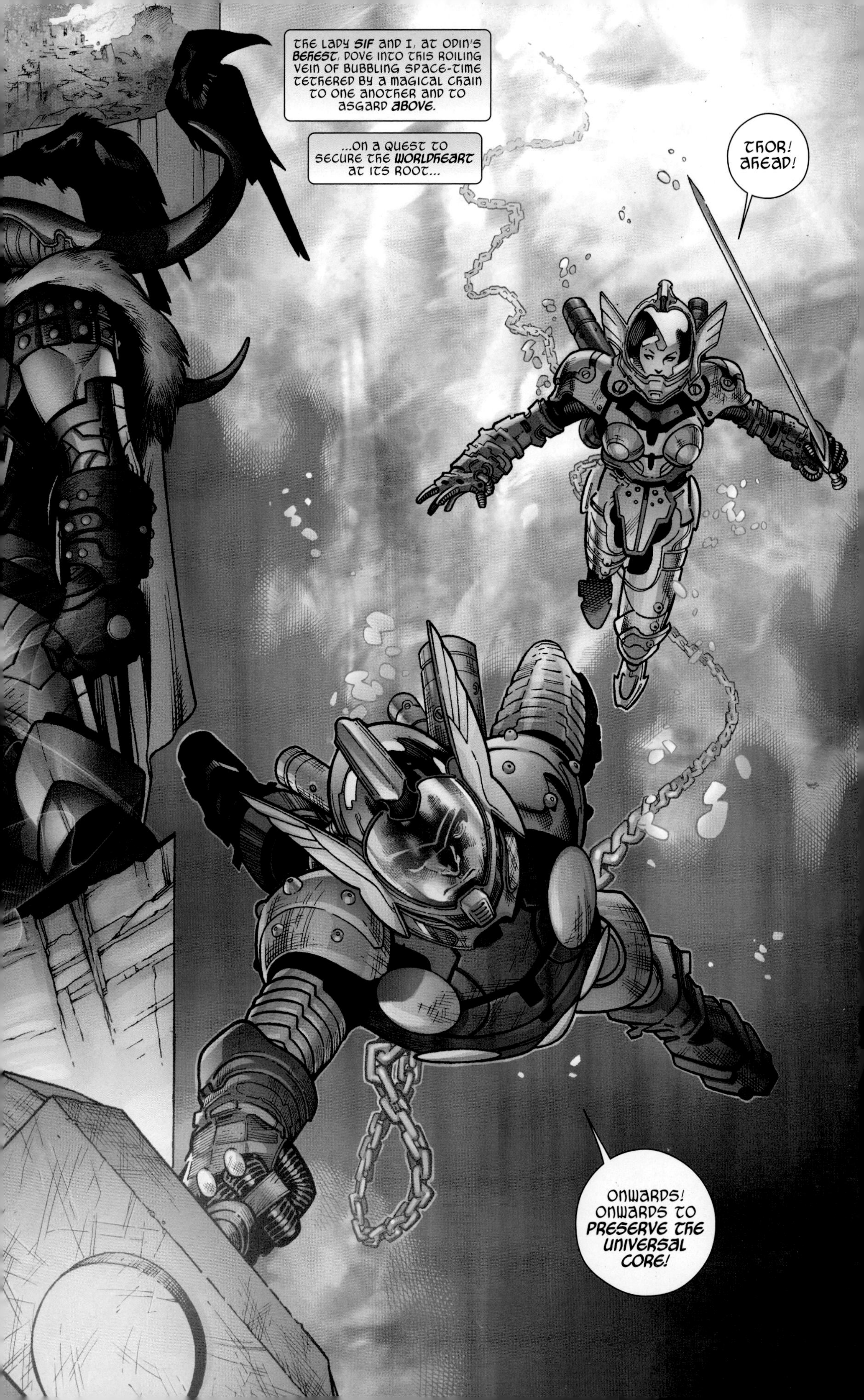
THE LADY SIF AND I, AT ODIN'S BEHEST, DOVE INTO THIS ROILING VEIN OF BUBBLING SPACE-TIME TETHERED BY A MAGICAL CHAIN TO ONE ANOTHER AND TO ASGARD ABOVE.
...ON A QUEST TO SECURE THE WORLDHEART AT ITS ROOT...
THOR! AHEAD!
ONWARDS! ONWARDS TO PRESERVE THE UNIVERSAL CORE!

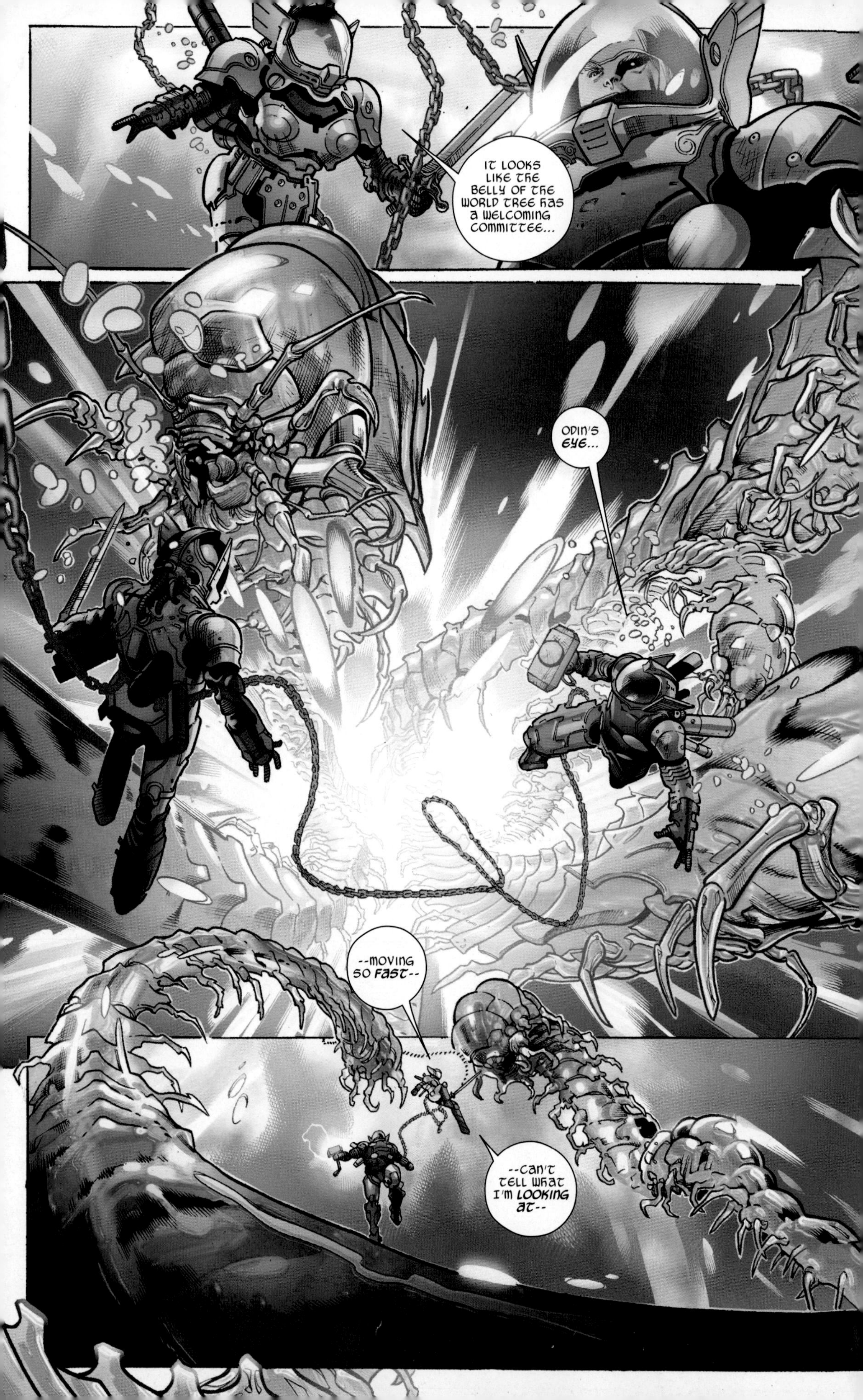
IT LOOKS LIKE THE BELLY OF THE WORLD TREE HAS A WELCOMING COMMITTEE...
ODIN'S EYE...
--MOVING SO FAST--
--CAN'T TELL WHAT I'M LOOKING AT--

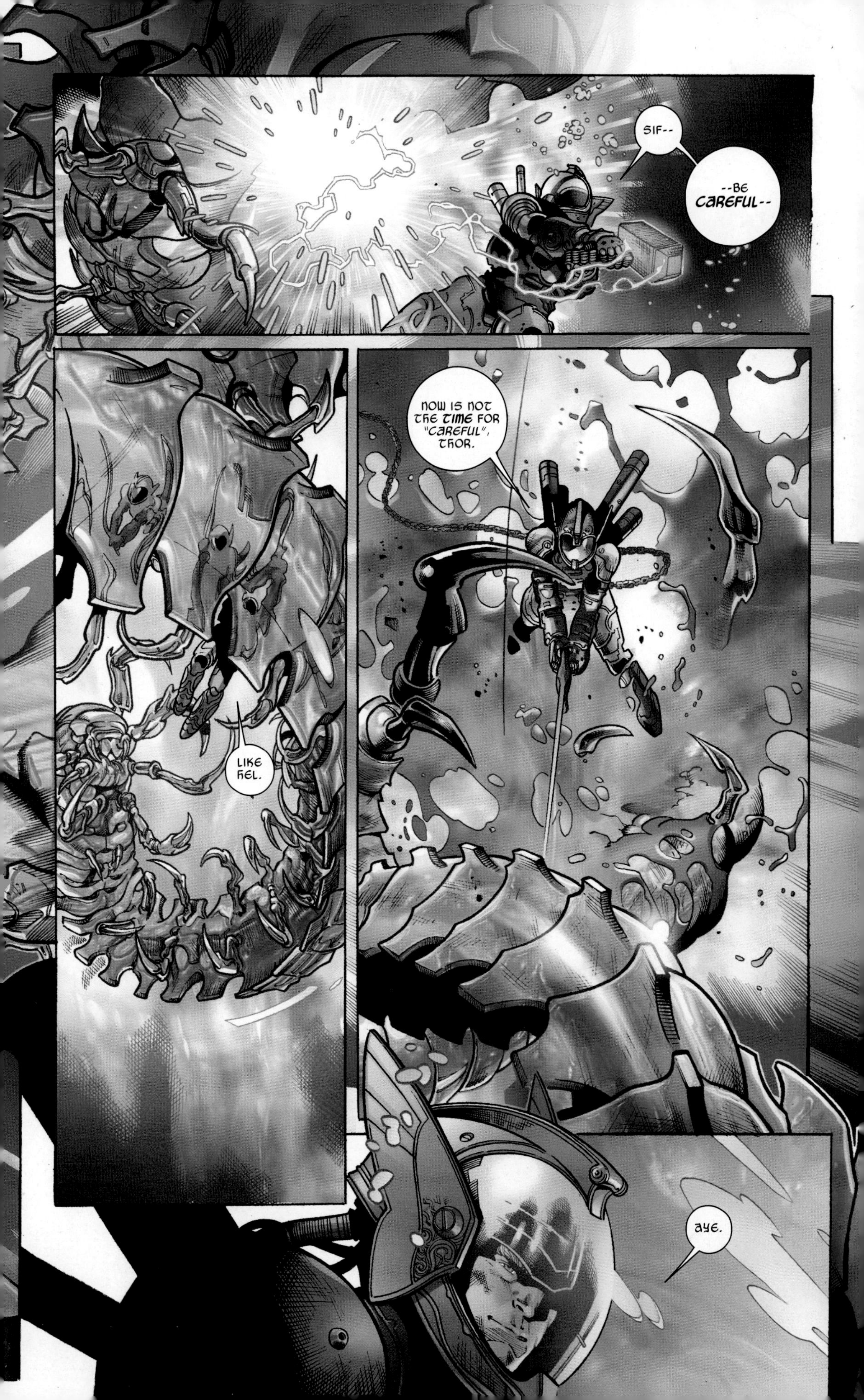
SIF--
--BE CAREFUL--
NOW IS NOT THE TIME FOR "CAREFUL", THOR.
LIKE HEL.
AYE.

FOR ASGARD!

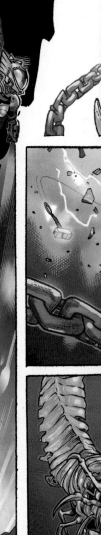

THE WORLD TREE SPANS SPACE AND TIME, GROWING IN DIRECTIONS OF WHICH WE CAN SCARCELY CONCEIVE.

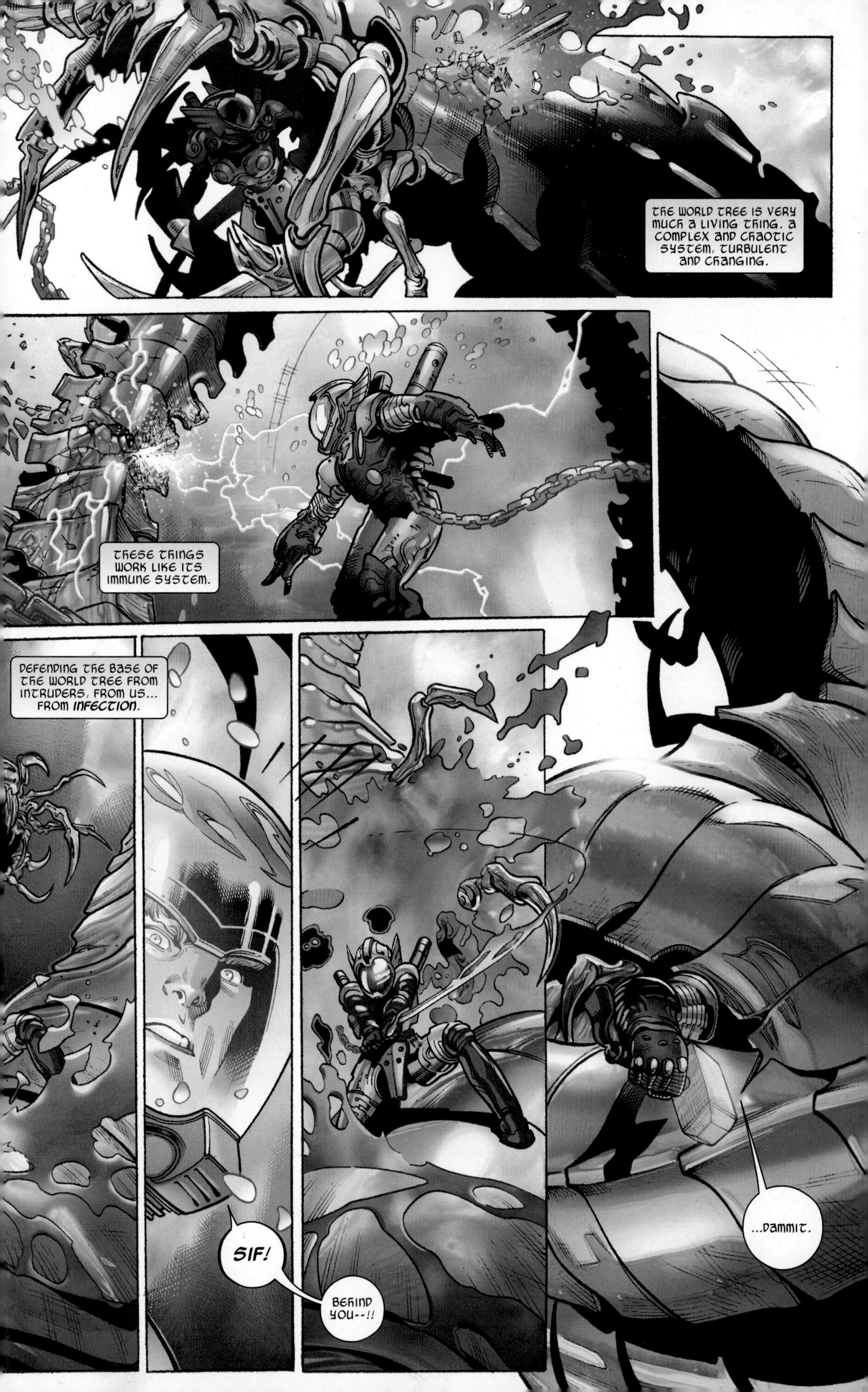
THE WORLD TREE IS VERY MUCH A LIVING THING. A COMPLEX AND CHAOTIC SYSTEM, TURBULENT AND CHANGING.
THESE THINGS WORK LIKE ITS IMMUNE SYSTEM.
DEFENDING THE BASE OF THE WORLD TREE FROM INTRUDERS, FROM US... FROM *INFECTION*.
SIF!
BEHIND YOU--!!
...DAMMIT.

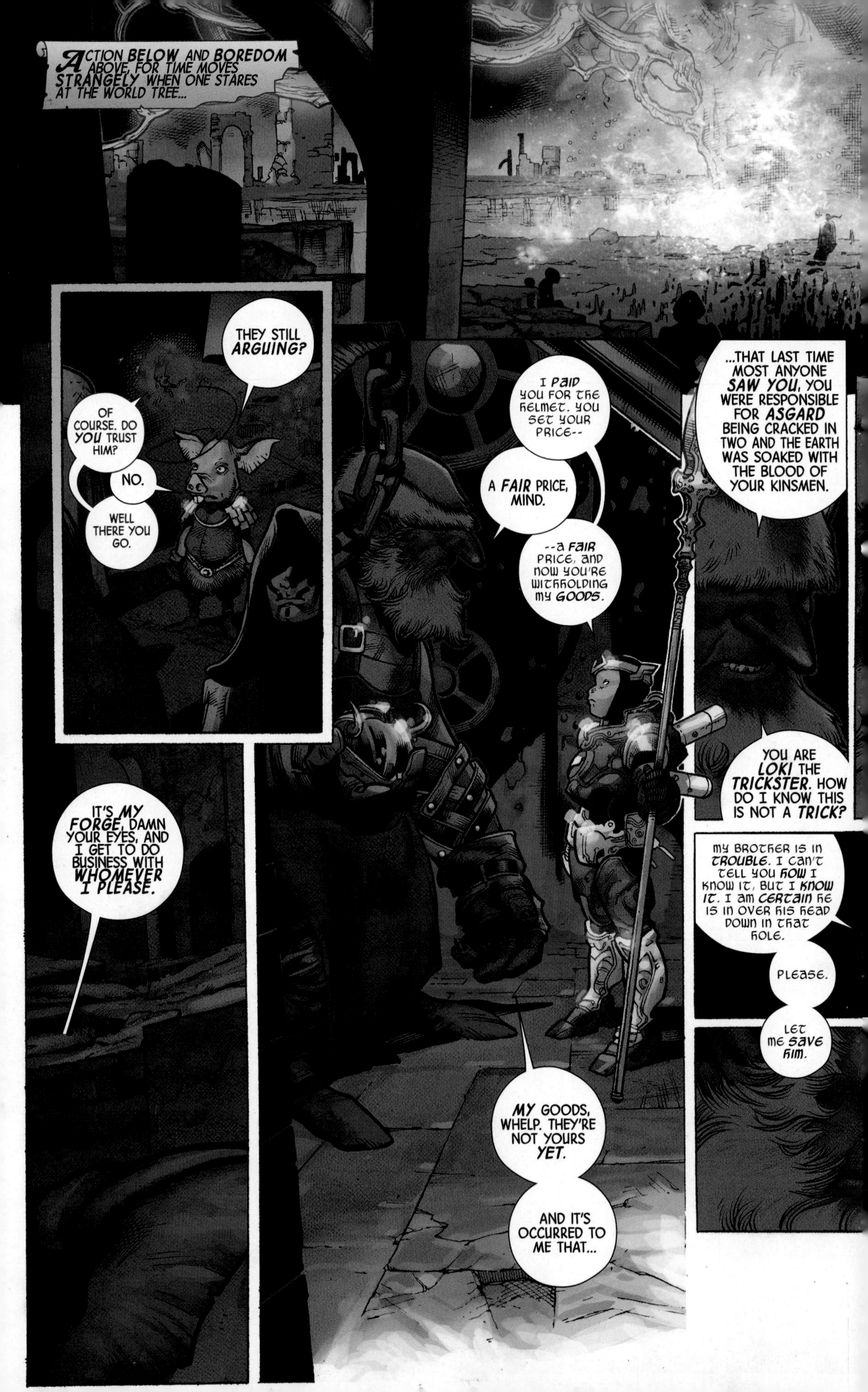
ACTION BELOW AND BOREDOM ABOVE, FOR TIME MOVES STRANGELY WHEN ONE STARES AT THE WORLD TREE...
THEY STILL ARGUING?
OF COURSE. DO YOU TRUST HIM?
NO.
WELL THERE YOU GO.
I PAID YOU FOR THE HELMET. YOU SET YOUR PRICE--
A FAIR PRICE, MIND.
--A FAIR PRICE, AND NOW YOU'RE WITHHOLDING MY GOODS.
IT'S MY FORGE, DAMN YOUR EYES, AND I GET TO DO BUSINESS WITH WHOMEVER I PLEASE.
MY GOODS, WHELP. THEY'RE NOT YOURS YET.
AND IT'S OCCURRED TO ME THAT...
...THAT LAST TIME MOST ANYONE SAW YOU, YOU WERE RESPONSIBLE FOR ASGARD BEING CRACKED IN TWO AND THE EARTH WAS SOAKED WITH THE BLOOD OF YOUR KINSMEN.
YOU ARE LOKI THE TRICKSTER. HOW DO I KNOW THIS IS NOT A TRICK?
MY BROTHER IS IN TROUBLE. I CAN'T TELL YOU HOW I KNOW IT, BUT I KNOW IT. I AM CERTAIN HE IS IN OVER HIS HEAD DOWN IN THAT HOLE.
PLEASE.
LET ME SAVE HIM.

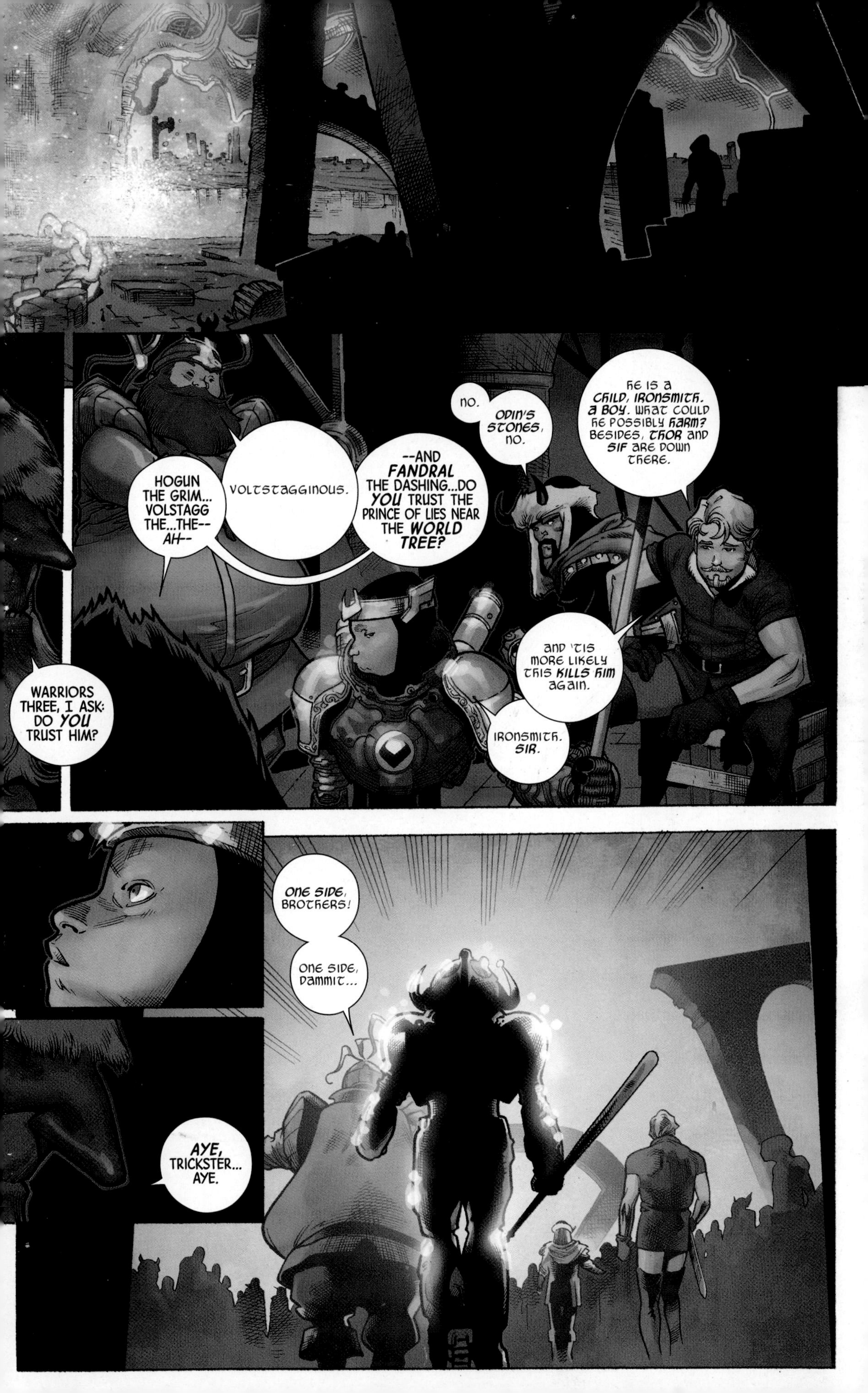
WARRIORS THREE, I ASK: DO *YOU* TRUST HIM?
HOGUN THE GRIM... VOLSTAGG THE...THE-- *AH*--
VOLTSTAGGINOUS.
--AND *FANDRAL* THE DASHING...DO *YOU* TRUST THE PRINCE OF LIES NEAR THE *WORLD TREE?*
NO.
ODIN'S STONES, NO.
HE IS A *CHILD, IRONSMITH. A BOY.* WHAT COULD HE POSSIBLY *HARM?* BESIDES, *THOR* AND *SIF* ARE DOWN THERE.
AND 'TIS MORE LIKELY THIS *KILLS* HIM AGAIN.
IRONSMITH. *SIR.*
ONE SIDE, BROTHERS!
ONE SIDE, DAMMIT...
AYE, TRICKSTER... AYE.

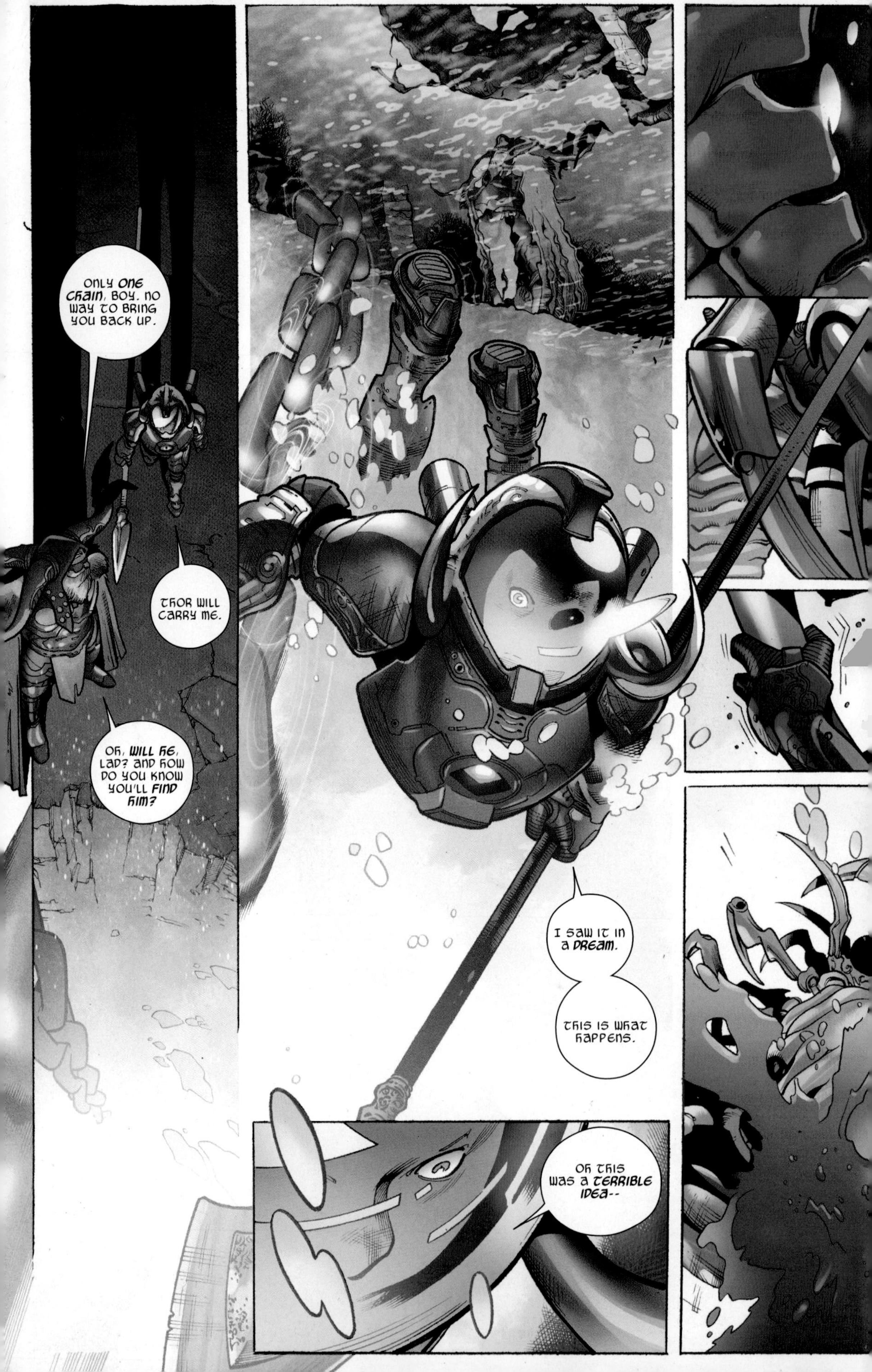
ONLY ONE CHAIN, BOY. NO WAY TO BRING YOU BACK UP.
THOR WILL CARRY ME.
OH, WILL HE, LAD? AND HOW DO YOU KNOW YOU'LL FIND HIM?
I SAW IT IN A DREAM.
THIS IS WHAT HAPPENS.
OH THIS WAS A TERRIBLE IDEA--

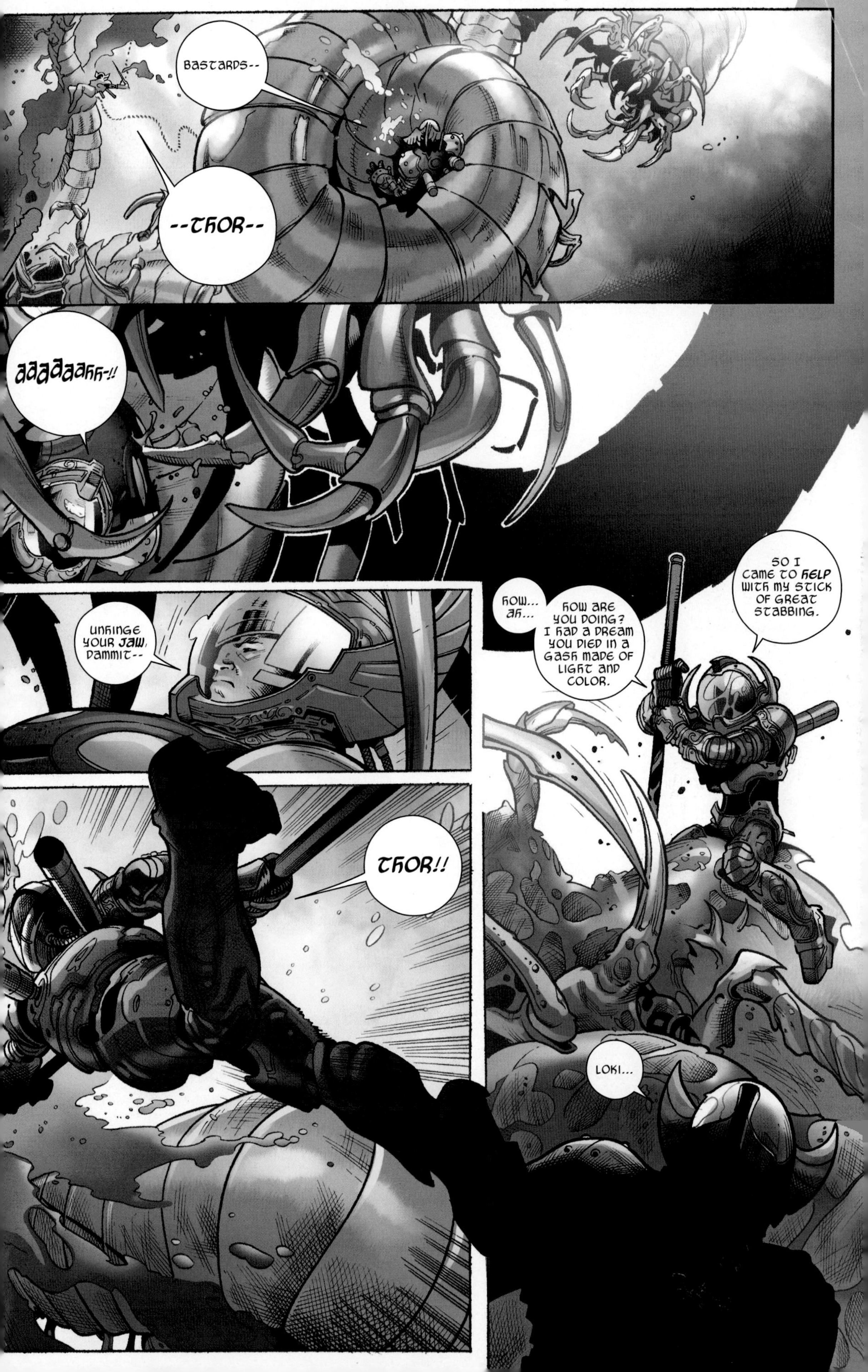
BASTARDS--
--THOR--
AAAAAAHH-!!
UNHINGE YOUR JAW, DAMMIT--
HOW... AH...
HOW ARE YOU DOING? I HAD A DREAM YOU DIED IN A GASH MADE OF LIGHT AND COLOR.
SO I CAME TO HELP WITH MY STICK OF GREAT STABBING.
THOR!!
LOKI...

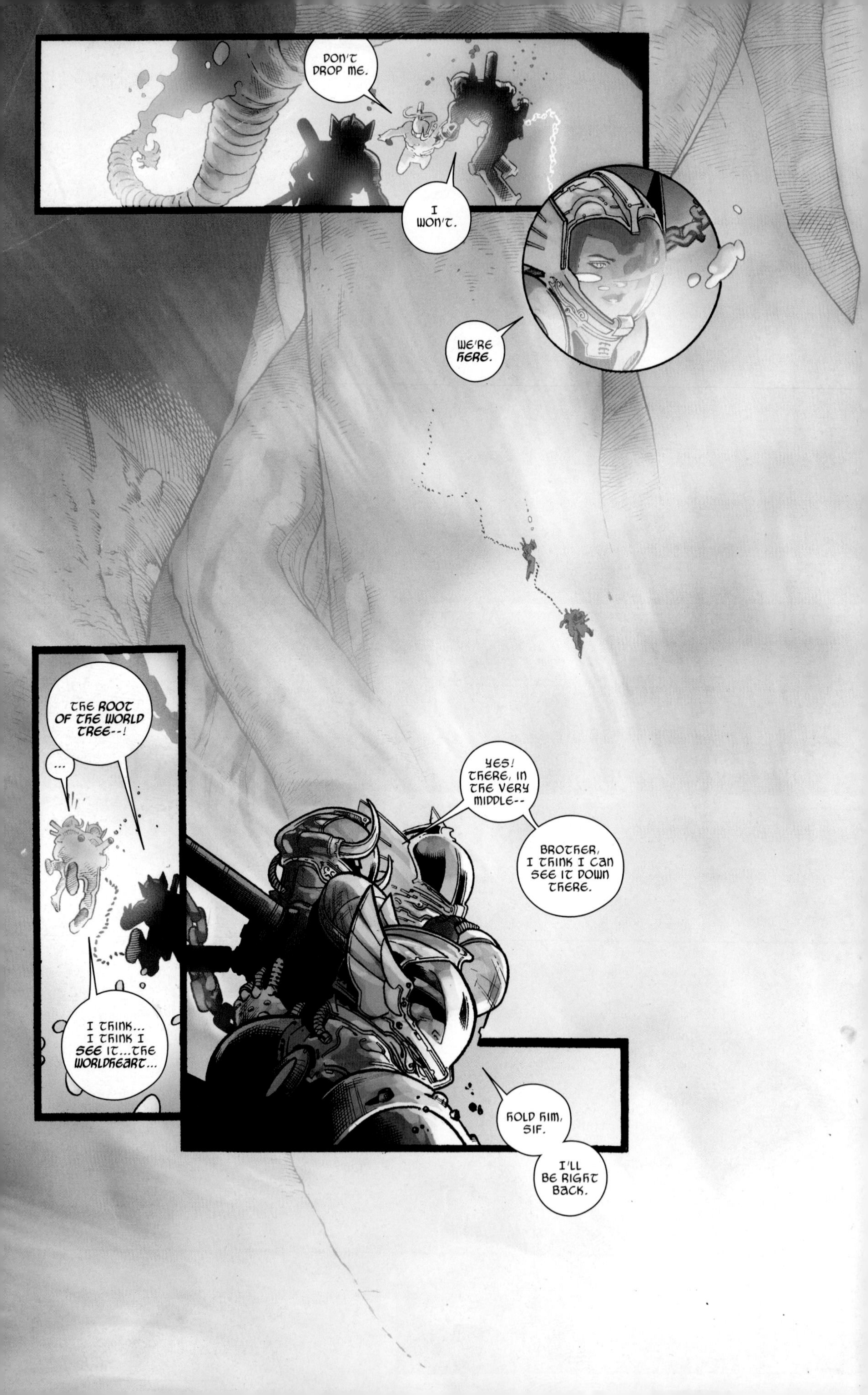
DON'T DROP ME.
I WON'T.
WE'RE HERE.
THE ROOT OF THE WORLD TREE--!
...
I THINK... I THINK I SEE IT...THE WORLDHEART...
YES! THERE, IN THE VERY MIDDLE--
BROTHER, I THINK I CAN SEE IT DOWN THERE.
HOLD HIM, SIF.
I'LL BE RIGHT BACK.

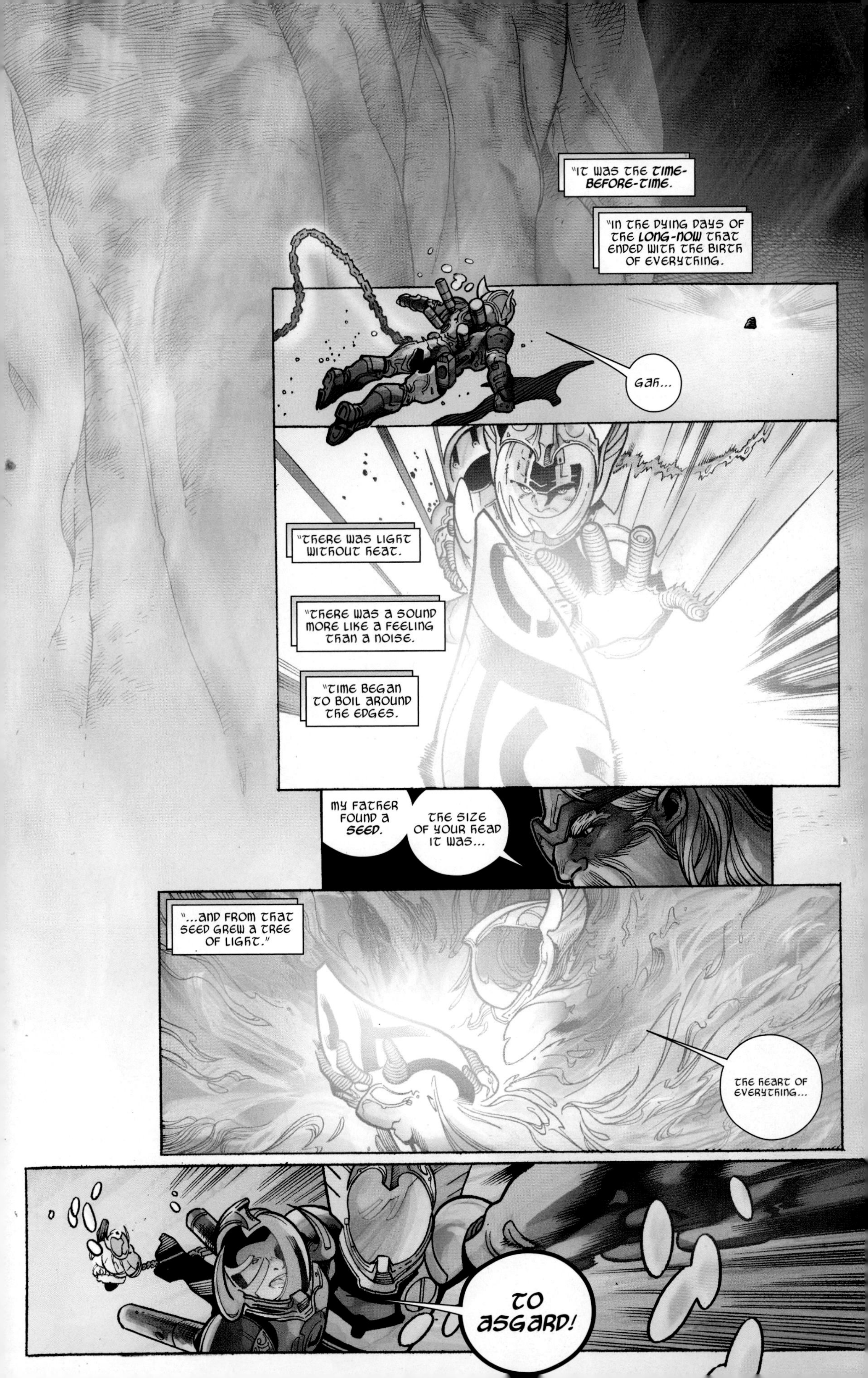
"IT WAS THE TIME-BEFORE-TIME.
"IN THE DYING DAYS OF THE LONG-NOW THAT ENDED WITH THE BIRTH OF EVERYTHING.
GAH...
"THERE WAS LIGHT WITHOUT HEAT.
"THERE WAS A SOUND MORE LIKE A FEELING THAN A NOISE.
"TIME BEGAN TO BOIL AROUND THE EDGES.
MY FATHER FOUND A SEED.
THE SIZE OF YOUR HEAD IT WAS...
"...AND FROM THAT SEED GREW A TREE OF LIGHT."
THE HEART OF EVERYTHING...
TO ASGARD!

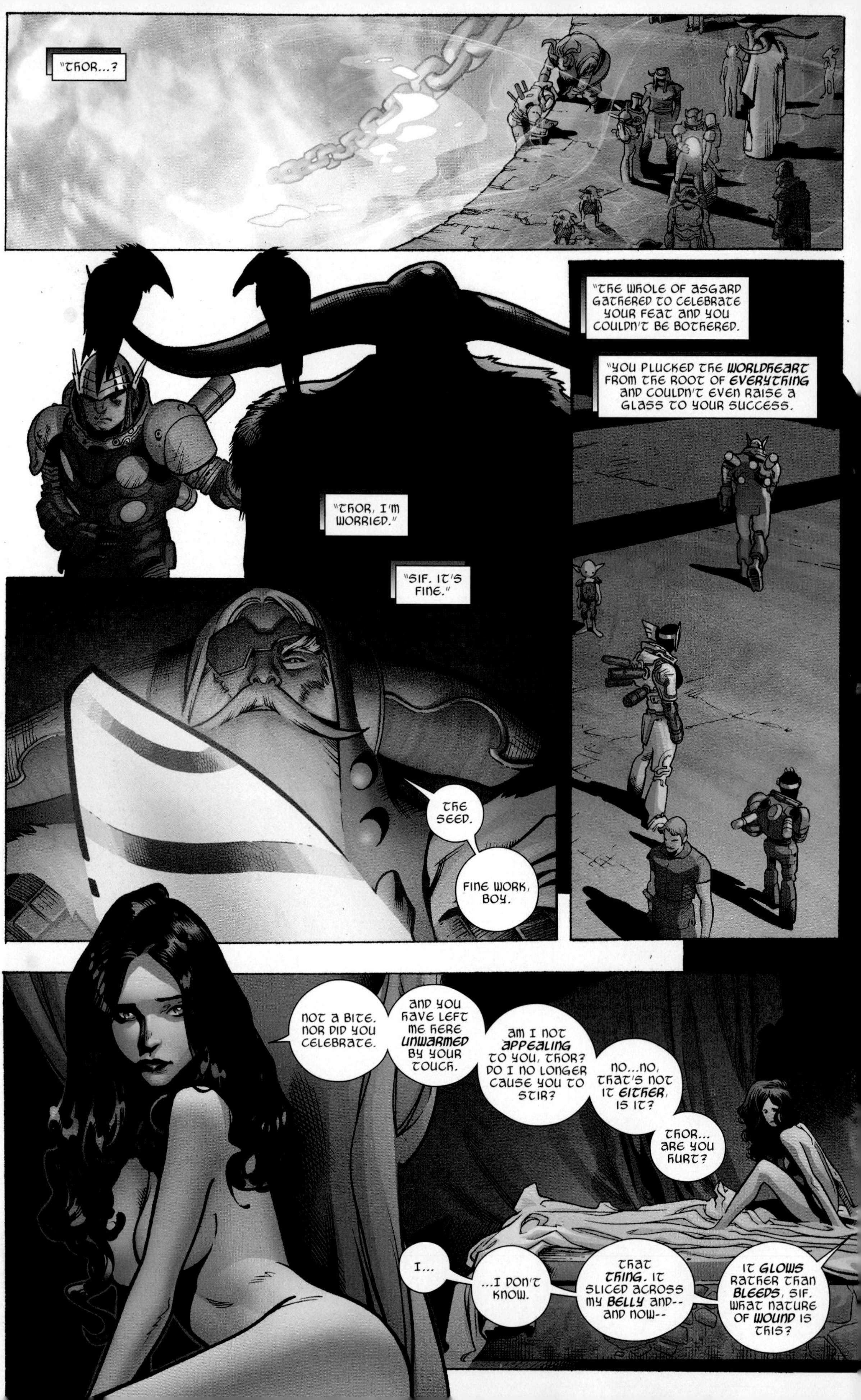
"THOR...?
"THE WHOLE OF ASGARD GATHERED TO CELEBRATE YOUR FEAT AND YOU COULDN'T BE BOTHERED.
"YOU PLUCKED THE WORLDHEART FROM THE ROOT OF EVERYTHING AND COULDN'T EVEN RAISE A GLASS TO YOUR SUCCESS.
"THOR, I'M WORRIED."
"SIF. IT'S FINE."
THE SEED.
FINE WORK, BOY.
NOT A BITE. NOR DID YOU CELEBRATE.
AND YOU HAVE LEFT ME HERE UNWARMED BY YOUR TOUCH.
AM I NOT APPEALING TO YOU, THOR? DO I NO LONGER CAUSE YOU TO STIR?
NO...NO, THAT'S NOT IT EITHER, IS IT?
THOR... ARE YOU HURT?
I...
...I DON'T KNOW.
THAT THING. IT SLICED ACROSS MY BELLY AND--AND NOW--
IT GLOWS RATHER THAN BLEEDS, SIF. WHAT NATURE OF WOUND IS THIS?

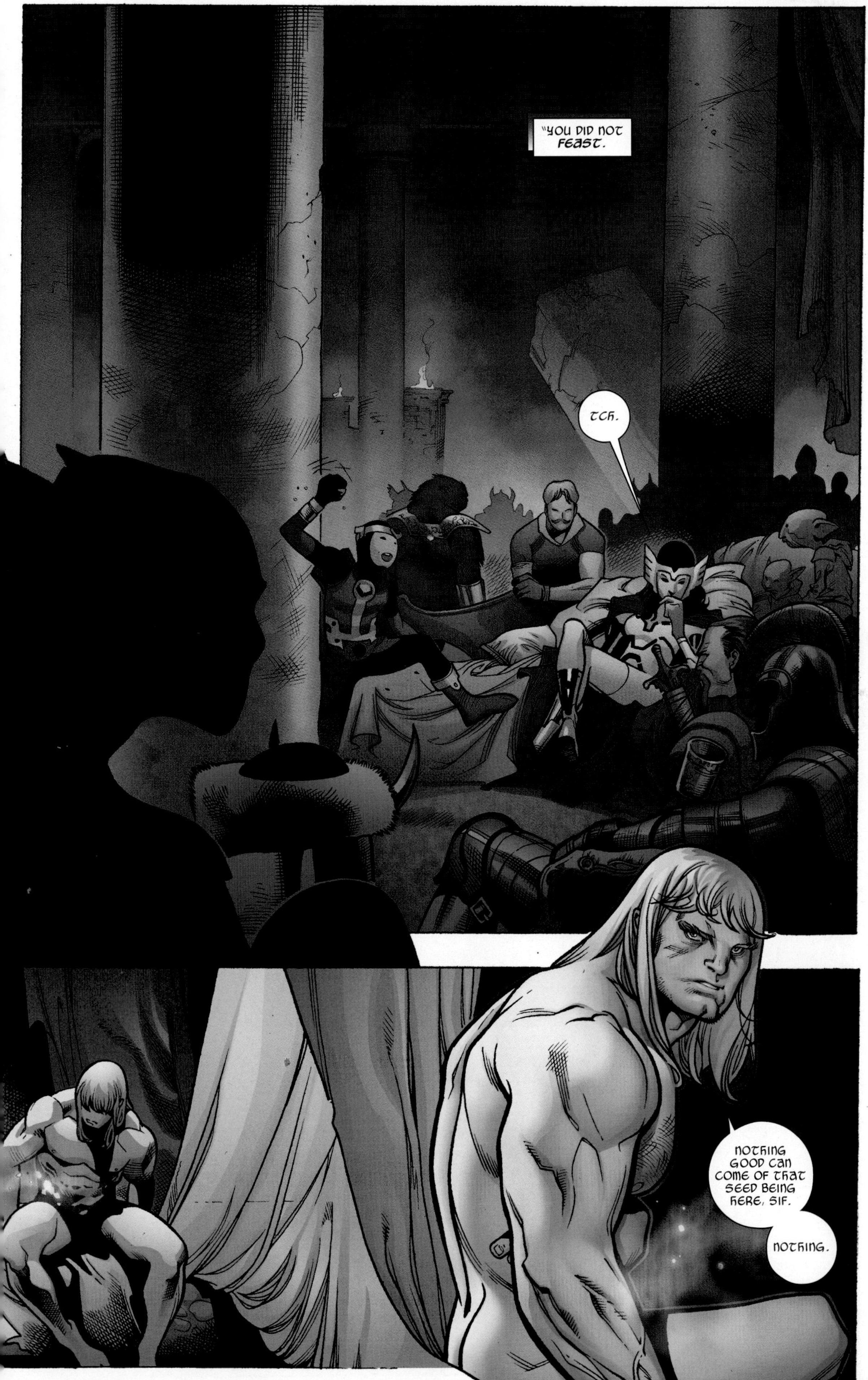
"YOU DID NOT FEAST.
TCH.
NOTHING GOOD CAN COME OF THAT SEED BEING HERE, SIF.
NOTHING.

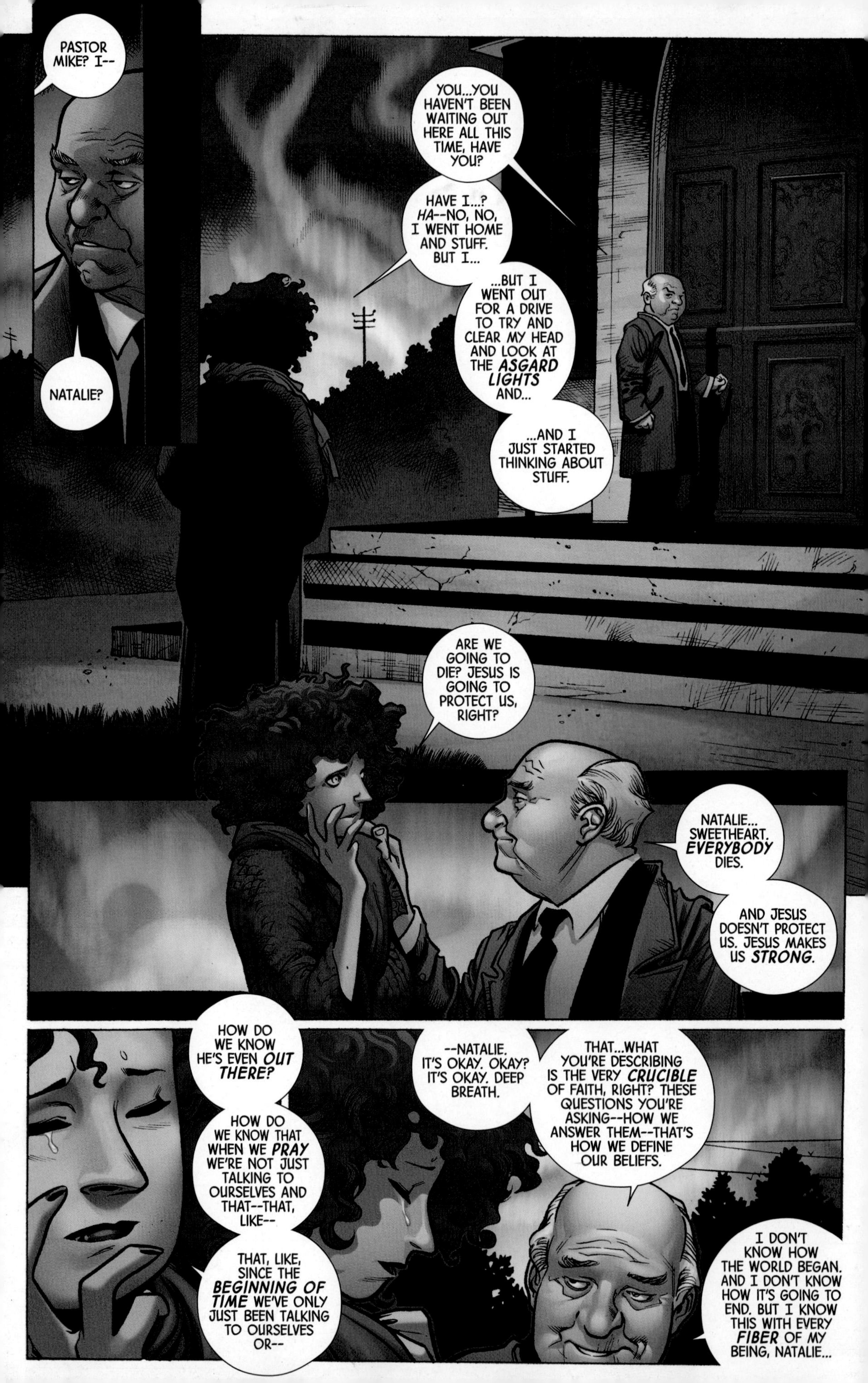
PASTOR MIKE? I--
NATALIE?
YOU...YOU HAVEN'T BEEN WAITING OUT HERE ALL THIS TIME, HAVE YOU?
HAVE I...? HA--NO, NO, I WENT HOME AND STUFF. BUT I...
...BUT I WENT OUT FOR A DRIVE TO TRY AND CLEAR MY HEAD AND LOOK AT THE ASGARD LIGHTS AND...
...AND I JUST STARTED THINKING ABOUT STUFF.
ARE WE GOING TO DIE? JESUS IS GOING TO PROTECT US, RIGHT?
NATALIE... SWEETHEART. EVERYBODY DIES.
AND JESUS DOESN'T PROTECT US. JESUS MAKES US STRONG.
HOW DO WE KNOW HE'S EVEN OUT THERE?
HOW DO WE KNOW THAT WHEN WE PRAY WE'RE NOT JUST TALKING TO OURSELVES AND THAT--THAT, LIKE--
THAT, LIKE, SINCE THE BEGINNING OF TIME WE'VE ONLY JUST BEEN TALKING TO OURSELVES OR--
--NATALIE. IT'S OKAY. OKAY? IT'S OKAY. DEEP BREATH.
THAT...WHAT YOU'RE DESCRIBING IS THE VERY CRUCIBLE OF FAITH, RIGHT? THESE QUESTIONS YOU'RE ASKING--HOW WE ANSWER THEM--THAT'S HOW WE DEFINE OUR BELIEFS.
I DON'T KNOW HOW THE WORLD BEGAN. AND I DON'T KNOW HOW IT'S GOING TO END. BUT I KNOW THIS WITH EVERY FIBER OF MY BEING, NATALIE...

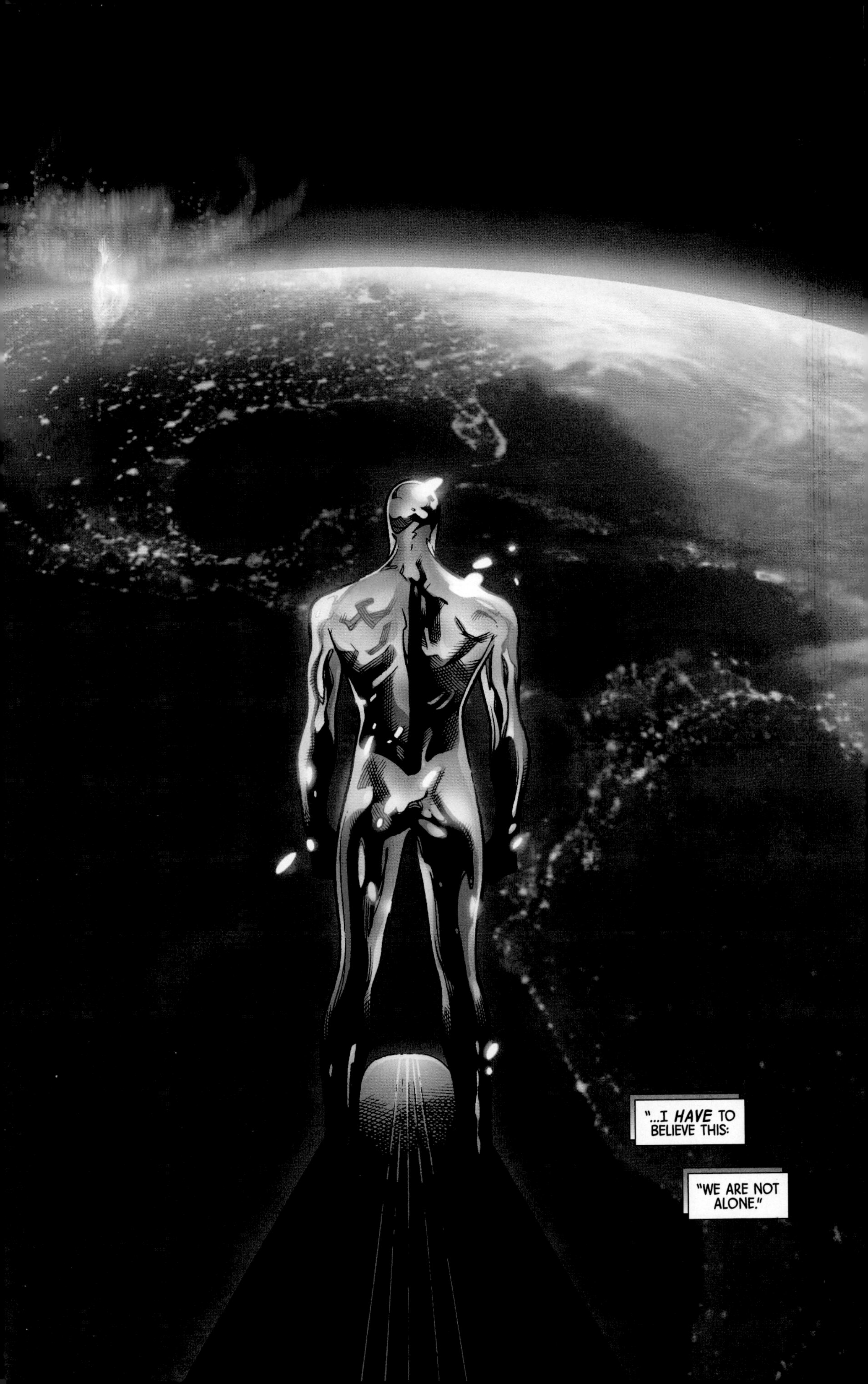
"...I HAVE TO BELIEVE THIS:
"WE ARE NOT ALONE."

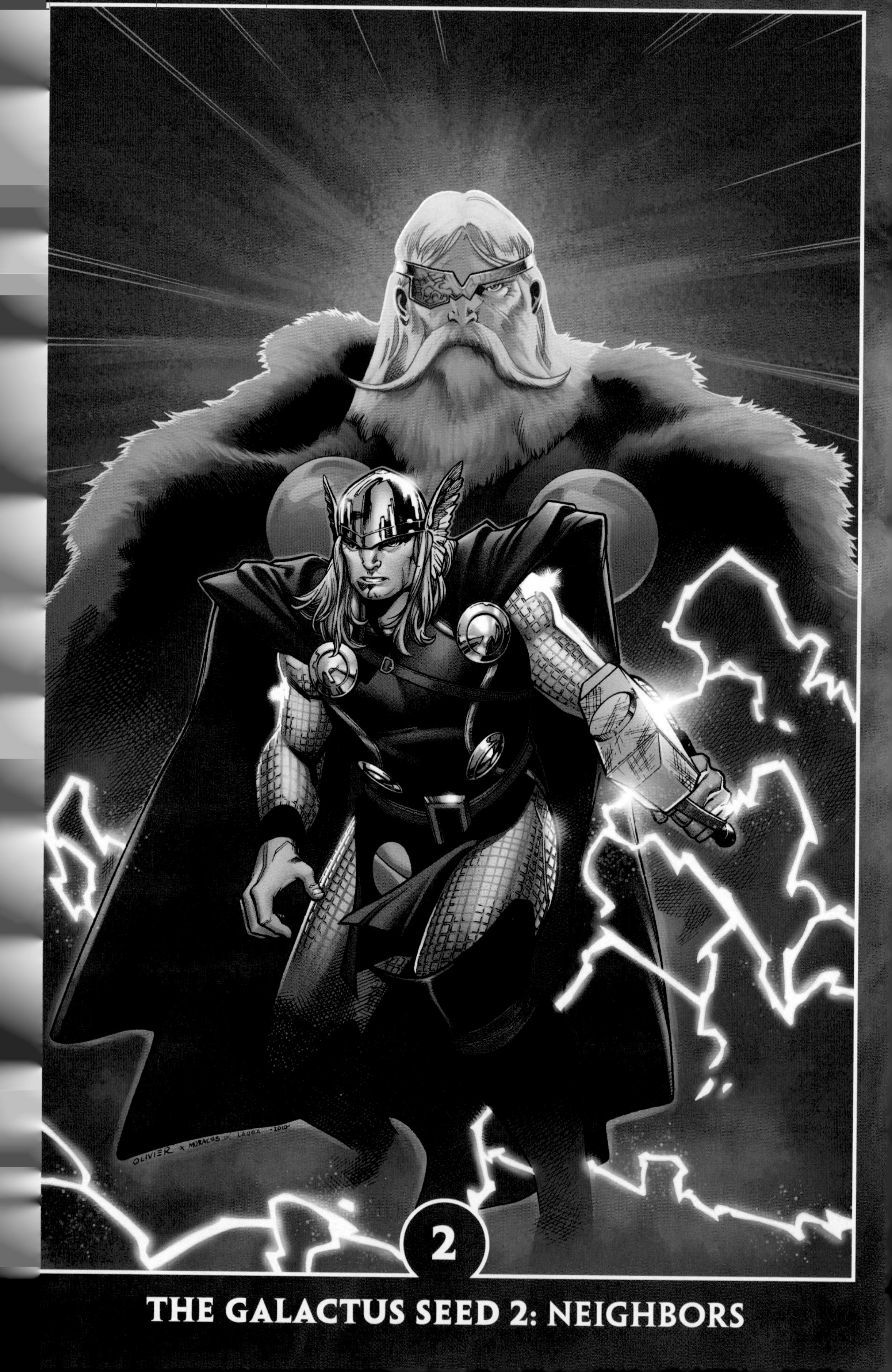

2

THE GALACTUS SEED 2: NEIGHBORS

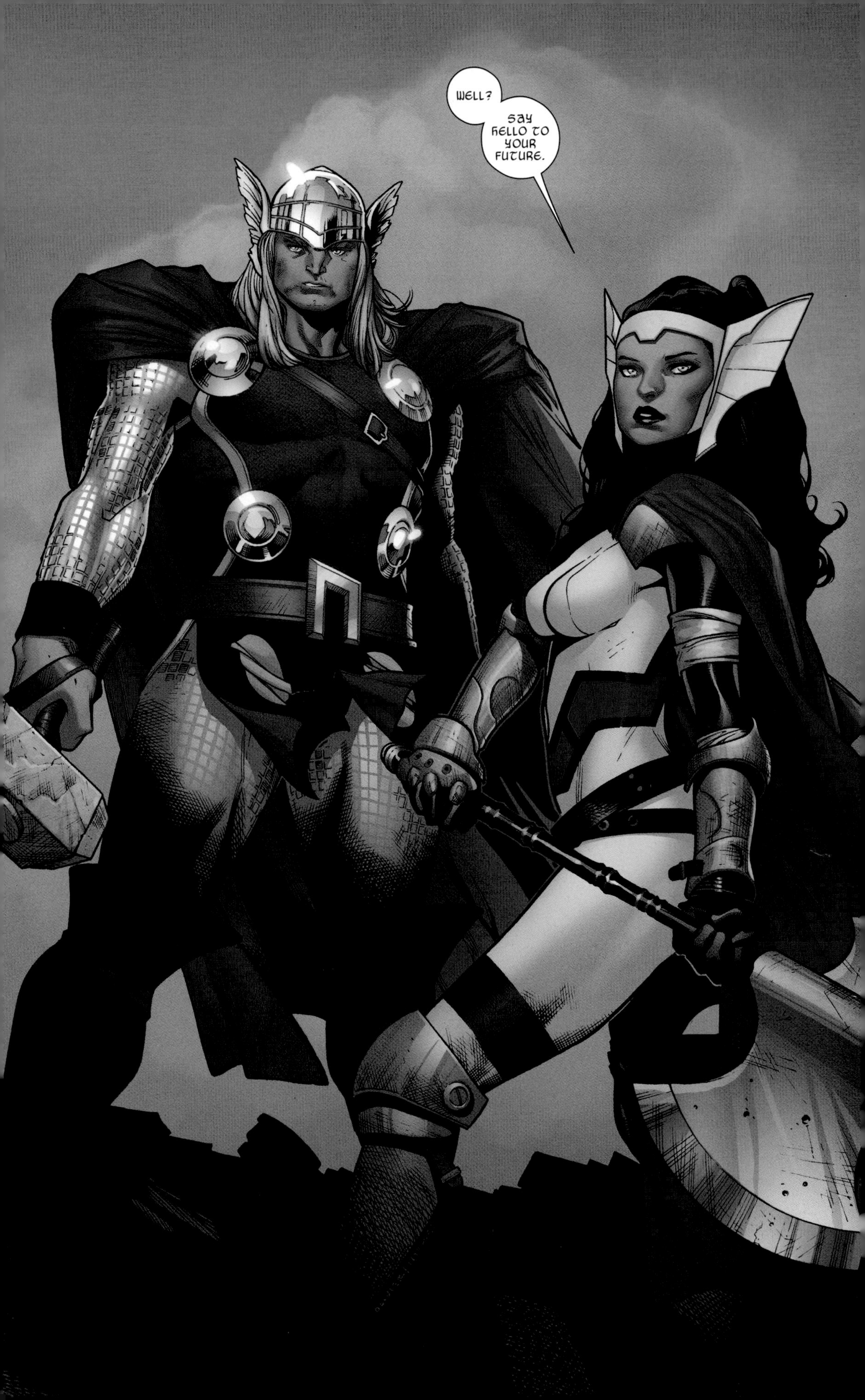
WELL?
SAY HELLO TO YOUR FUTURE.

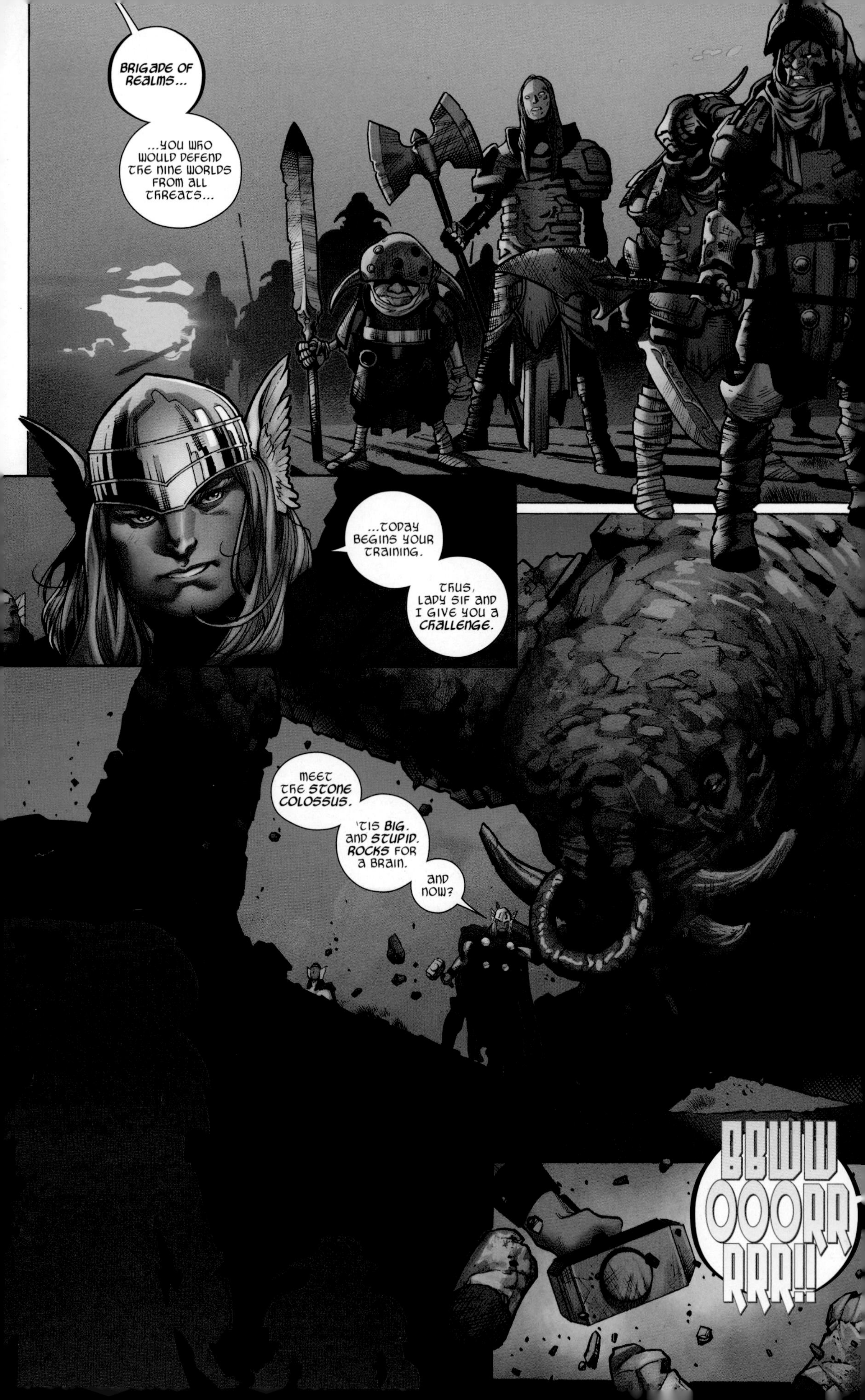
BRIGADE OF REALMS...
...YOU WHO WOULD DEFEND THE NINE WORLDS FROM ALL THREATS...
...TODAY BEGINS YOUR TRAINING.
THUS, LADY SIF AND I GIVE YOU A CHALLENGE.
MEET THE STONE COLOSSUS.
'TIS BIG. AND STUPID. ROCKS FOR A BRAIN.
AND NOW?
BBWWOOORRRRR!!

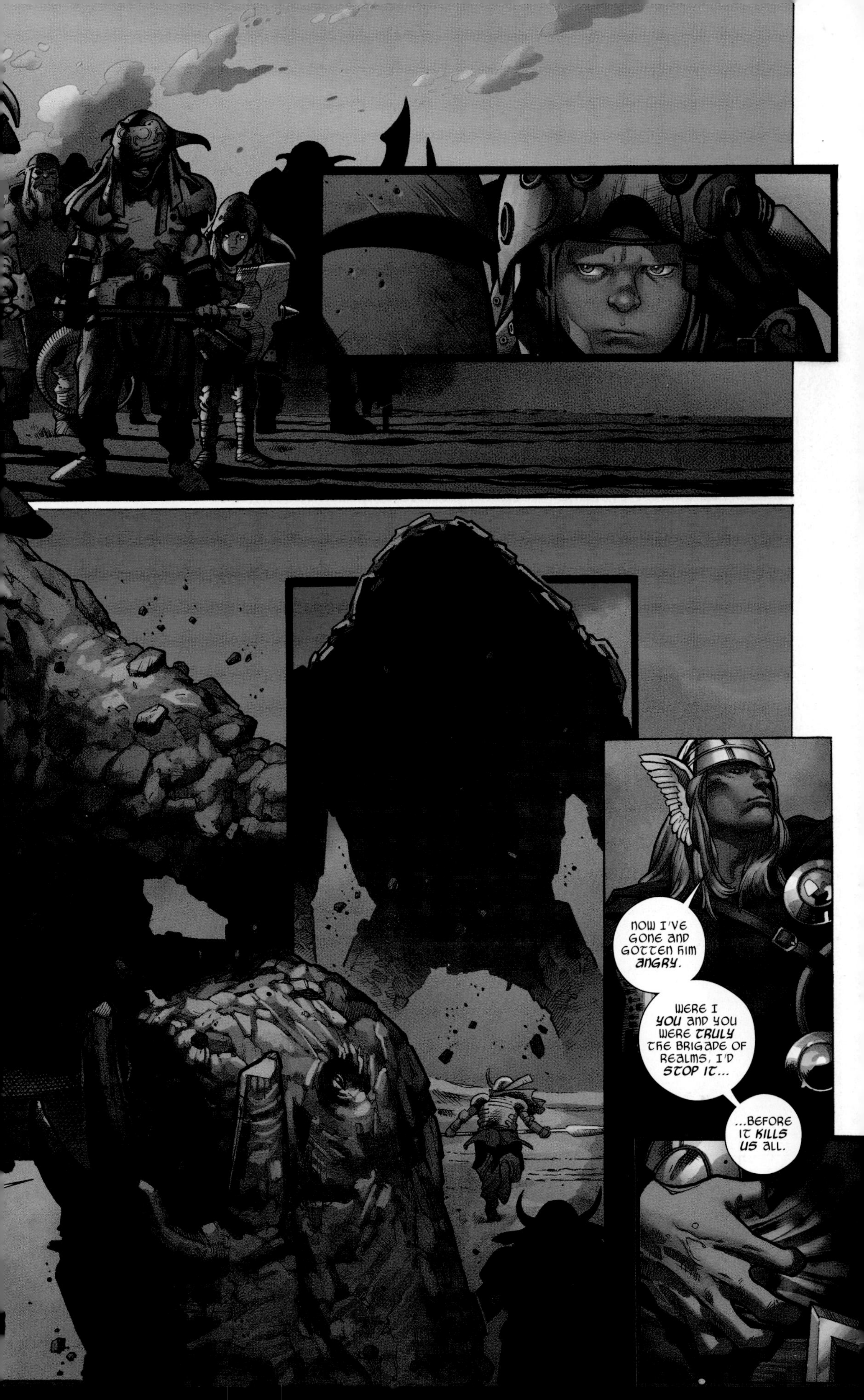
NOW I'VE GONE AND GOTTEN HIM ANGRY.
WERE I YOU AND YOU WERE TRULY THE BRIGADE OF REALMS, I'D STOP IT...
...BEFORE IT KILLS US ALL.

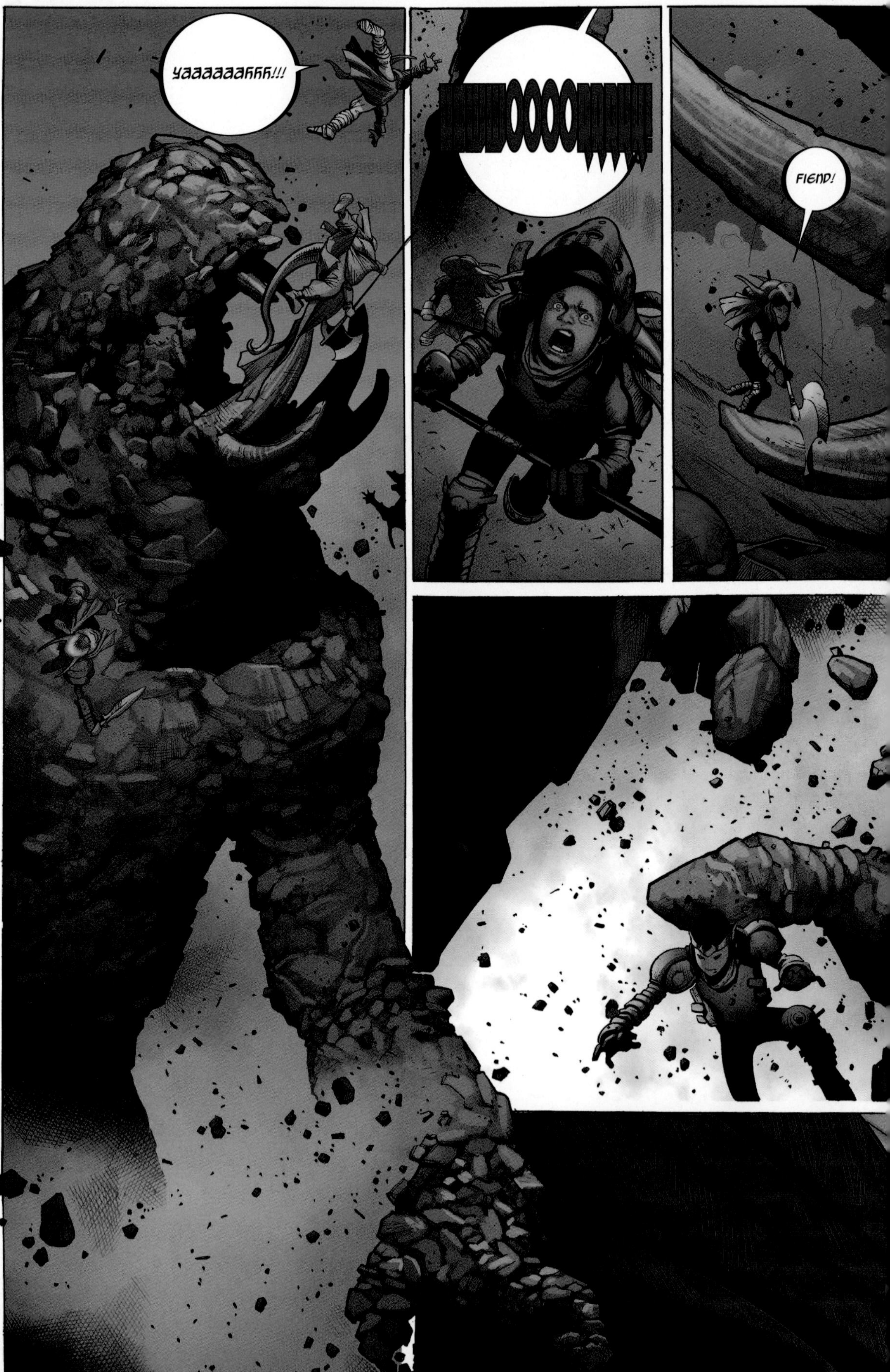
YAAAAAAAHHH!!!
FIEND!

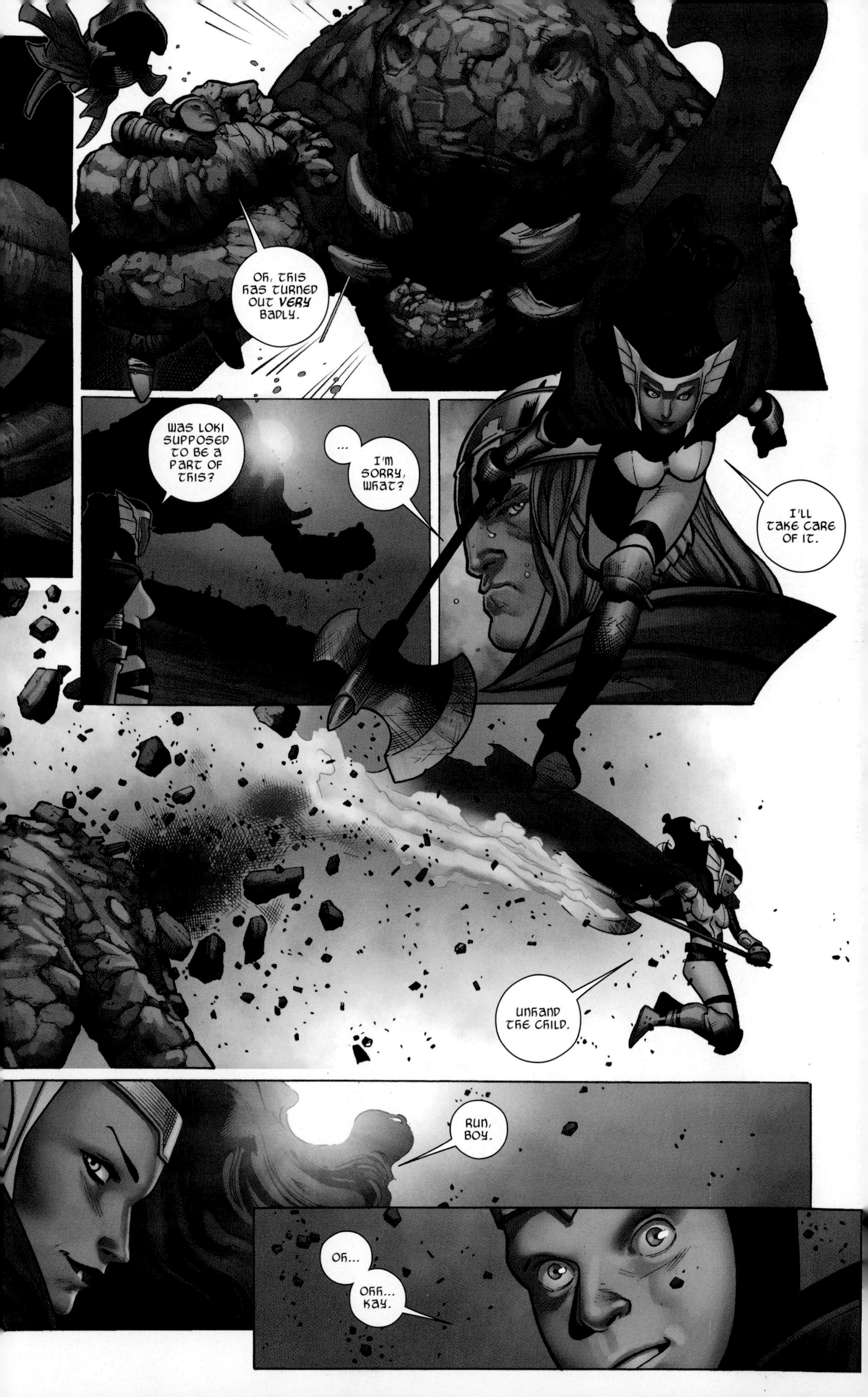
OH, THIS HAS TURNED OUT VERY BADLY.
WAS LOKI SUPPOSED TO BE A PART OF THIS?
... I'M SORRY, WHAT?
I'LL TAKE CARE OF IT.
UNHAND THE CHILD.
RUN, BOY.
OH...
OHH... KAY.

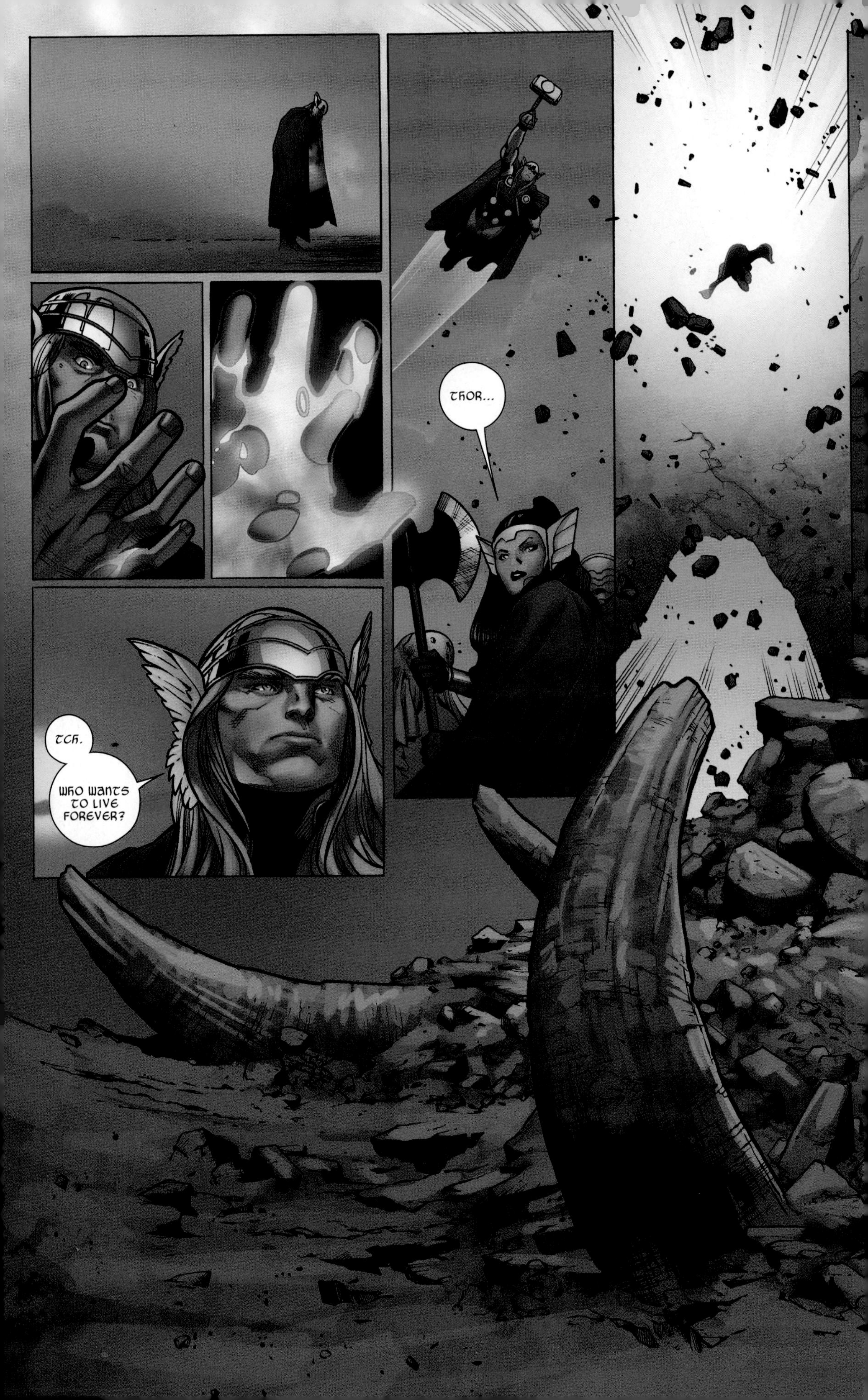
TCH.
WHO WANTS TO LIVE FOREVER?
THOR...

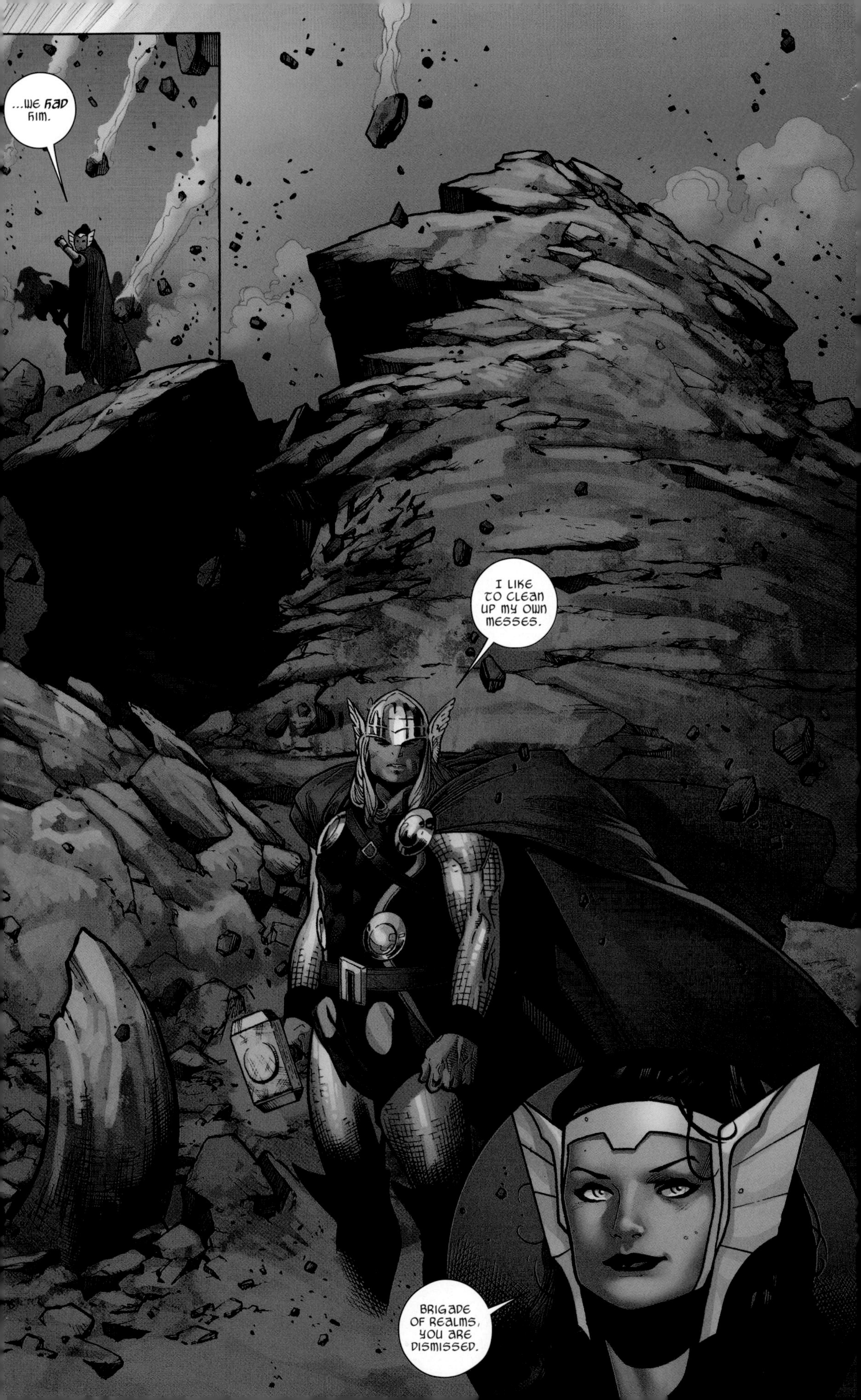
...WE HAD HIM.
I LIKE TO CLEAN UP MY OWN MESSES.
BRIGADE OF REALMS, YOU ARE DISMISSED.

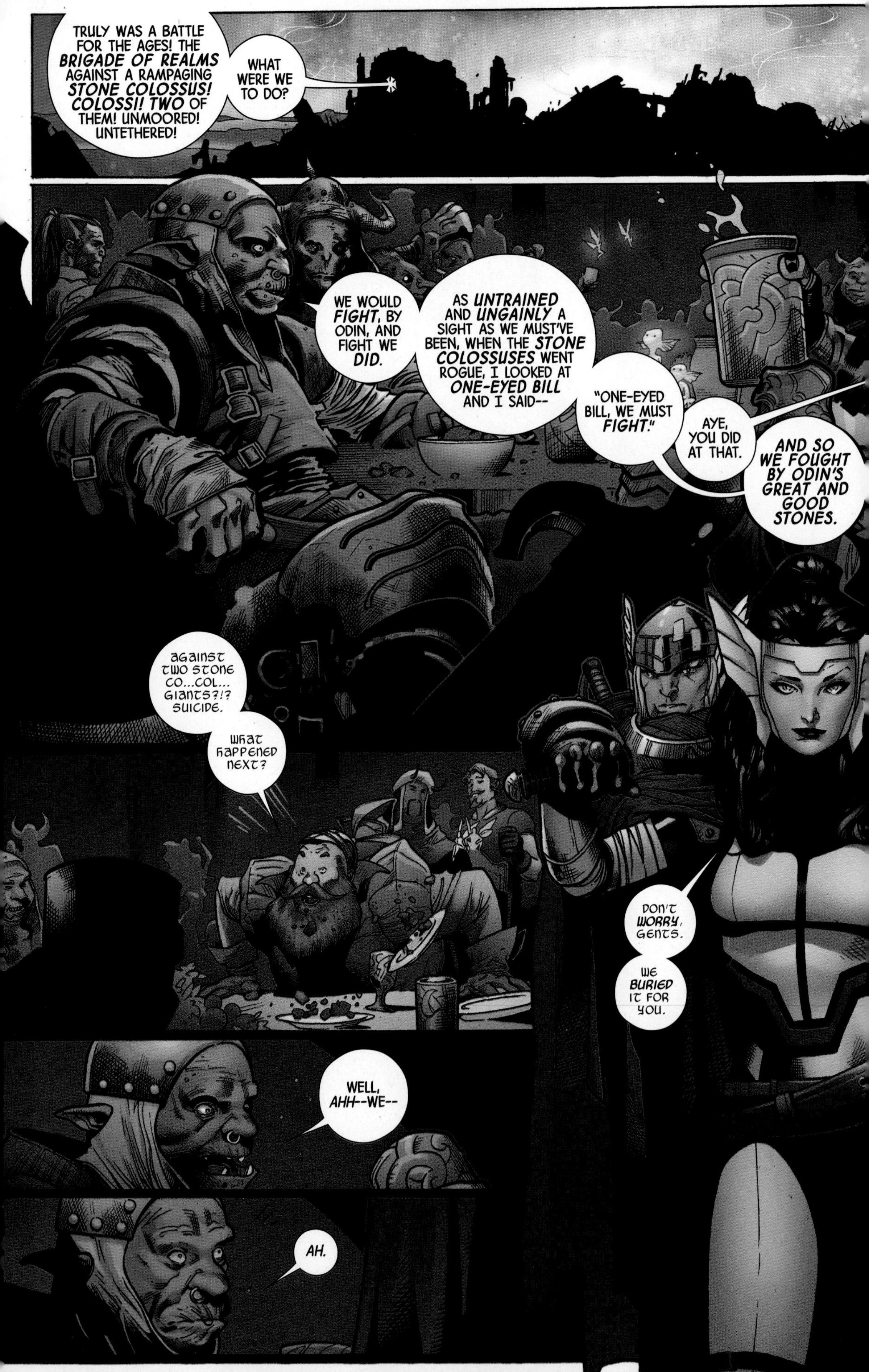
TRULY WAS A BATTLE FOR THE AGES! THE BRIGADE OF REALMS AGAINST A RAMPAGING STONE COLOSSUS! COLOSSI! TWO OF THEM! UNMOORED! UNTETHERED!
WHAT WERE WE TO DO?
WE WOULD FIGHT, BY ODIN, AND FIGHT WE DID.
AS UNTRAINED AND UNGAINLY A SIGHT AS WE MUST'VE BEEN, WHEN THE STONE COLOSSUSES WENT ROGUE, I LOOKED AT ONE-EYED BILL AND I SAID--
"ONE-EYED BILL, WE MUST FIGHT."
AYE, YOU DID AT THAT.
AND SO WE FOUGHT BY ODIN'S GREAT AND GOOD STONES.
AGAINST TWO STONE CO...COL... GIANTS?!? SUICIDE.
WHAT HAPPENED NEXT?
DON'T WORRY, GENTS.
WE BURIED IT FOR YOU.
WELL, AHH--WE--
AH.

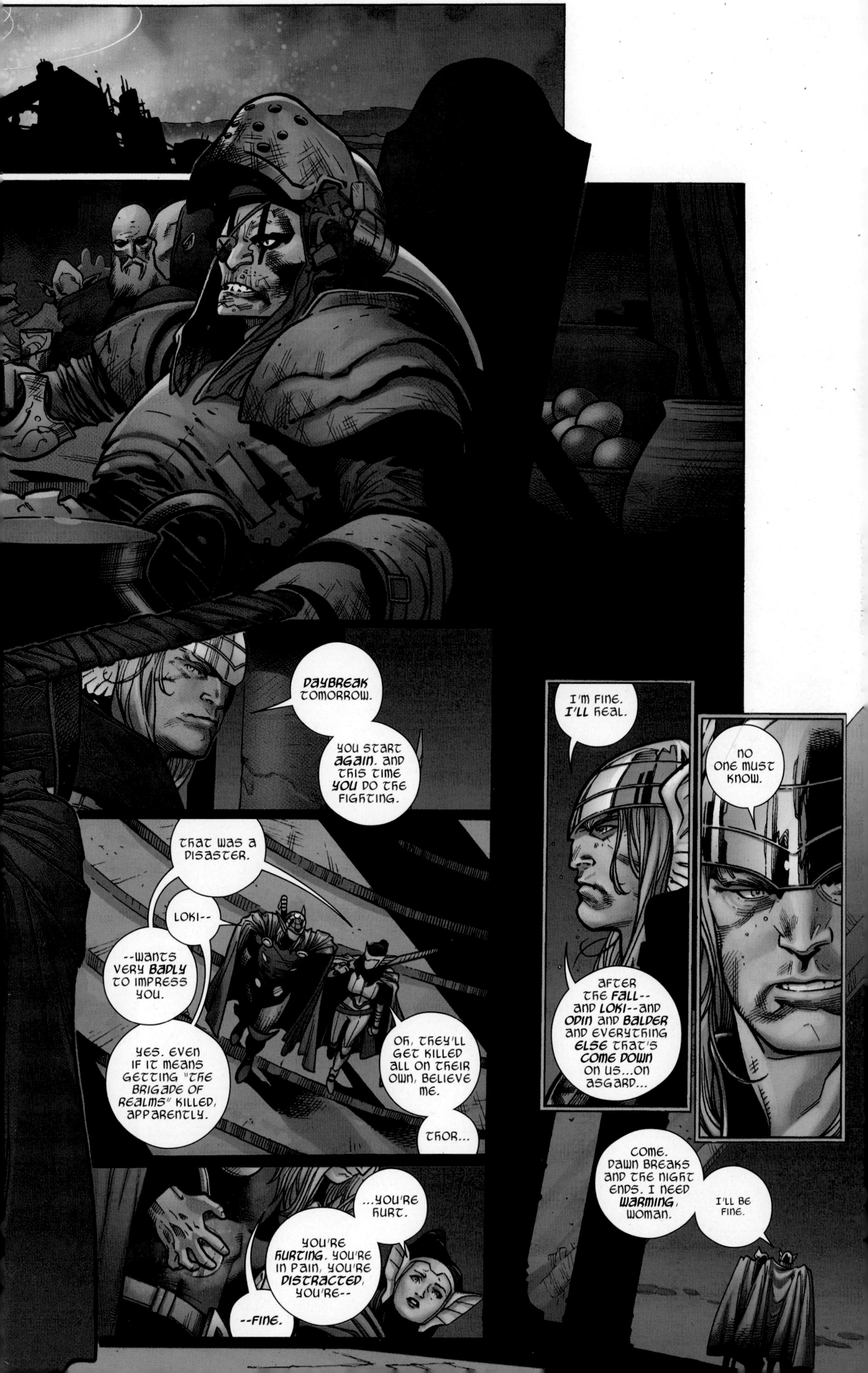

DAYBREAK TOMORROW.
YOU START AGAIN. AND THIS TIME YOU DO THE FIGHTING.
THAT WAS A DISASTER.
LOKI--
--WANTS VERY BADLY TO IMPRESS YOU.
YES. EVEN IF IT MEANS GETTING "THE BRIGADE OF REALMS" KILLED, APPARENTLY.
OH, THEY'LL GET KILLED ALL ON THEIR OWN, BELIEVE ME.
THOR...
...YOU'RE HURT.
YOU'RE HURTING. YOU'RE IN PAIN, YOU'RE DISTRACTED, YOU'RE--
--FINE.
I'M FINE. I'LL HEAL.
AFTER THE FALL--AND LOKI--AND ODIN AND BALDER AND EVERYTHING ELSE THAT'S COME DOWN ON US...ON ASGARD...
NO ONE MUST KNOW.
COME. DAWN BREAKS AND THE NIGHT ENDS. I NEED WARMING, WOMAN.
I'LL BE FINE.

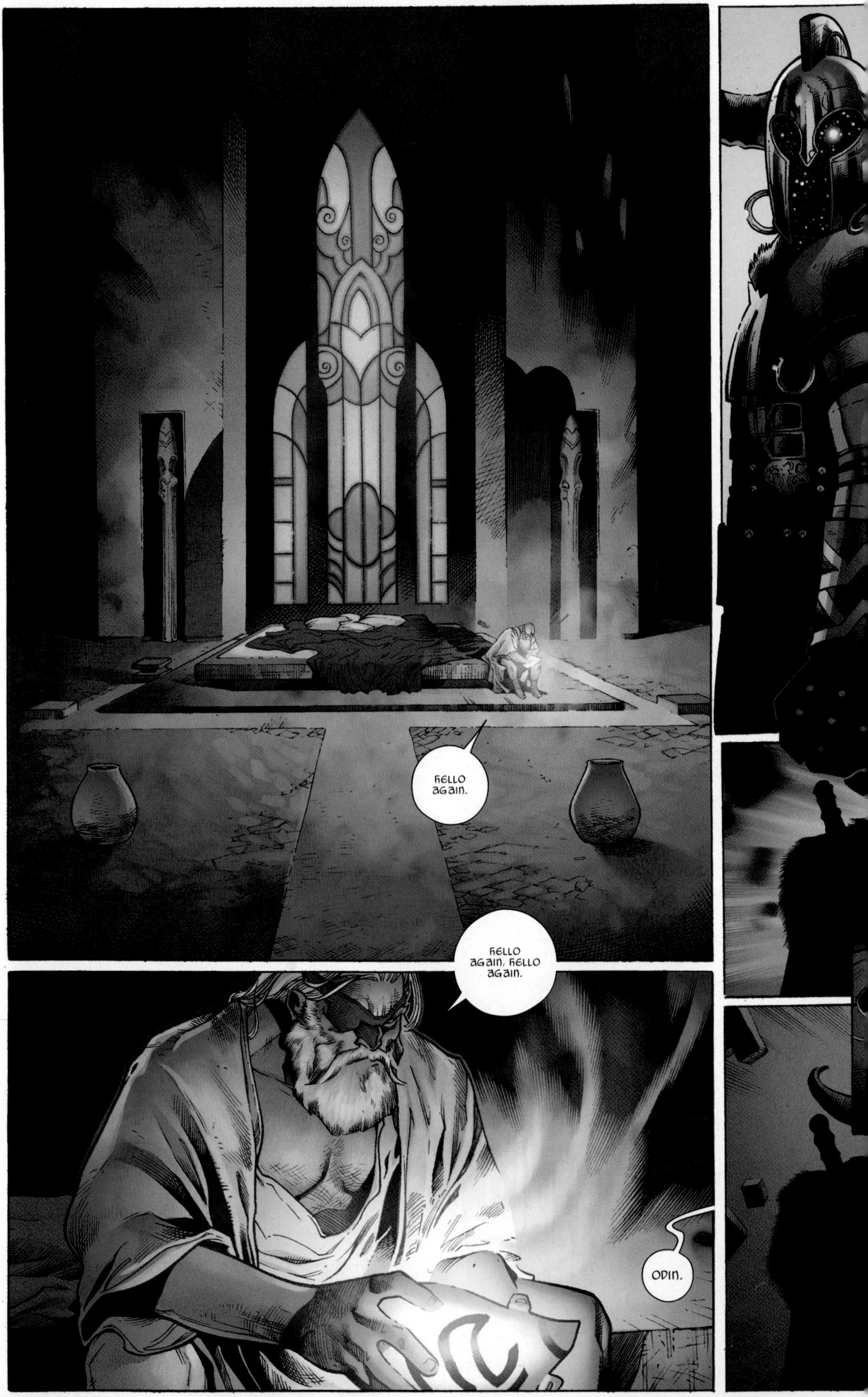
HELLO AGAIN.
HELLO AGAIN, HELLO AGAIN.
ODIN.

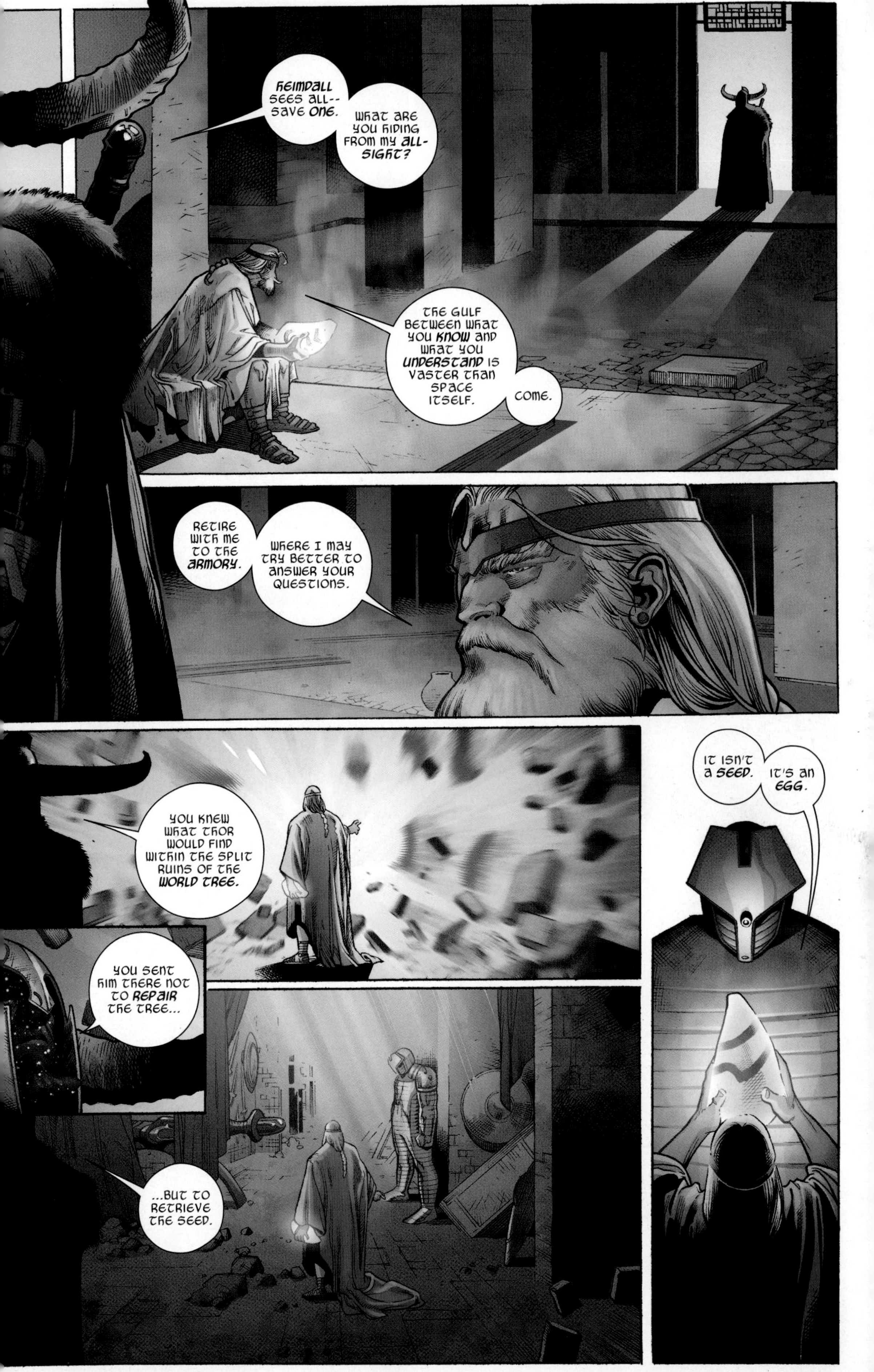
HEIMDALL SEES ALL-- SAVE ONE.
WHAT ARE YOU HIDING FROM MY ALL-SIGHT?
THE GULF BETWEEN WHAT YOU KNOW AND WHAT YOU UNDERSTAND IS VASTER THAN SPACE ITSELF.
COME.
RETIRE WITH ME TO THE ARMORY.
WHERE I MAY TRY BETTER TO ANSWER YOUR QUESTIONS.
YOU KNEW WHAT THOR WOULD FIND WITHIN THE SPLIT RUINS OF THE WORLD TREE.
YOU SENT HIM THERE NOT TO REPAIR THE TREE...
...BUT TO RETRIEVE THE SEED.
IT ISN'T A SEED.
IT'S AN EGG.

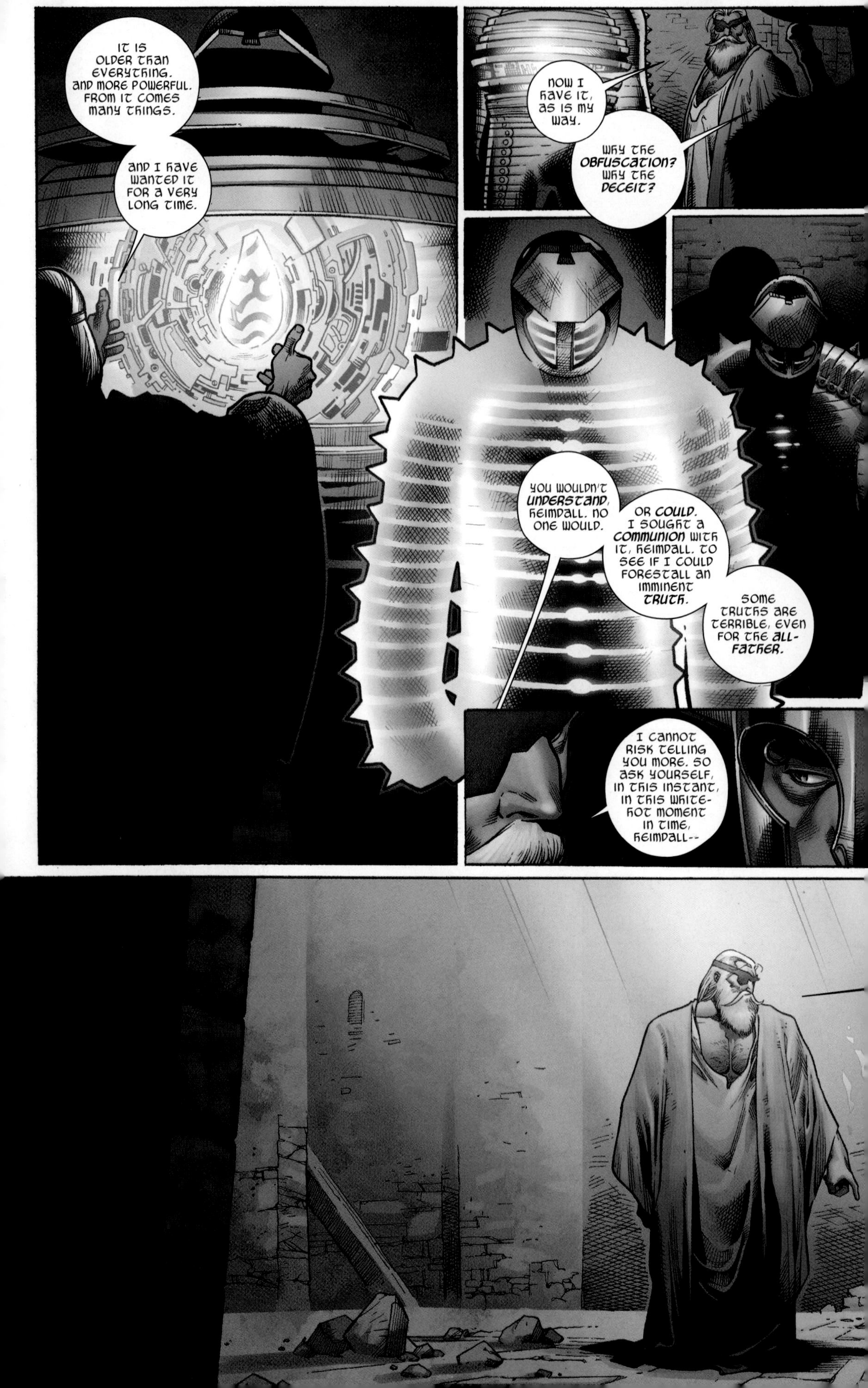
IT IS OLDER THAN EVERYTHING. AND MORE POWERFUL. FROM IT COMES MANY THINGS.
AND I HAVE WANTED IT FOR A VERY LONG TIME.
NOW I HAVE IT, AS IS MY WAY.
WHY THE OBFUSCATION? WHY THE DECEIT?
YOU WOULDN'T UNDERSTAND, HEIMDALL. NO ONE WOULD.
OR COULD. I SOUGHT A COMMUNION WITH IT, HEIMDALL. TO SEE IF I COULD FORESTALL AN IMMINENT TRUTH.
SOME TRUTHS ARE TERRIBLE, EVEN FOR THE ALL-FATHER.
I CANNOT RISK TELLING YOU MORE. SO ASK YOURSELF, IN THIS INSTANT, IN THIS WHITE-HOT MOMENT IN TIME, HEIMDALL--

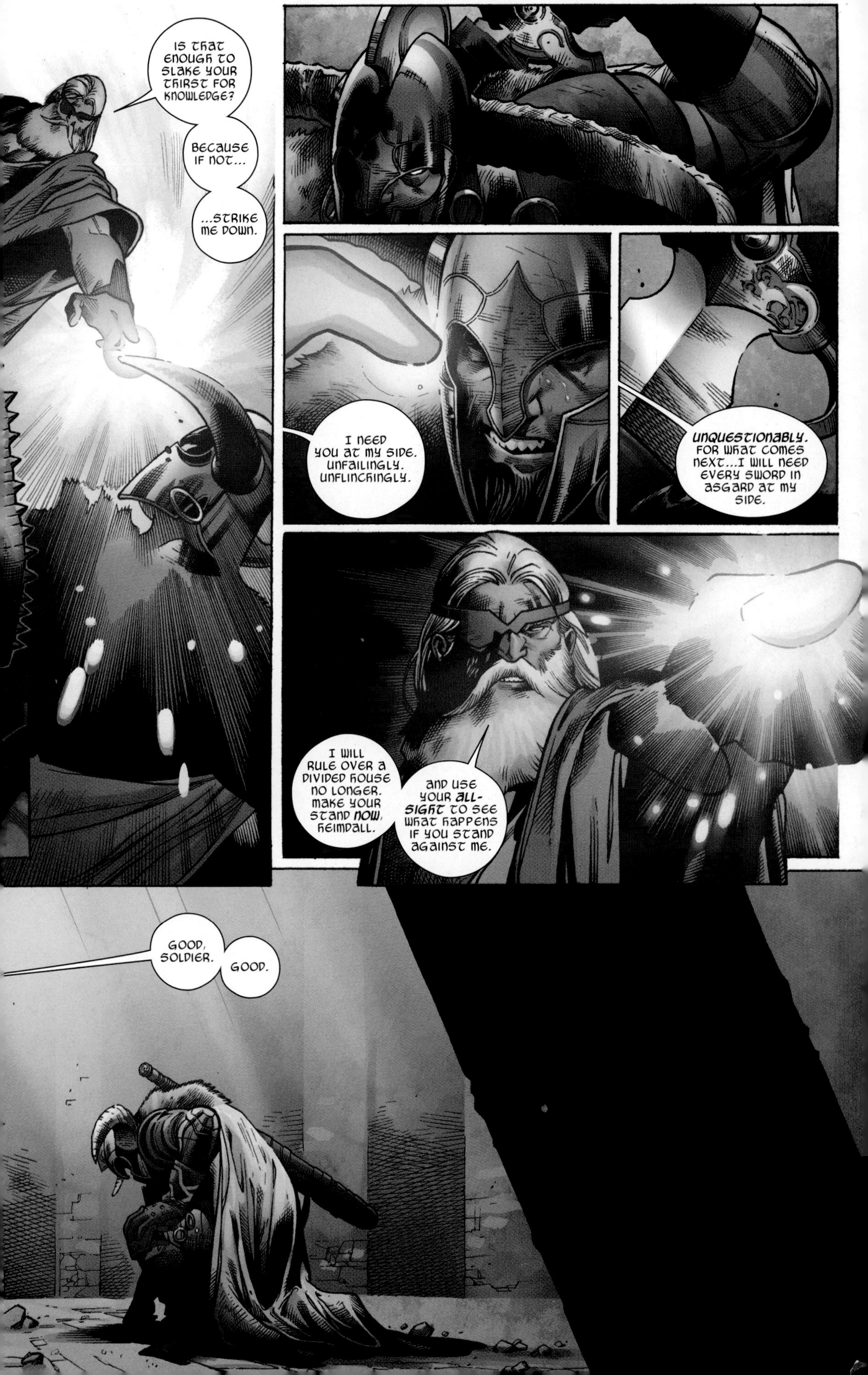

IS THAT ENOUGH TO SLAKE YOUR THIRST FOR KNOWLEDGE?
BECAUSE IF NOT...
...STRIKE ME DOWN.
I NEED YOU AT MY SIDE. UNFAILINGLY. UNFLINCHINGLY.
UNQUESTIONABLY. FOR WHAT COMES NEXT...I WILL NEED EVERY SWORD IN ASGARD AT MY SIDE.
I WILL RULE OVER A DIVIDED HOUSE NO LONGER. MAKE YOUR STAND NOW, HEIMDALL.
AND USE YOUR ALL-SIGHT TO SEE WHAT HAPPENS IF YOU STAND AGAINST ME.
GOOD, SOLDIER.
GOOD.

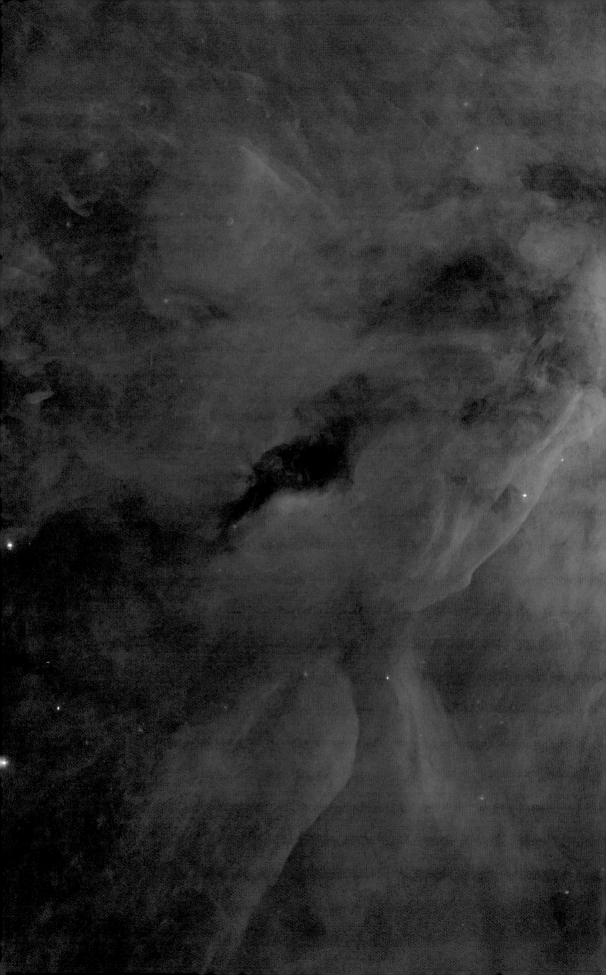

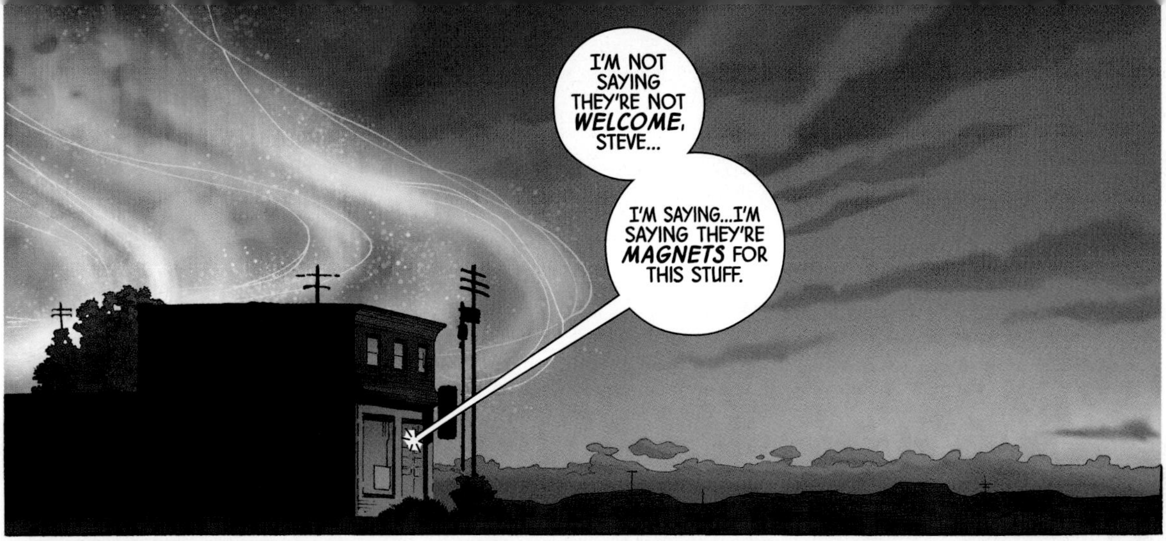
I'M NOT SAYING THEY'RE NOT WELCOME, STEVE...
I'M SAYING...I'M SAYING THEY'RE MAGNETS FOR THIS STUFF.

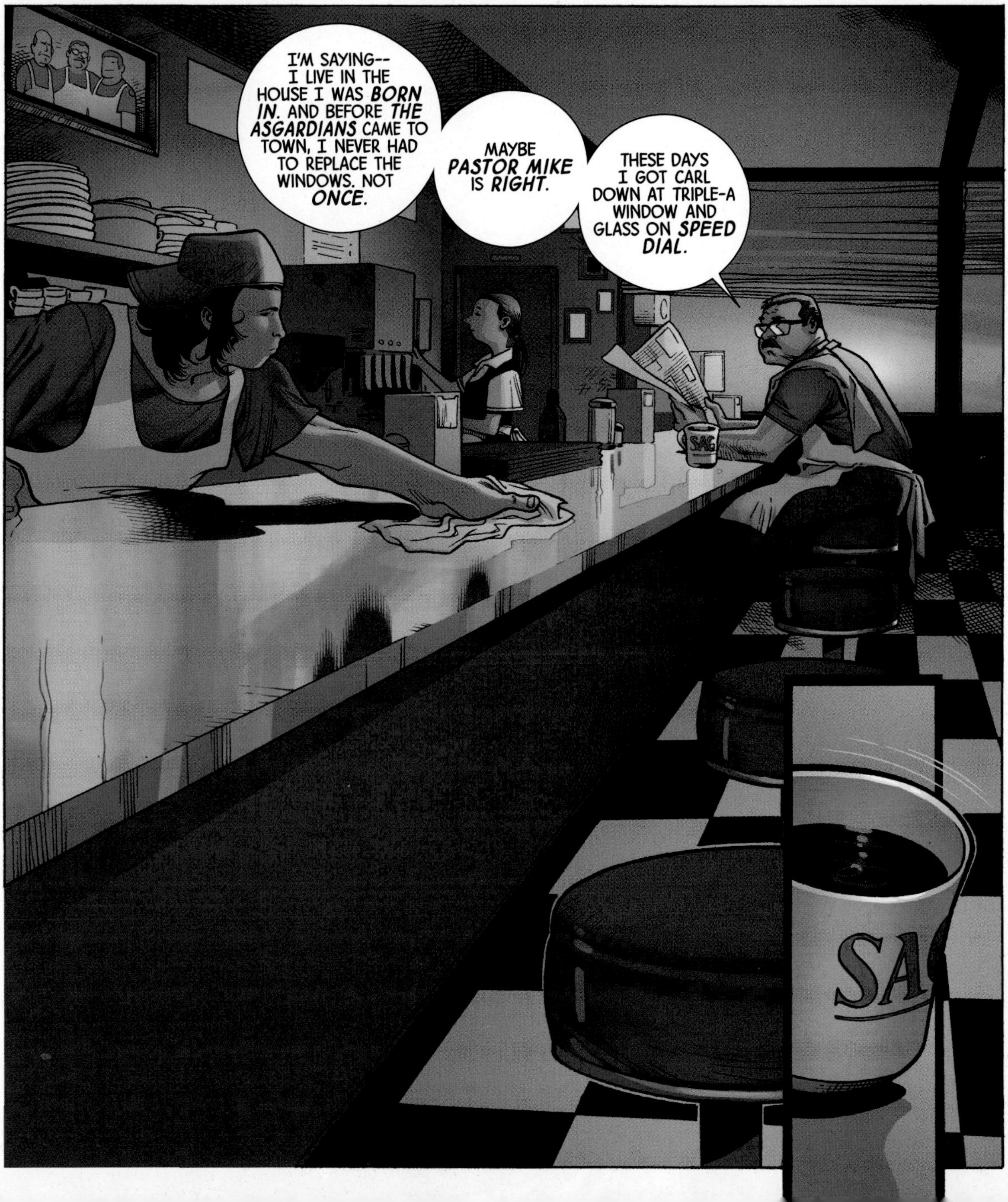
I'M SAYING-- I LIVE IN THE HOUSE I WAS BORN IN. AND BEFORE THE ASGARDIANS CAME TO TOWN, I NEVER HAD TO REPLACE THE WINDOWS. NOT ONCE.
MAYBE PASTOR MIKE IS RIGHT.
THESE DAYS I GOT CARL DOWN AT TRIPLE-A WINDOW AND GLASS ON SPEED DIAL.
SAG

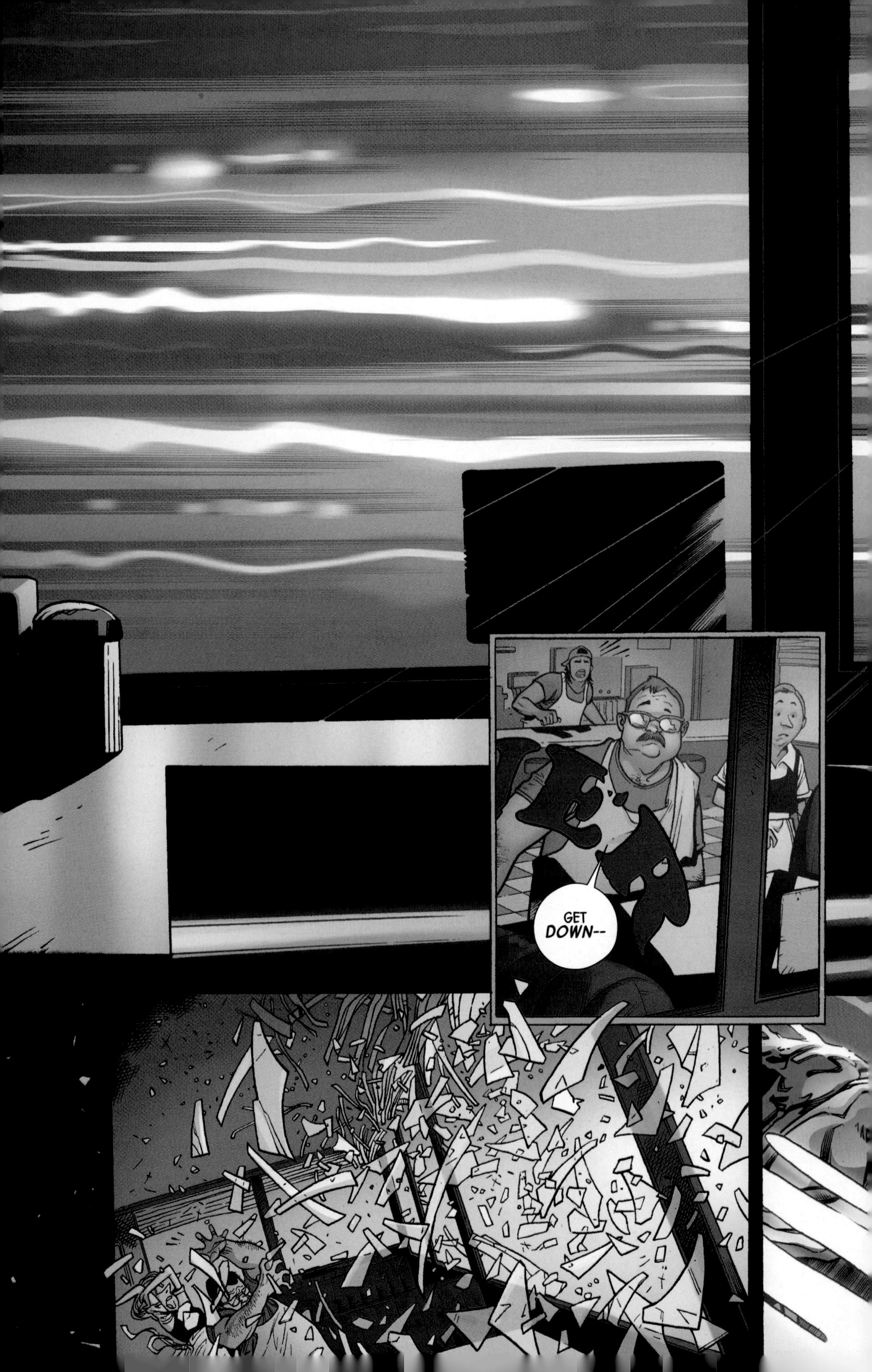
GET DOWN--

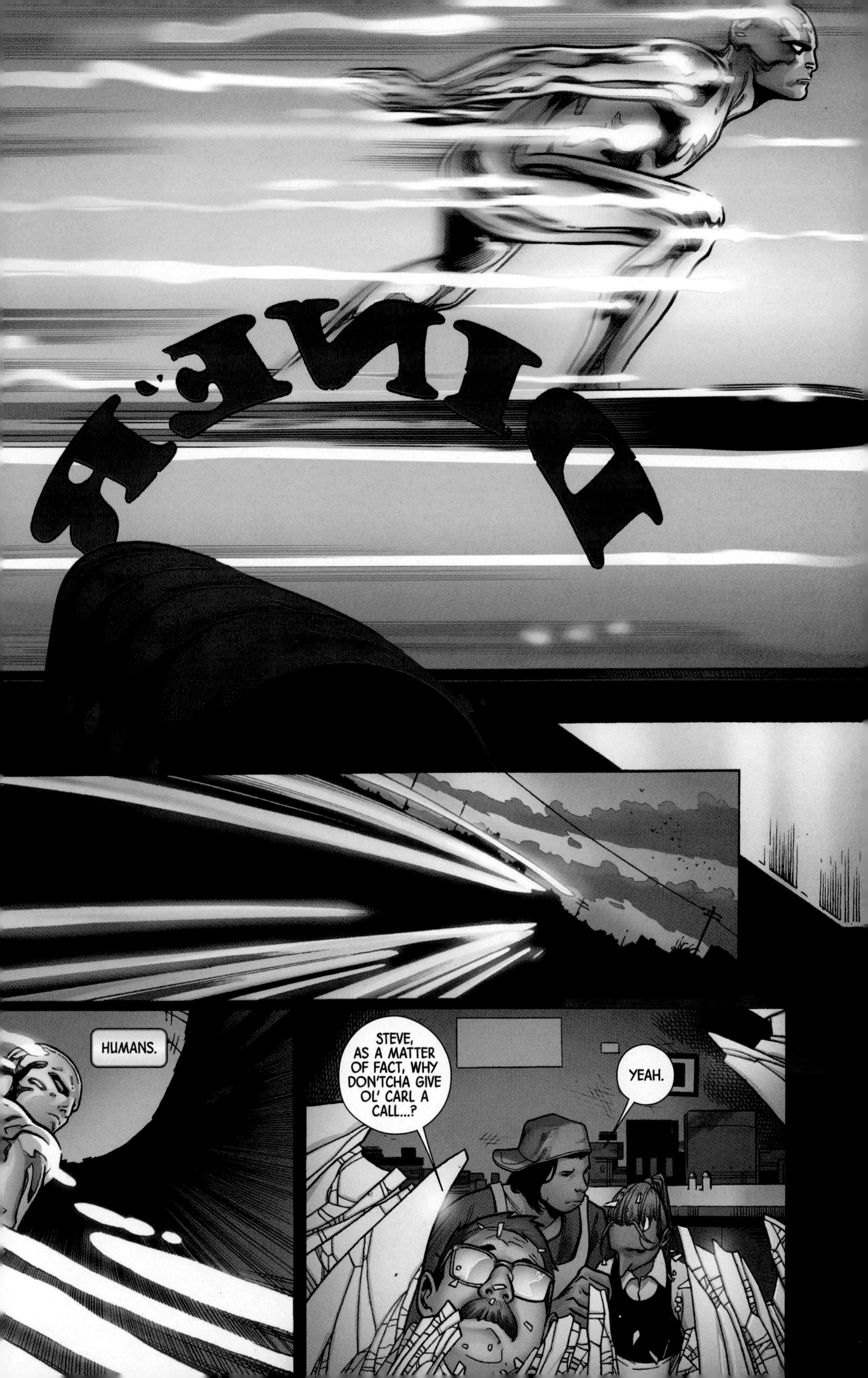
HUMANS.
STEVE, AS A MATTER OF FACT, WHY DON'TCHA GIVE OL' CARL A CALL...?
YEAH.

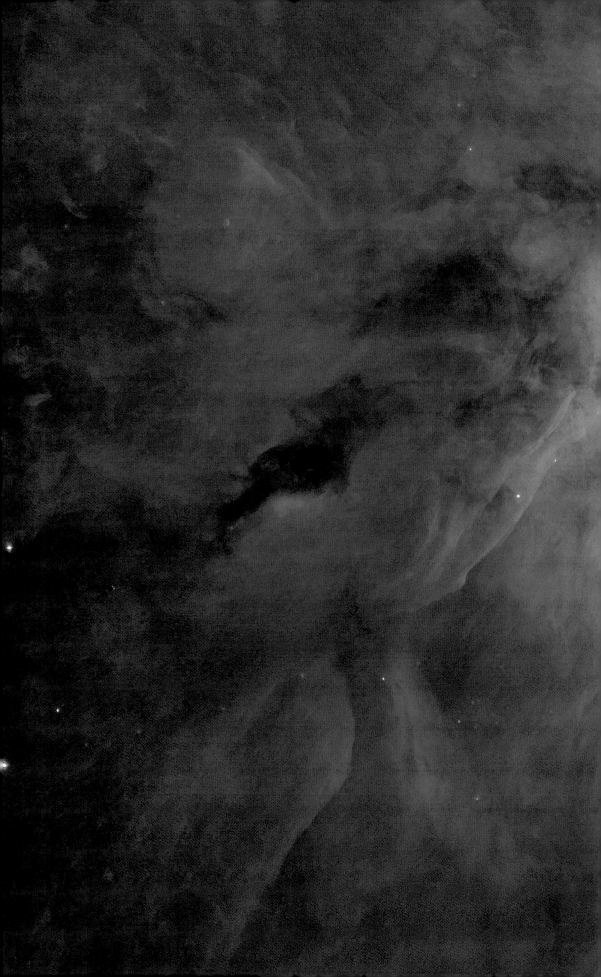

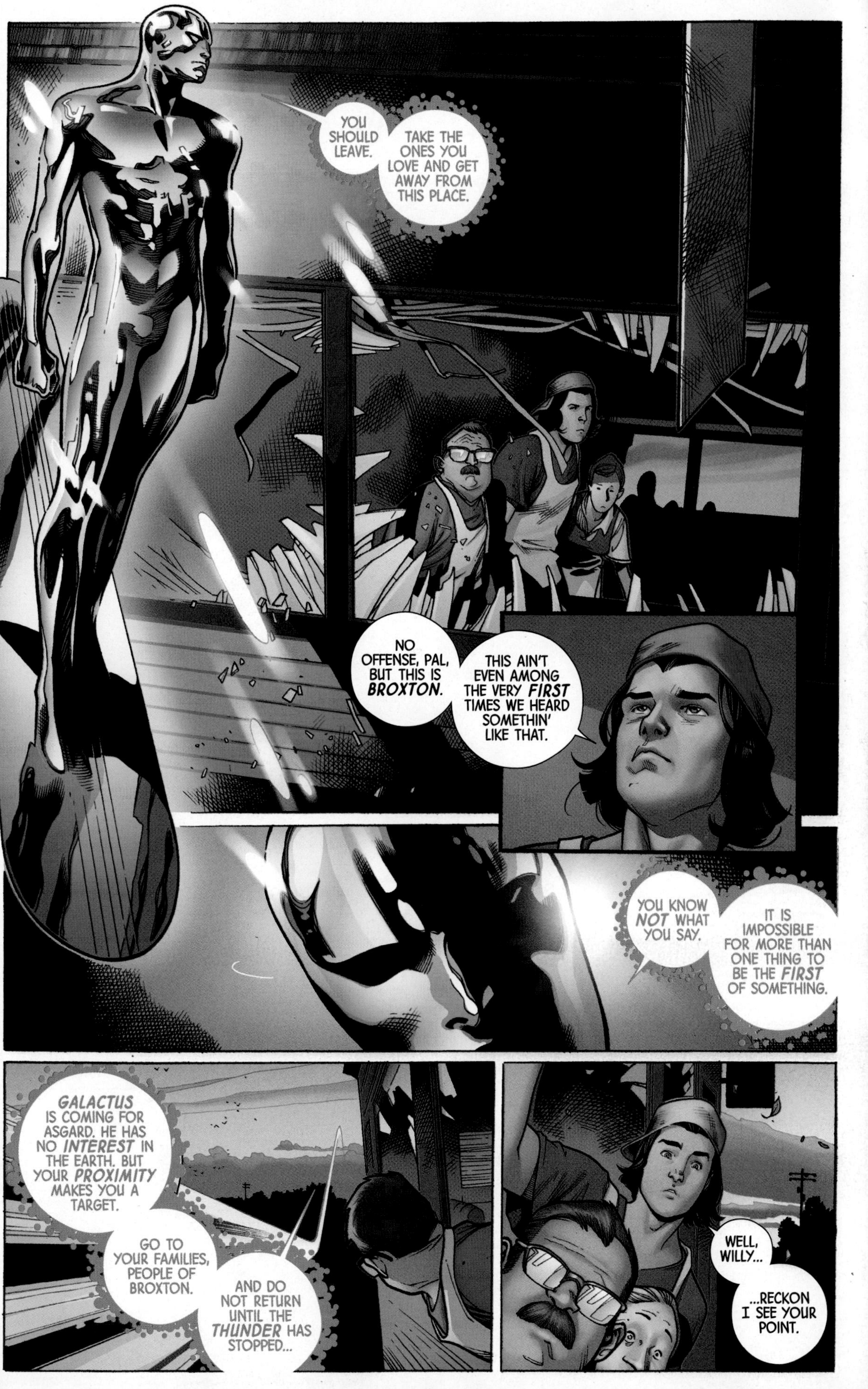
YOU SHOULD LEAVE.
TAKE THE ONES YOU LOVE AND GET AWAY FROM THIS PLACE.
NO OFFENSE, PAL, BUT THIS IS BROXTON.
THIS AIN'T EVEN AMONG THE VERY FIRST TIMES WE HEARD SOMETHIN' LIKE THAT.
YOU KNOW NOT WHAT YOU SAY.
IT IS IMPOSSIBLE FOR MORE THAN ONE THING TO BE THE FIRST OF SOMETHING.
GALACTUS IS COMING FOR ASGARD. HE HAS NO INTEREST IN THE EARTH. BUT YOUR PROXIMITY MAKES YOU A TARGET.
GO TO YOUR FAMILIES, PEOPLE OF BROXTON.
AND DO NOT RETURN UNTIL THE THUNDER HAS STOPPED...
WELL, WILLY...
...RECKON I SEE YOUR POINT.

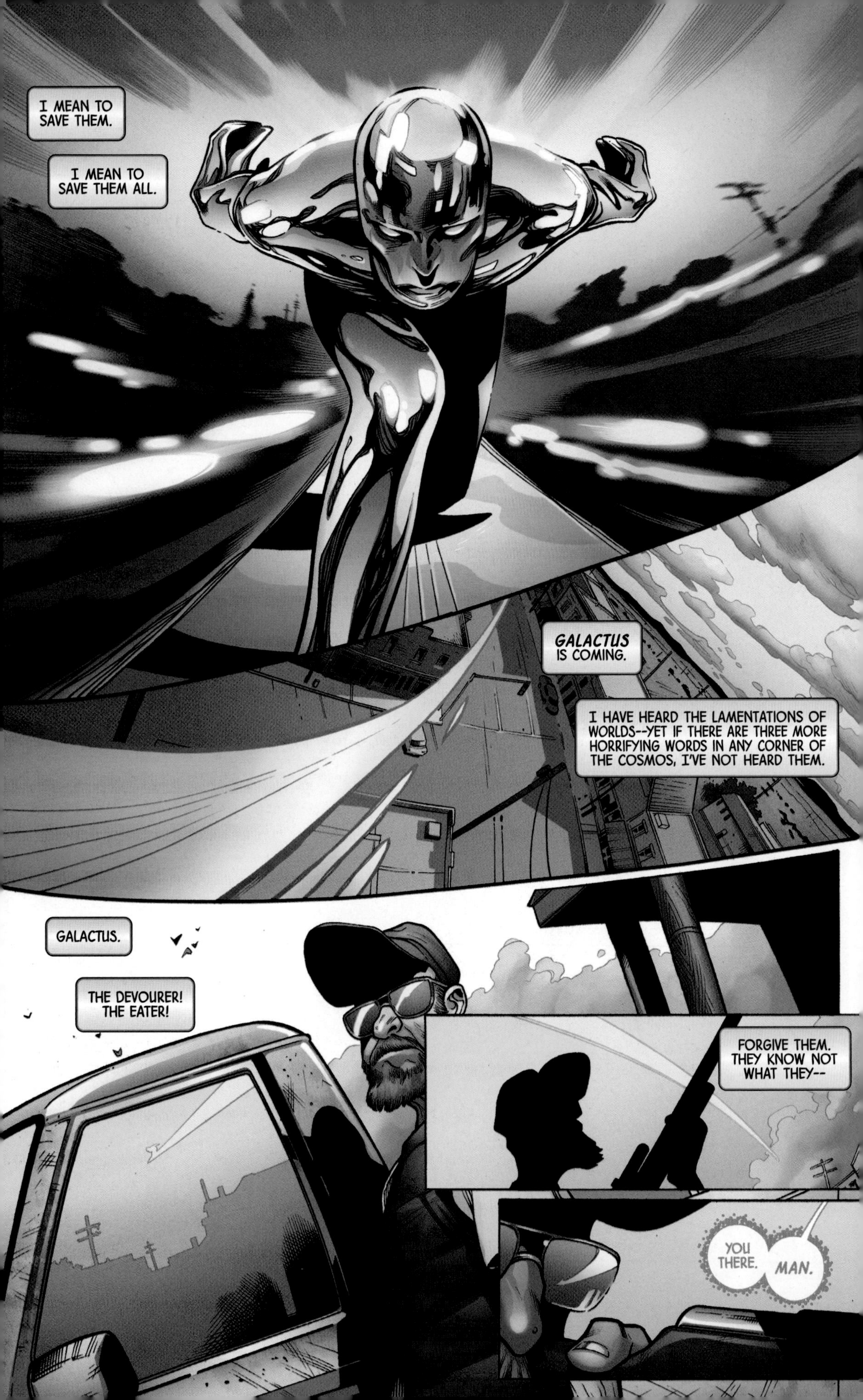

I MEAN TO SAVE THEM.
I MEAN TO SAVE THEM ALL.
GALACTUS IS COMING.
I HAVE HEARD THE LAMENTATIONS OF WORLDS--YET IF THERE ARE THREE MORE HORRIFYING WORDS IN ANY CORNER OF THE COSMOS, I'VE NOT HEARD THEM.
GALACTUS.
THE DEVOURER! THE EATER!
FORGIVE THEM. THEY KNOW NOT WHAT THEY--
YOU THERE.
MAN.

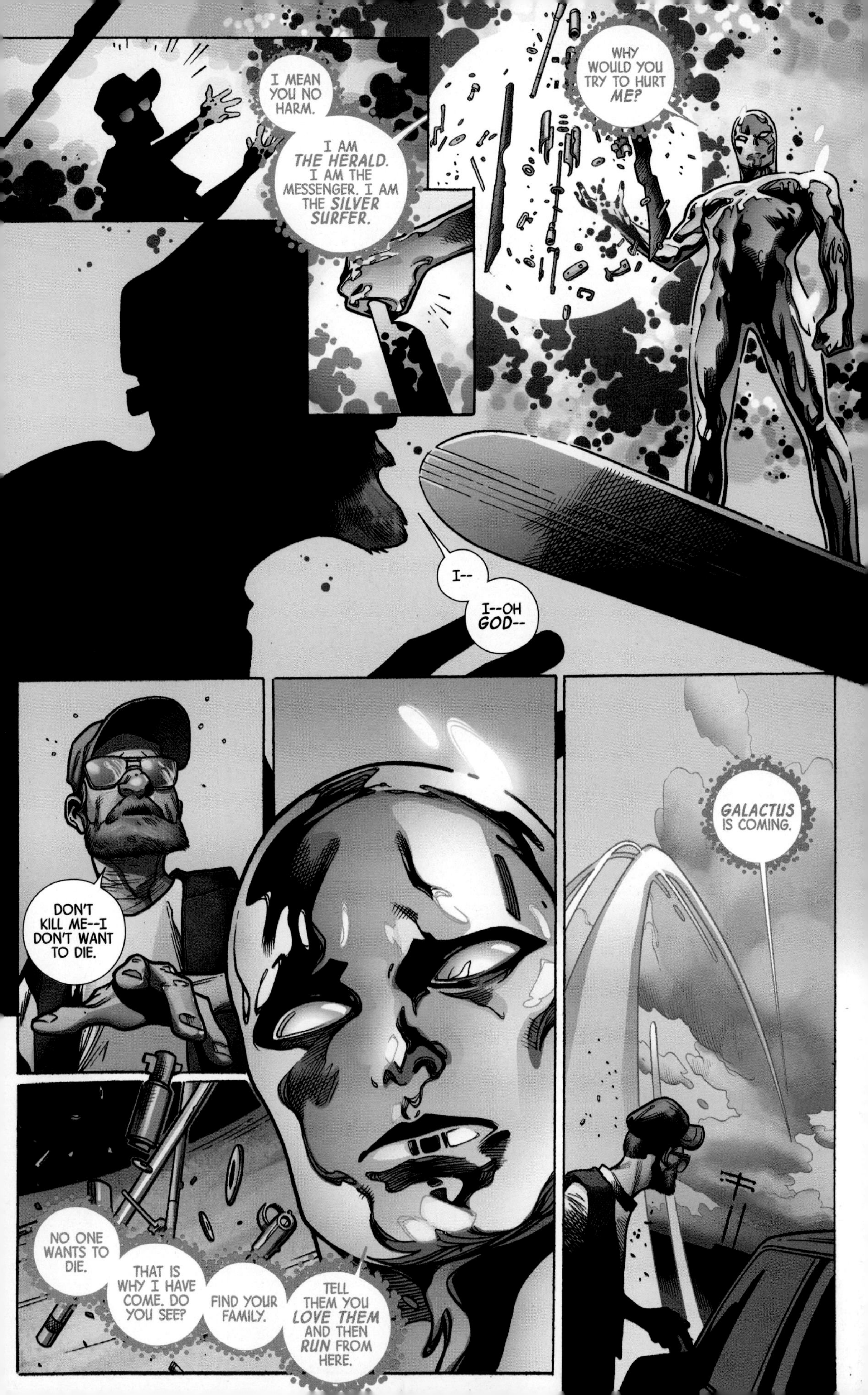
I MEAN YOU NO HARM.
I AM THE HERALD. I AM THE MESSENGER. I AM THE SILVER SURFER.
WHY WOULD YOU TRY TO HURT ME?
I--
I--OH GOD--
DON'T KILL ME--I DON'T WANT TO DIE.
NO ONE WANTS TO DIE.
THAT IS WHY I HAVE COME. DO YOU SEE?
FIND YOUR FAMILY.
TELL THEM YOU LOVE THEM AND THEN RUN FROM HERE.
GALACTUS IS COMING.

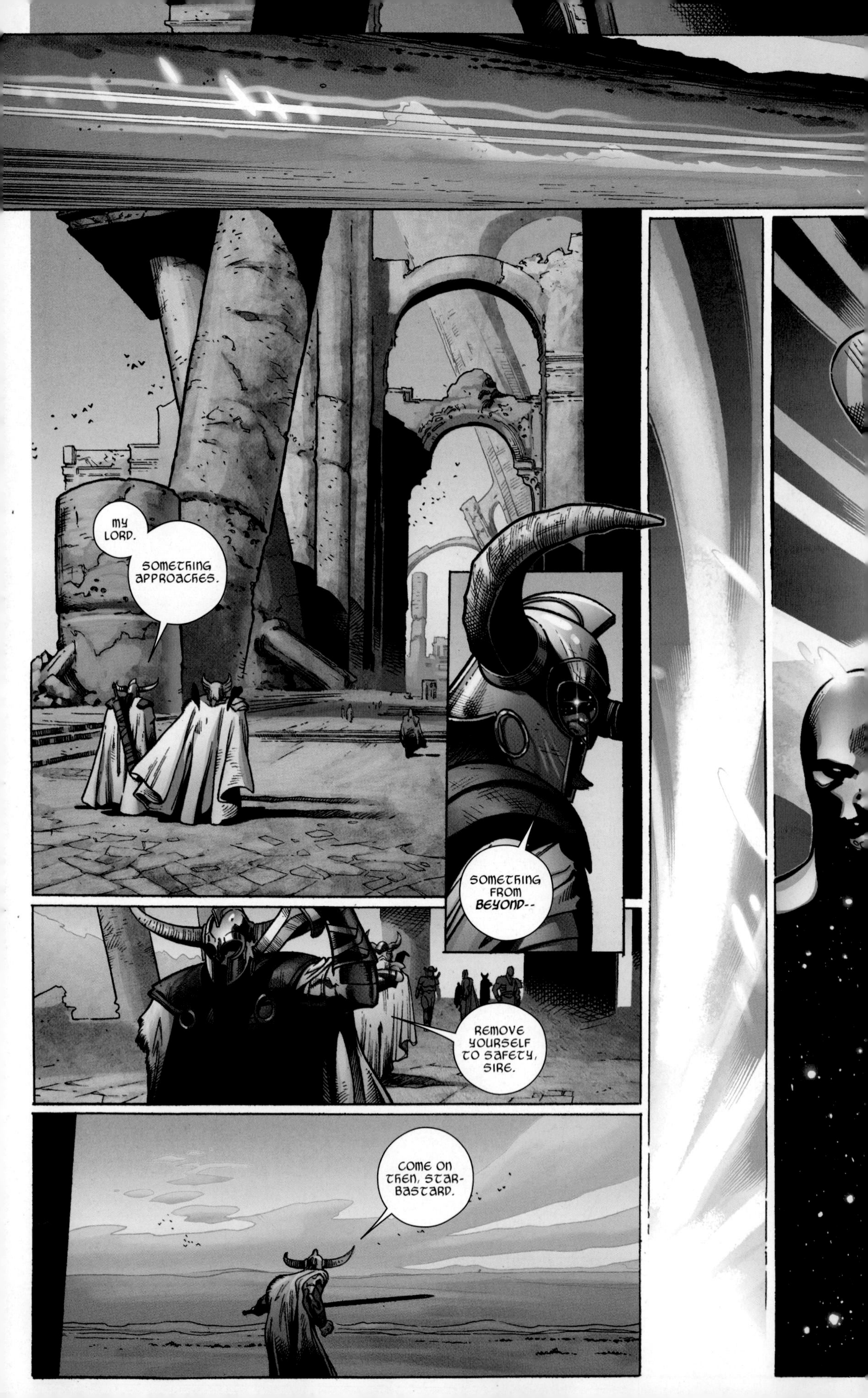
MY LORD.
SOMETHING APPROACHES.
SOMETHING FROM BEYOND--
REMOVE YOURSELF TO SAFETY, SIRE.
COME ON THEN, STAR-BASTARD.

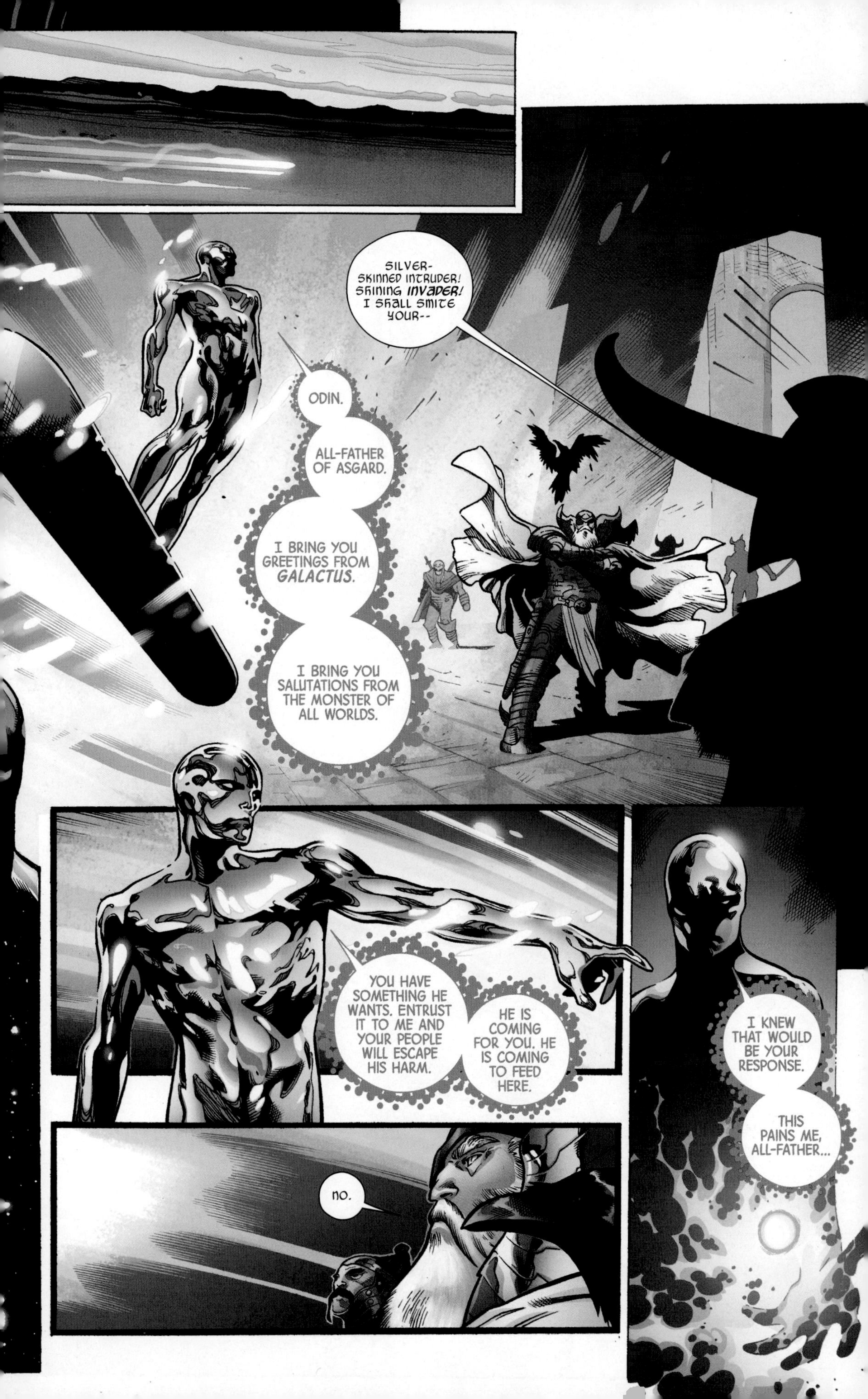
SILVER-SKINNED INTRUDER! SHINING INVADER! I SHALL SMITE YOUR--
ODIN.
ALL-FATHER OF ASGARD.
I BRING YOU GREETINGS FROM GALACTUS.
I BRING YOU SALUTATIONS FROM THE MONSTER OF ALL WORLDS.
YOU HAVE SOMETHING HE WANTS. ENTRUST IT TO ME AND YOUR PEOPLE WILL ESCAPE HIS HARM.
HE IS COMING FOR YOU. HE IS COMING TO FEED HERE.
no.
I KNEW THAT WOULD BE YOUR RESPONSE.
THIS PAINS ME, ALL-FATHER...

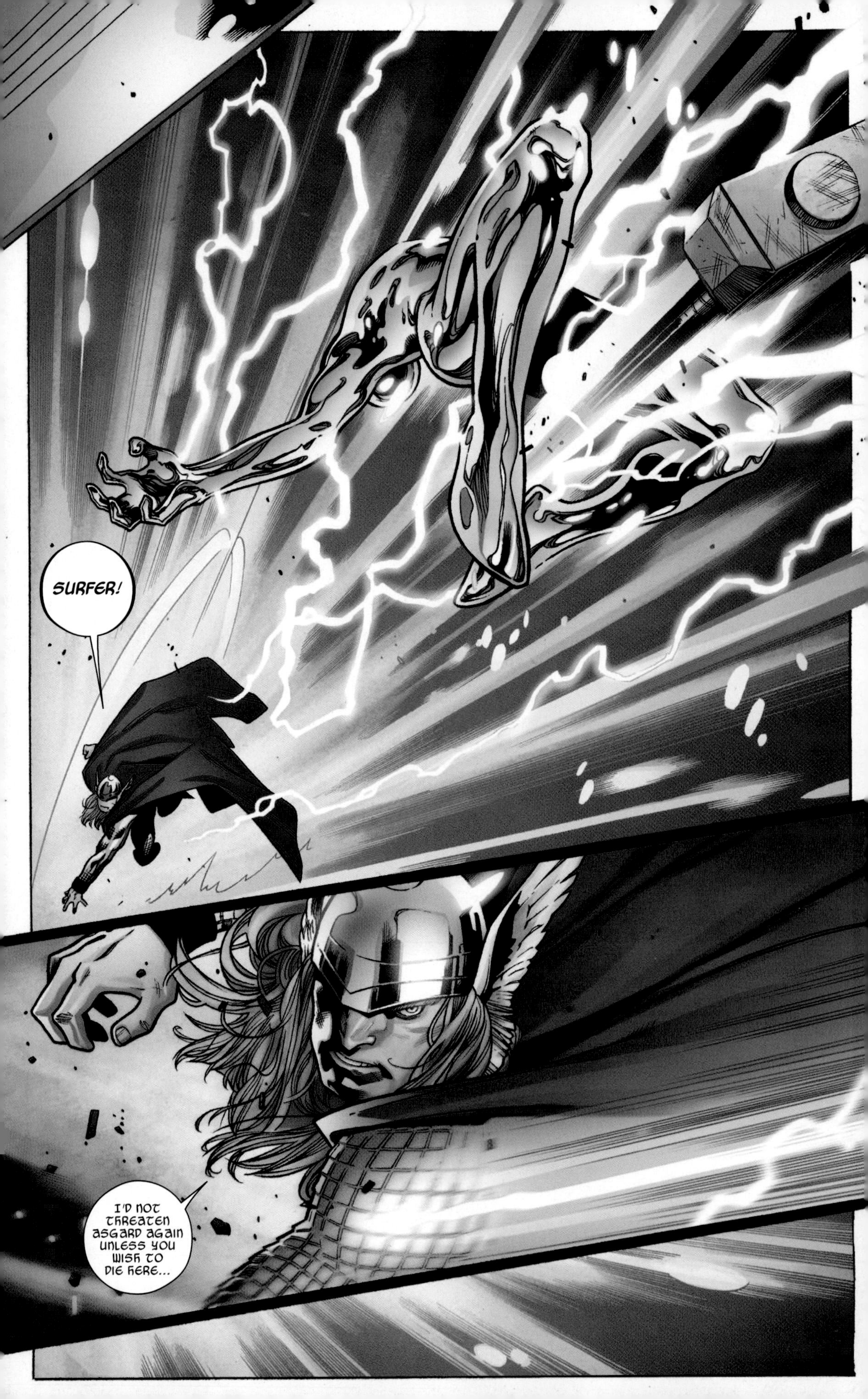
SURFER!
I'D NOT THREATEN ASGARD AGAIN UNLESS YOU WISH TO DIE HERE...

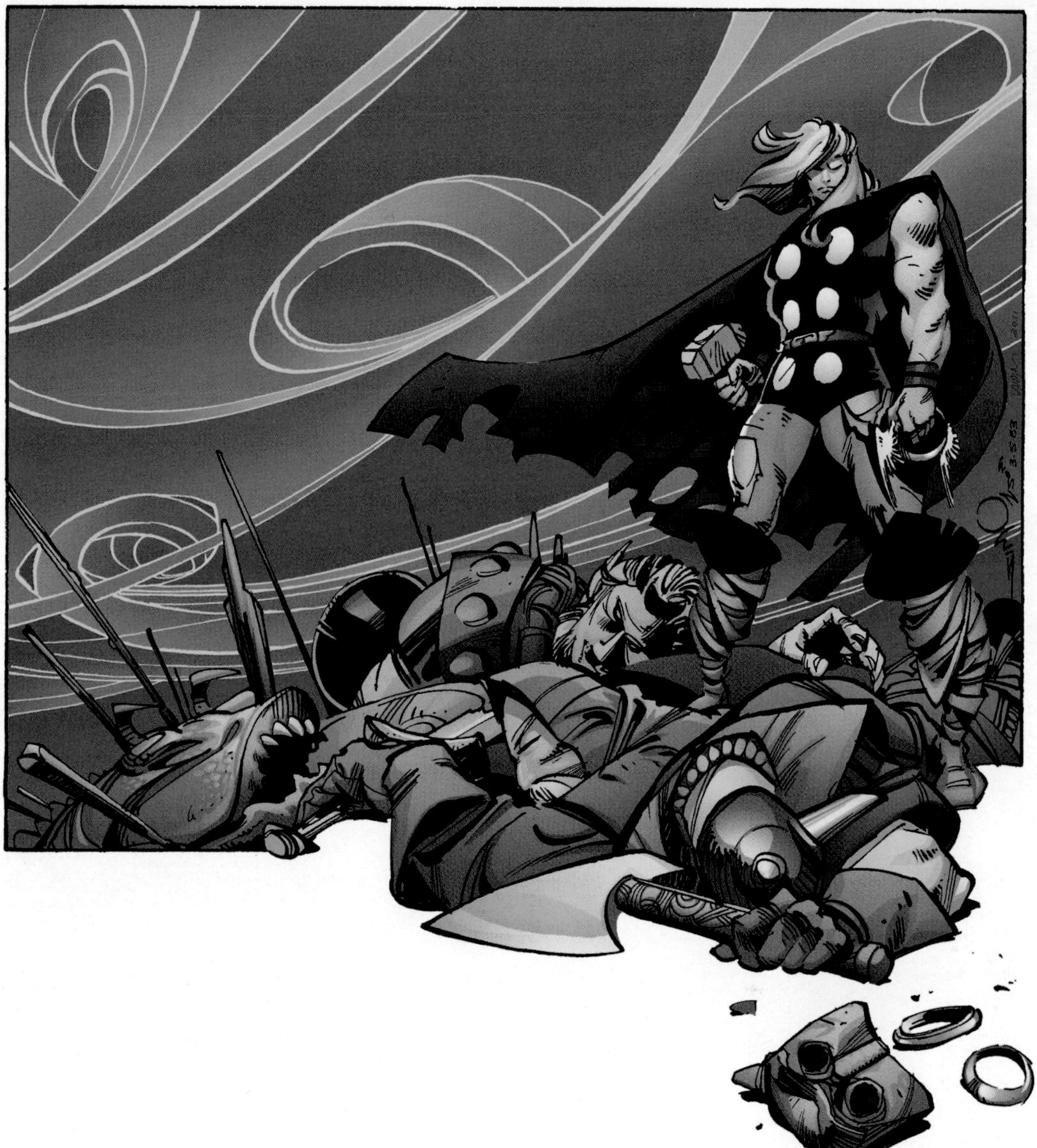

#1 VARIANT BY **WALTER SIMONSON & LAURA MARTIN**

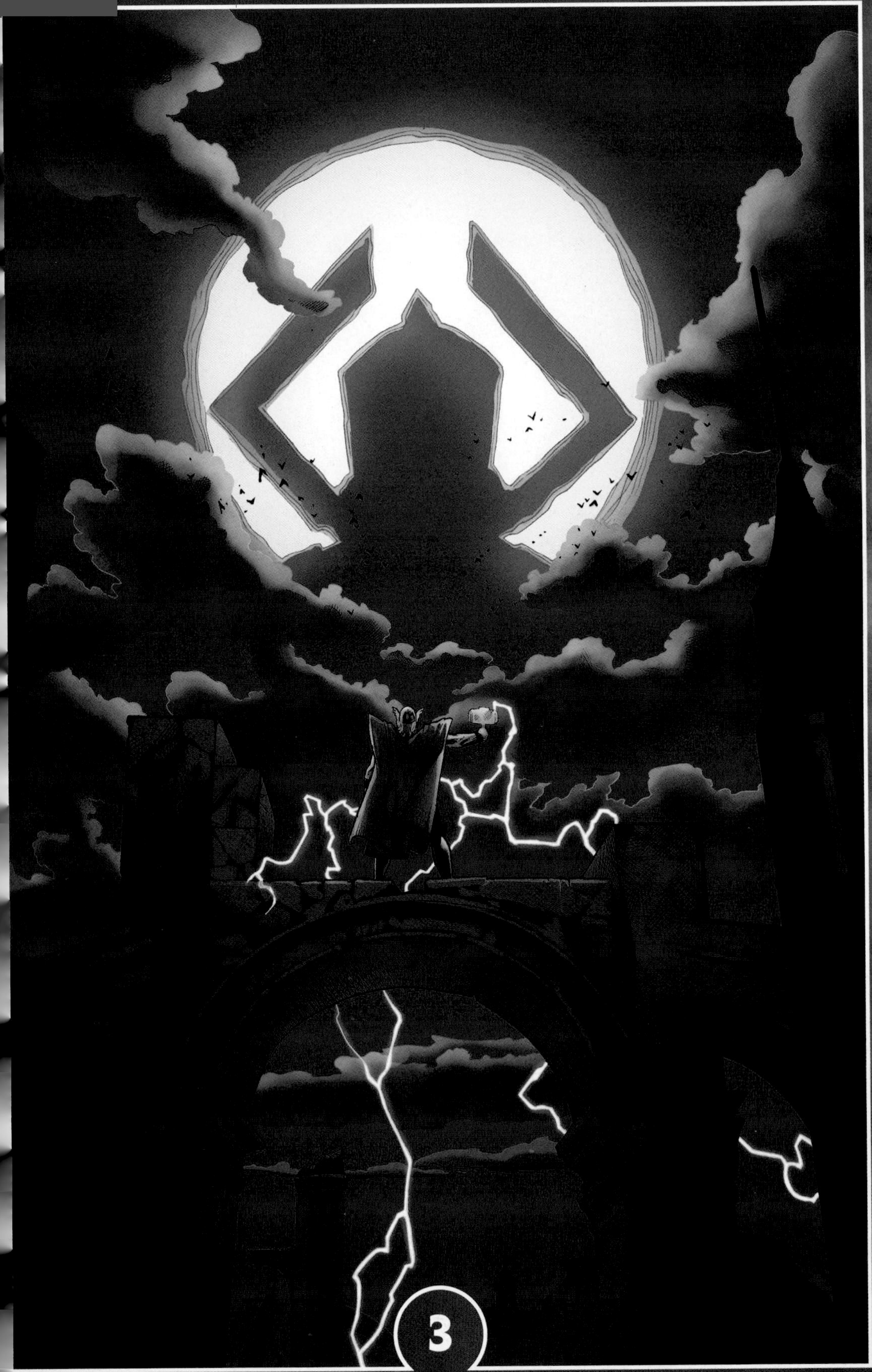
3

THE GALACTUS SEED 3: THE STRANGER

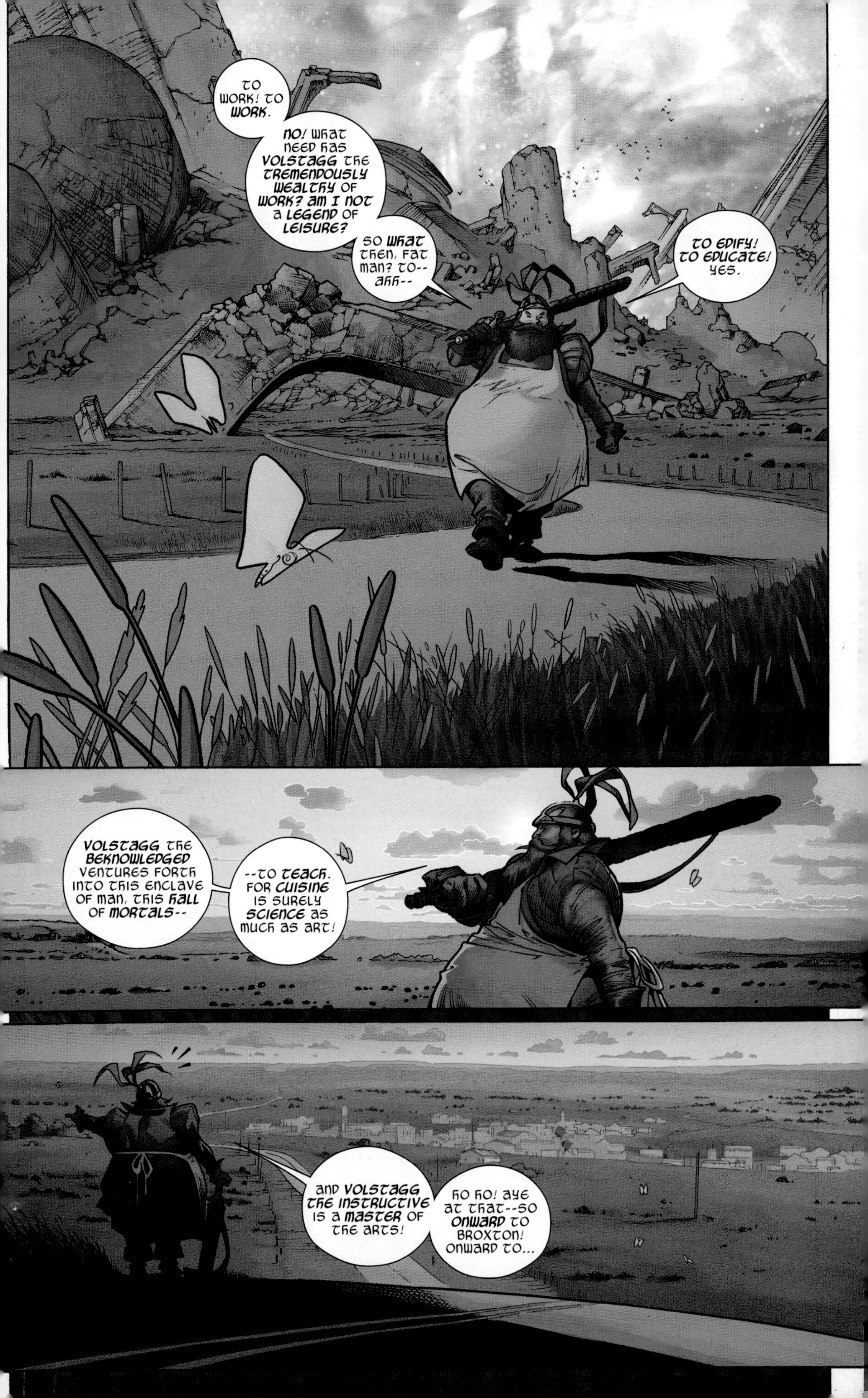
TO WORK! TO WORK.
NO! WHAT NEED HAS VOLSTAGG THE TREMENDOUSLY WEALTHY OF WORK? AM I NOT A LEGEND OF LEISURE?
SO WHAT THEN, FAT MAN? TO-- AHH--
TO EDIFY! TO EDUCATE! YES.
VOLSTAGG THE BEKNOWLEDGED VENTURES FORTH INTO THIS ENCLAVE OF MAN, THIS HALL OF MORTALS--
--TO TEACH. FOR CUISINE IS SURELY SCIENCE AS MUCH AS ART!
AND VOLSTAGG THE INSTRUCTIVE IS A MASTER OF THE ARTS!
HO HO! AYE AT THAT--SO ONWARD TO BROXTON! ONWARD TO...

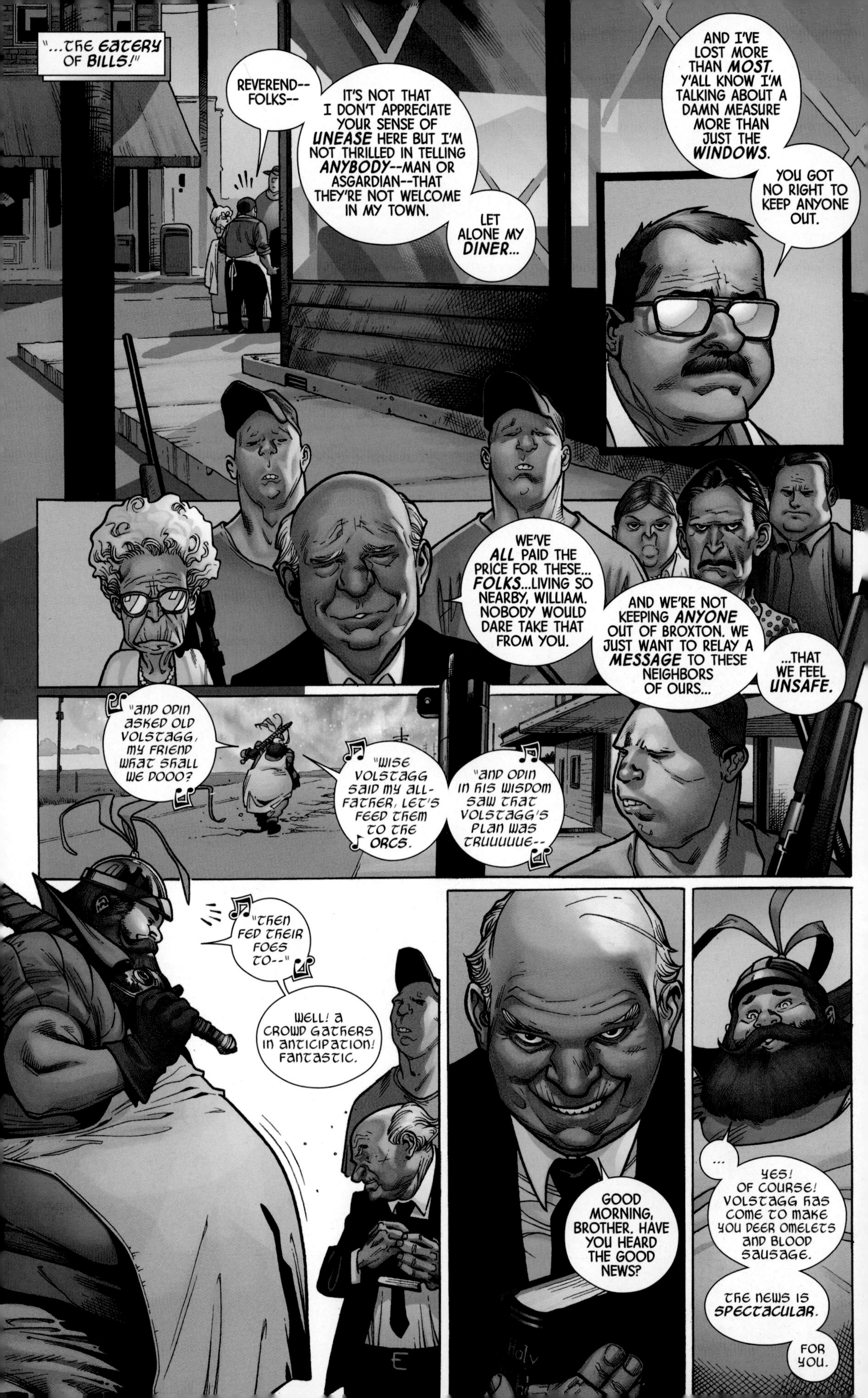
"...THE EATERY OF BILLS!"
REVEREND-- FOLKS--
IT'S NOT THAT I DON'T APPRECIATE YOUR SENSE OF UNEASE HERE BUT I'M NOT THRILLED IN TELLING ANYBODY--MAN OR ASGARDIAN--THAT THEY'RE NOT WELCOME IN MY TOWN.
LET ALONE MY DINER...
AND I'VE LOST MORE THAN MOST. Y'ALL KNOW I'M TALKING ABOUT A DAMN MEASURE MORE THAN JUST THE WINDOWS.
YOU GOT NO RIGHT TO KEEP ANYONE OUT.
WE'VE ALL PAID THE PRICE FOR THESE... FOLKS...LIVING SO NEARBY, WILLIAM. NOBODY WOULD DARE TAKE THAT FROM YOU.
AND WE'RE NOT KEEPING ANYONE OUT OF BROXTON. WE JUST WANT TO RELAY A MESSAGE TO THESE NEIGHBORS OF OURS...
...THAT WE FEEL UNSAFE.
"AND ODIN ASKED OLD VOLSTAGG, MY FRIEND WHAT SHALL WE DOOO?
"WISE VOLSTAGG SAID MY ALL-FATHER, LET'S FEED THEM TO THE ORCS.
"AND ODIN IN HIS WISDOM SAW THAT VOLSTAGG'S PLAN WAS TRUUUUUE--
"THEN FED THEIR FOES TO--"
WELL! A CROWD GATHERS IN ANTICIPATION! FANTASTIC.
GOOD MORNING, BROTHER. HAVE YOU HEARD THE GOOD NEWS?
...
YES! OF COURSE! VOLSTAGG HAS COME TO MAKE YOU DEER OMELETS AND BLOOD SAUSAGE.
THE NEWS IS SPECTACULAR.
FOR YOU.

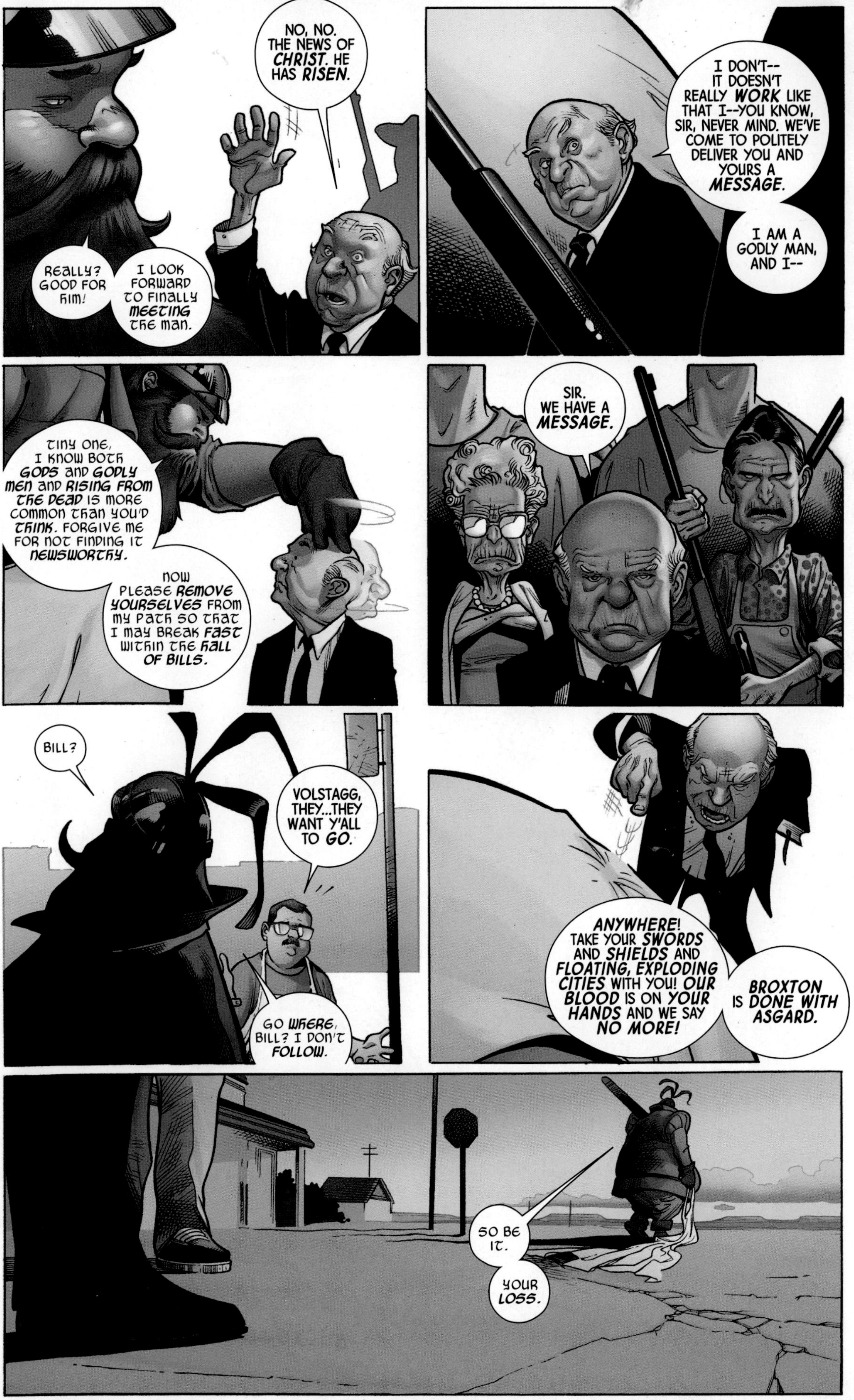
NO, NO. THE NEWS OF CHRIST. HE HAS RISEN.
REALLY? GOOD FOR HIM!
I LOOK FORWARD TO FINALLY MEETING THE MAN.
I DON'T-- IT DOESN'T REALLY WORK LIKE THAT I--YOU KNOW, SIR, NEVER MIND. WE'VE COME TO POLITELY DELIVER YOU AND YOURS A MESSAGE.
I AM A GODLY MAN, AND I--
TINY ONE, I KNOW BOTH GODS AND GODLY MEN AND RISING FROM THE DEAD IS MORE COMMON THAN YOU'D THINK. FORGIVE ME FOR NOT FINDING IT NEWSWORTHY.
NOW PLEASE REMOVE YOURSELVES FROM MY PATH SO THAT I MAY BREAK FAST WITHIN THE HALL OF BILLS.
SIR. WE HAVE A MESSAGE.
BILL?
VOLSTAGG, THEY...THEY WANT Y'ALL TO GO.
GO WHERE, BILL? I DON'T FOLLOW.
ANYWHERE! TAKE YOUR SWORDS AND SHIELDS AND FLOATING, EXPLODING CITIES WITH YOU! OUR BLOOD IS ON YOUR HANDS AND WE SAY NO MORE!
BROXTON IS DONE WITH ASGARD.
SO BE IT.
YOUR LOSS.

TOO LATE.

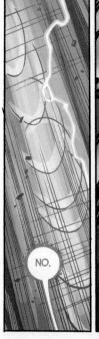

NO.

IT'S *NEVER* TOO LATE.

GGRRAA--

--WAIT--

--RRRAAAHH!

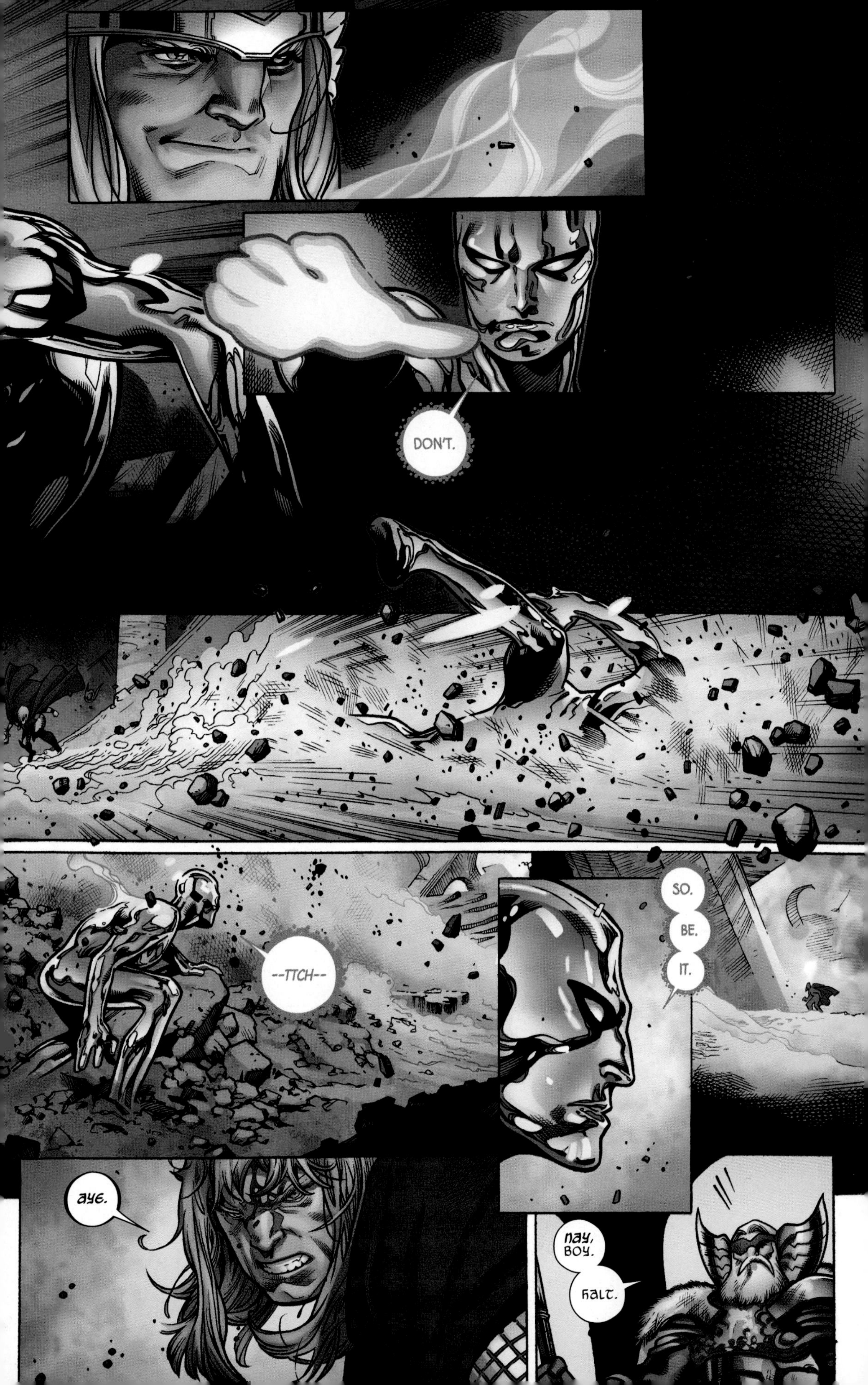
DON'T.
--TTCH--
SO.
BE.
IT.
AYE.
NAY, BOY.
HALT.

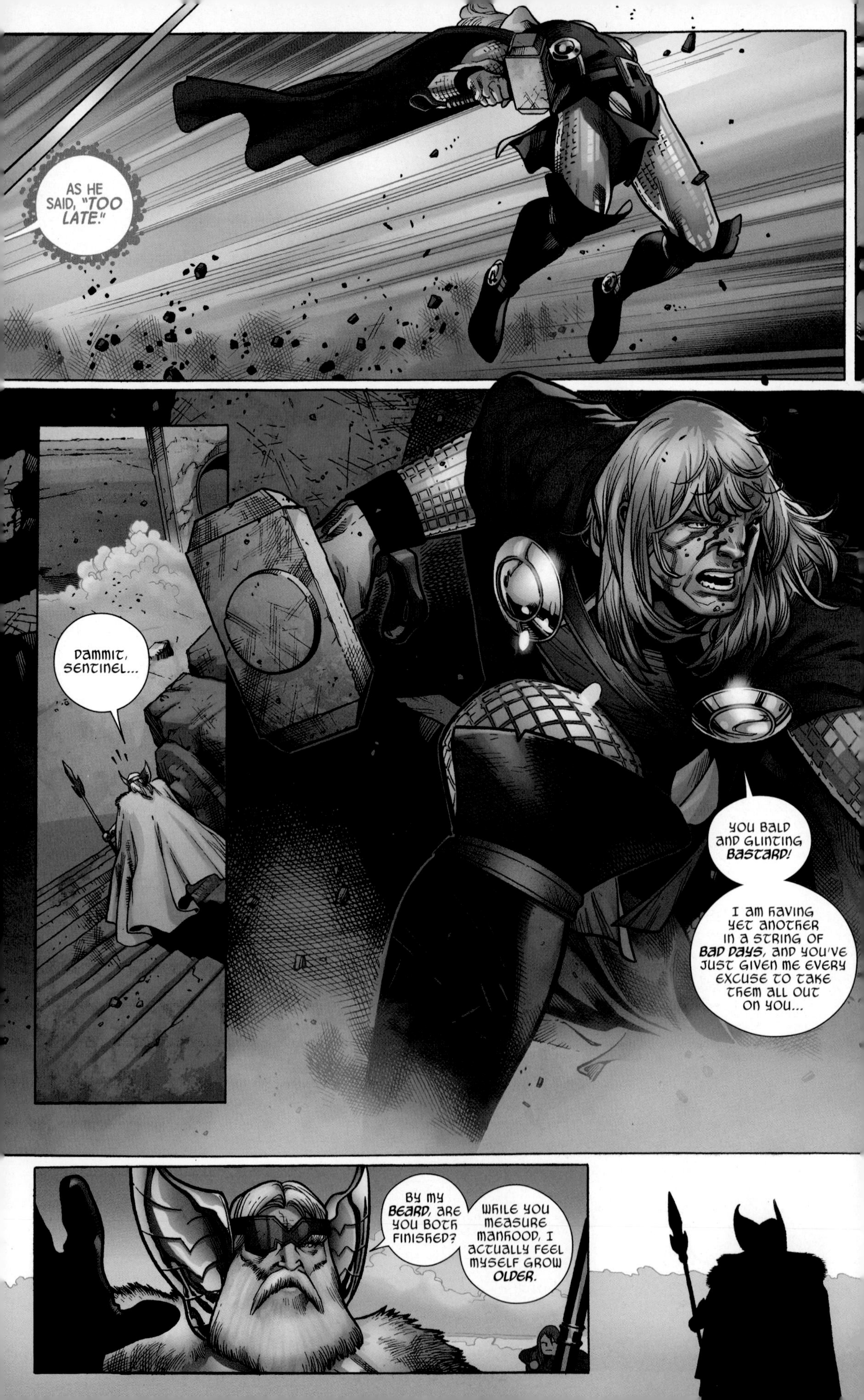
AS HE SAID, "TOO LATE."
DAMMIT, SENTINEL...
YOU BALD AND GLINTING BASTARD!
I AM HAVING YET ANOTHER IN A STRING OF BAD DAYS, AND YOU'VE JUST GIVEN ME EVERY EXCUSE TO TAKE THEM ALL OUT ON YOU...
BY MY BEARD, ARE YOU BOTH FINISHED?
WHILE YOU MEASURE MANHOOD, I ACTUALLY FEEL MYSELF GROW OLDER.

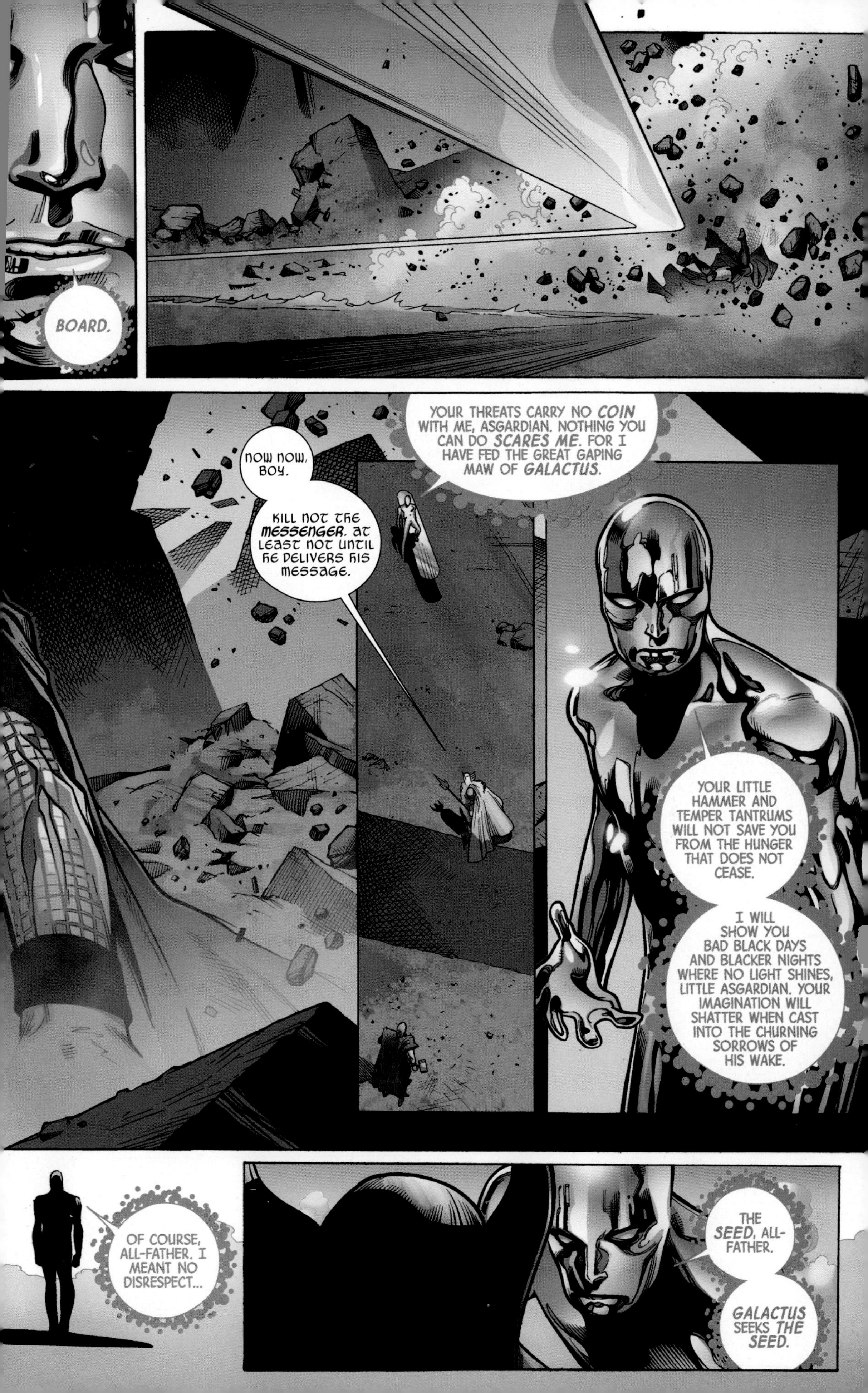
BOARD.
NOW NOW, BOY.
KILL NOT THE MESSENGER. AT LEAST NOT UNTIL HE DELIVERS HIS MESSAGE.
YOUR THREATS CARRY NO COIN WITH ME, ASGARDIAN. NOTHING YOU CAN DO SCARES ME. FOR I HAVE FED THE GREAT GAPING MAW OF GALACTUS.
YOUR LITTLE HAMMER AND TEMPER TANTRUMS WILL NOT SAVE YOU FROM THE HUNGER THAT DOES NOT CEASE.
I WILL SHOW YOU BAD BLACK DAYS AND BLACKER NIGHTS WHERE NO LIGHT SHINES, LITTLE ASGARDIAN. YOUR IMAGINATION WILL SHATTER WHEN CAST INTO THE CHURNING SORROWS OF HIS WAKE.
OF COURSE, ALL-FATHER. I MEANT NO DISRESPECT...
THE SEED, ALL-FATHER.
GALACTUS SEEKS THE SEED.

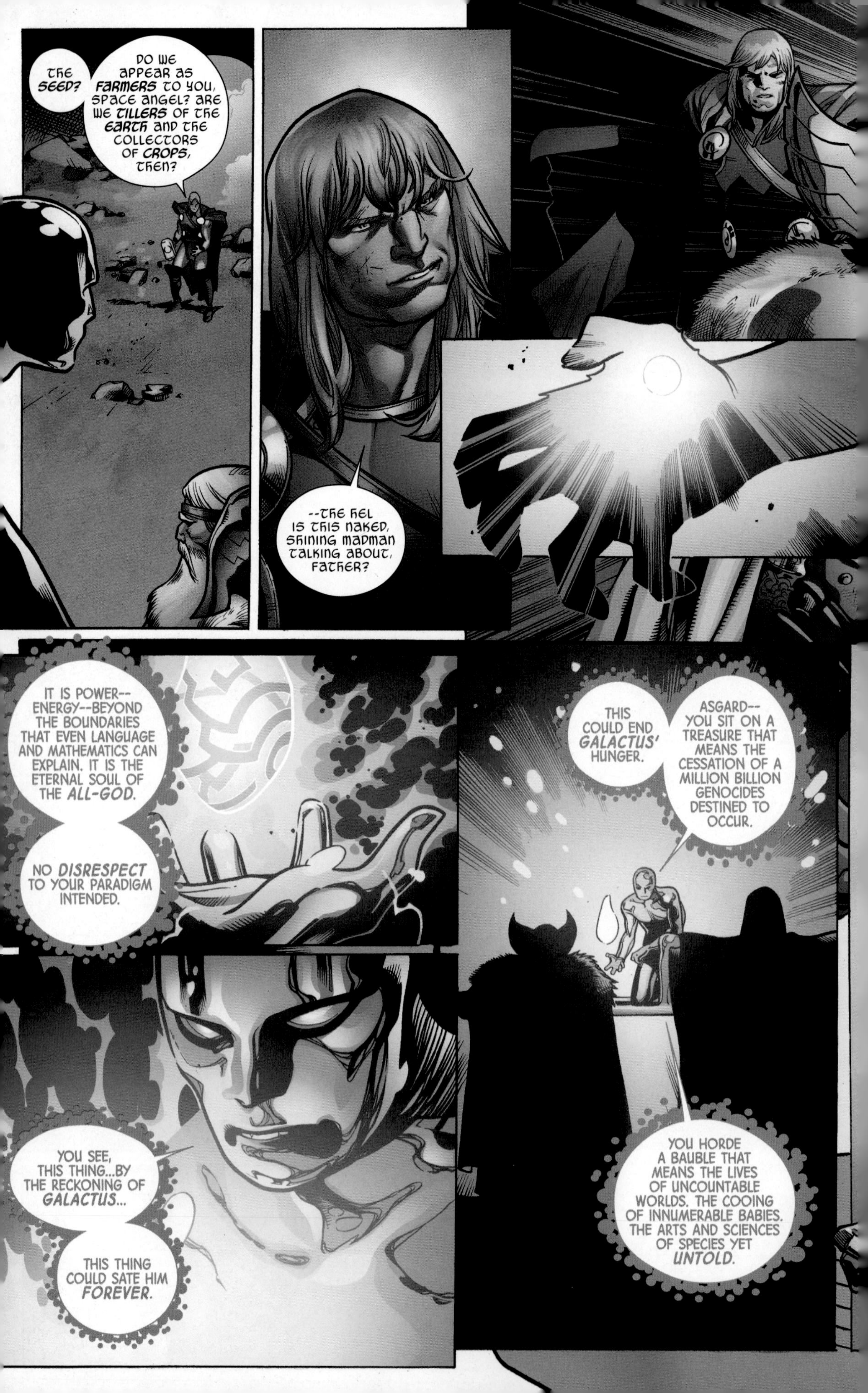
THE SEED?
DO WE APPEAR AS FARMERS TO YOU, SPACE ANGEL? ARE WE TILLERS OF THE EARTH AND THE COLLECTORS OF CROPS, THEN?
--THE HEL IS THIS NAKED, SHINING MADMAN TALKING ABOUT, FATHER?
IT IS POWER--ENERGY--BEYOND THE BOUNDARIES THAT EVEN LANGUAGE AND MATHEMATICS CAN EXPLAIN. IT IS THE ETERNAL SOUL OF THE ALL-GOD.
NO DISRESPECT TO YOUR PARADIGM INTENDED.
YOU SEE, THIS THING...BY THE RECKONING OF GALACTUS...
THIS THING COULD SATE HIM FOREVER.
THIS COULD END GALACTUS' HUNGER.
ASGARD--YOU SIT ON A TREASURE THAT MEANS THE CESSATION OF A MILLION BILLION GENOCIDES DESTINED TO OCCUR.
YOU HORDE A BAUBLE THAT MEANS THE LIVES OF UNCOUNTABLE WORLDS, THE COOING OF INNUMERABLE BABIES. THE ARTS AND SCIENCES OF SPECIES YET UNTOLD.

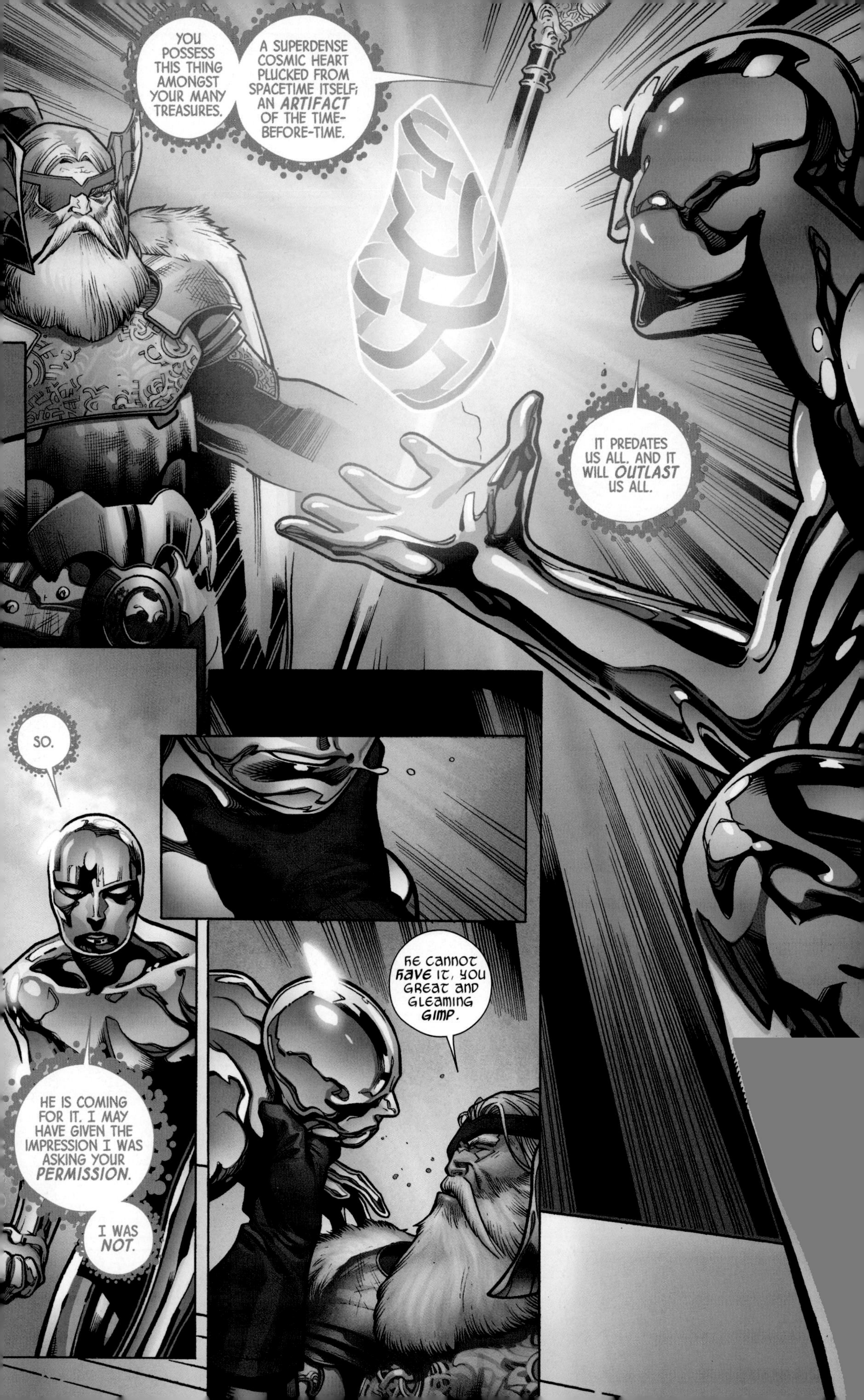
YOU POSSESS THIS THING AMONGST YOUR MANY TREASURES.
A SUPERDENSE COSMIC HEART PLUCKED FROM SPACETIME ITSELF; AN ARTIFACT OF THE TIME-BEFORE-TIME.
IT PREDATES US ALL. AND IT WILL OUTLAST US ALL.
SO.
HE IS COMING FOR IT. I MAY HAVE GIVEN THE IMPRESSION I WAS ASKING YOUR PERMISSION.
I WAS NOT.
HE CANNOT HAVE IT, YOU GREAT AND GLEAMING GIMP.

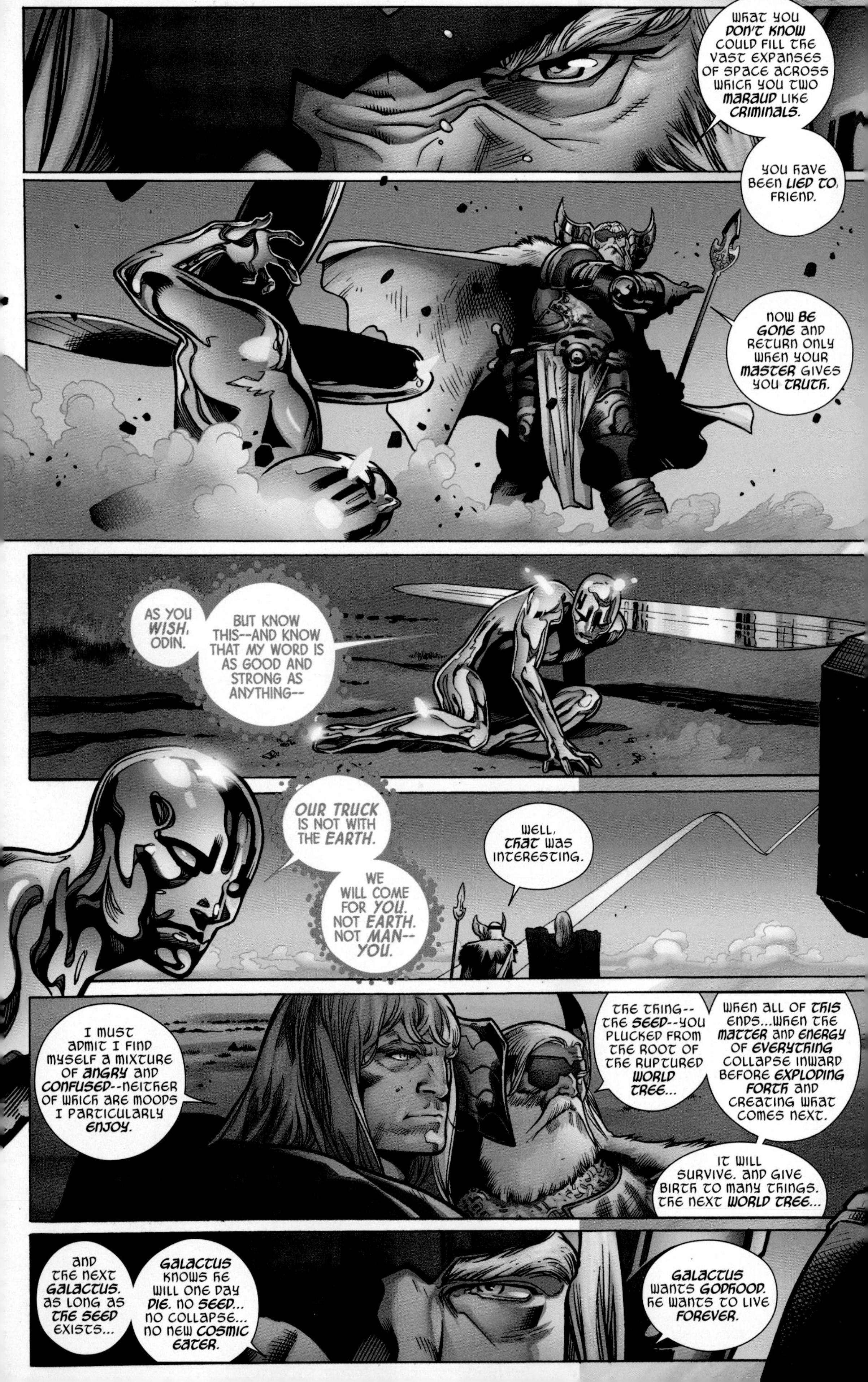
WHAT YOU DON'T KNOW COULD FILL THE VAST EXPANSES OF SPACE ACROSS WHICH YOU TWO MARAUD LIKE CRIMINALS.
YOU HAVE BEEN LIED TO, FRIEND.
NOW BE GONE AND RETURN ONLY WHEN YOUR MASTER GIVES YOU TRUTH.
AS YOU WISH, ODIN.
BUT KNOW THIS--AND KNOW THAT MY WORD IS AS GOOD AND STRONG AS ANYTHING--
OUR TRUCK IS NOT WITH THE EARTH.
WE WILL COME FOR YOU. NOT EARTH. NOT MAN--YOU.
WELL, THAT WAS INTERESTING.
I MUST ADMIT I FIND MYSELF A MIXTURE OF ANGRY AND CONFUSED--NEITHER OF WHICH ARE MOODS I PARTICULARLY ENJOY.
THE THING--THE SEED--YOU PLUCKED FROM THE ROOT OF THE RUPTURED WORLD TREE...
WHEN ALL OF THIS ENDS...WHEN THE MATTER AND ENERGY OF EVERYTHING COLLAPSE INWARD BEFORE EXPLODING FORTH AND CREATING WHAT COMES NEXT.
IT WILL SURVIVE. AND GIVE BIRTH TO MANY THINGS. THE NEXT WORLD TREE...
AND THE NEXT GALACTUS. AS LONG AS THE SEED EXISTS...
GALACTUS KNOWS HE WILL ONE DAY DIE. NO SEED... NO COLLAPSE... NO NEW COSMIC EATER.
GALACTUS WANTS GODHOOD. HE WANTS TO LIVE FOREVER.

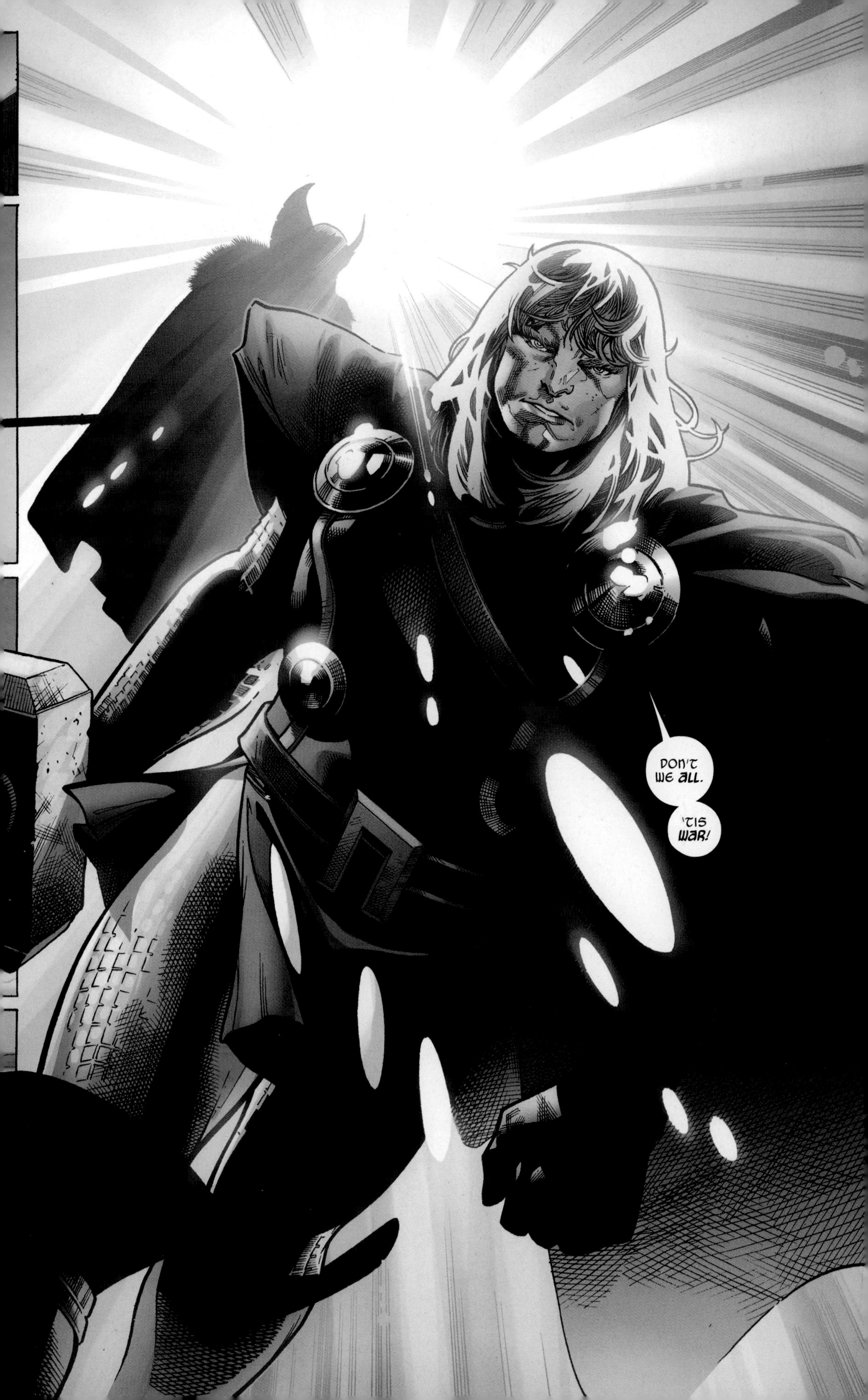
DON'T WE ALL.
'TIS WAR!

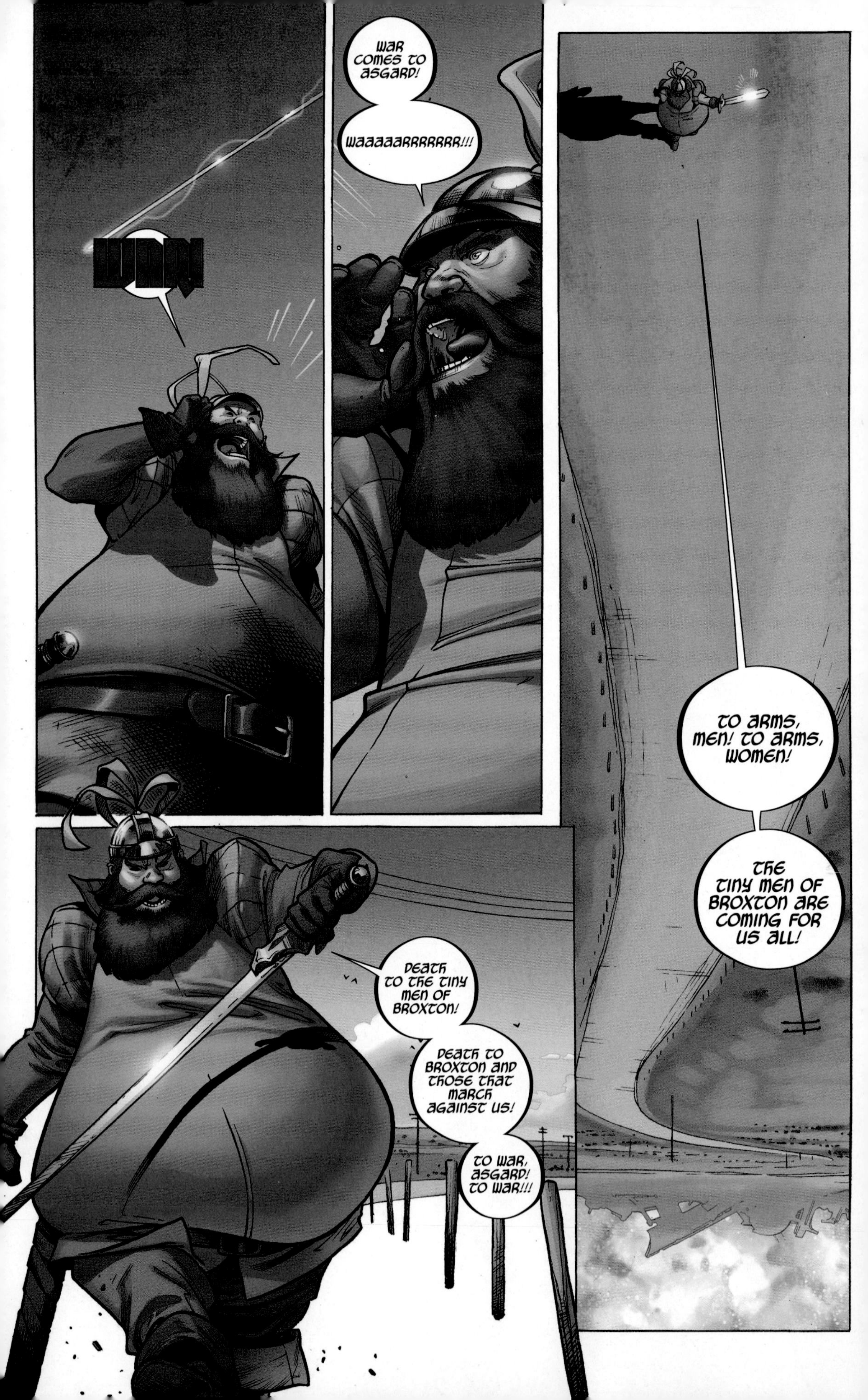
WAR!
WAR COMES TO ASGARD!
WAAAAARRRRRRR!!!
TO ARMS, MEN! TO ARMS, WOMEN!
THE TINY MEN OF BROXTON ARE COMING FOR US ALL!
DEATH TO THE TINY MEN OF BROXTON!
DEATH TO BROXTON AND THOSE THAT MARCH AGAINST US!
TO WAR, ASGARD! TO WAR!!!

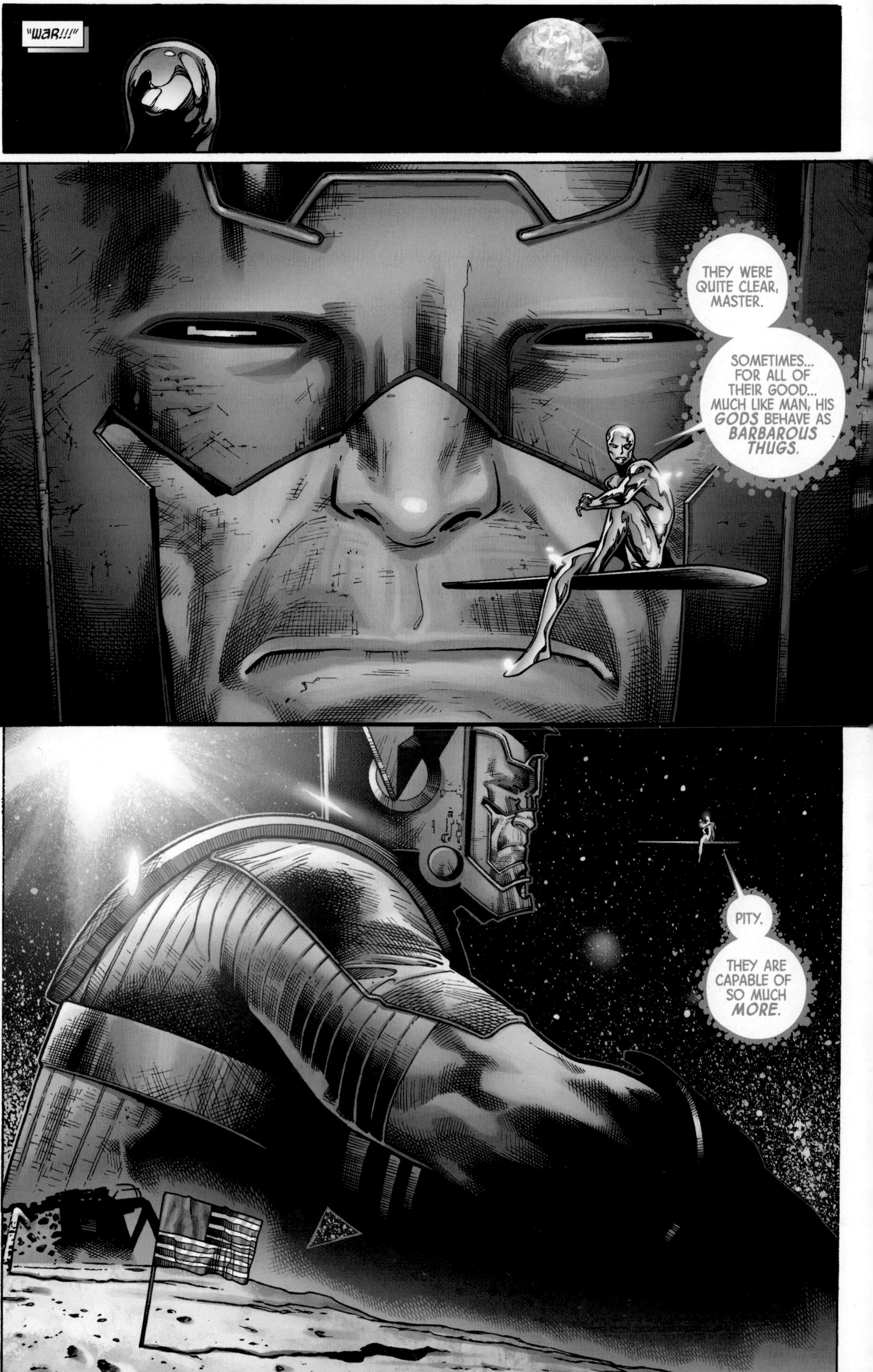
"WAR!!!"
THEY WERE QUITE CLEAR, MASTER.
SOMETIMES... FOR ALL OF THEIR GOOD... MUCH LIKE MAN, HIS GODS BEHAVE AS BARBAROUS THUGS.
PITY.
THEY ARE CAPABLE OF SO MUCH MORE.

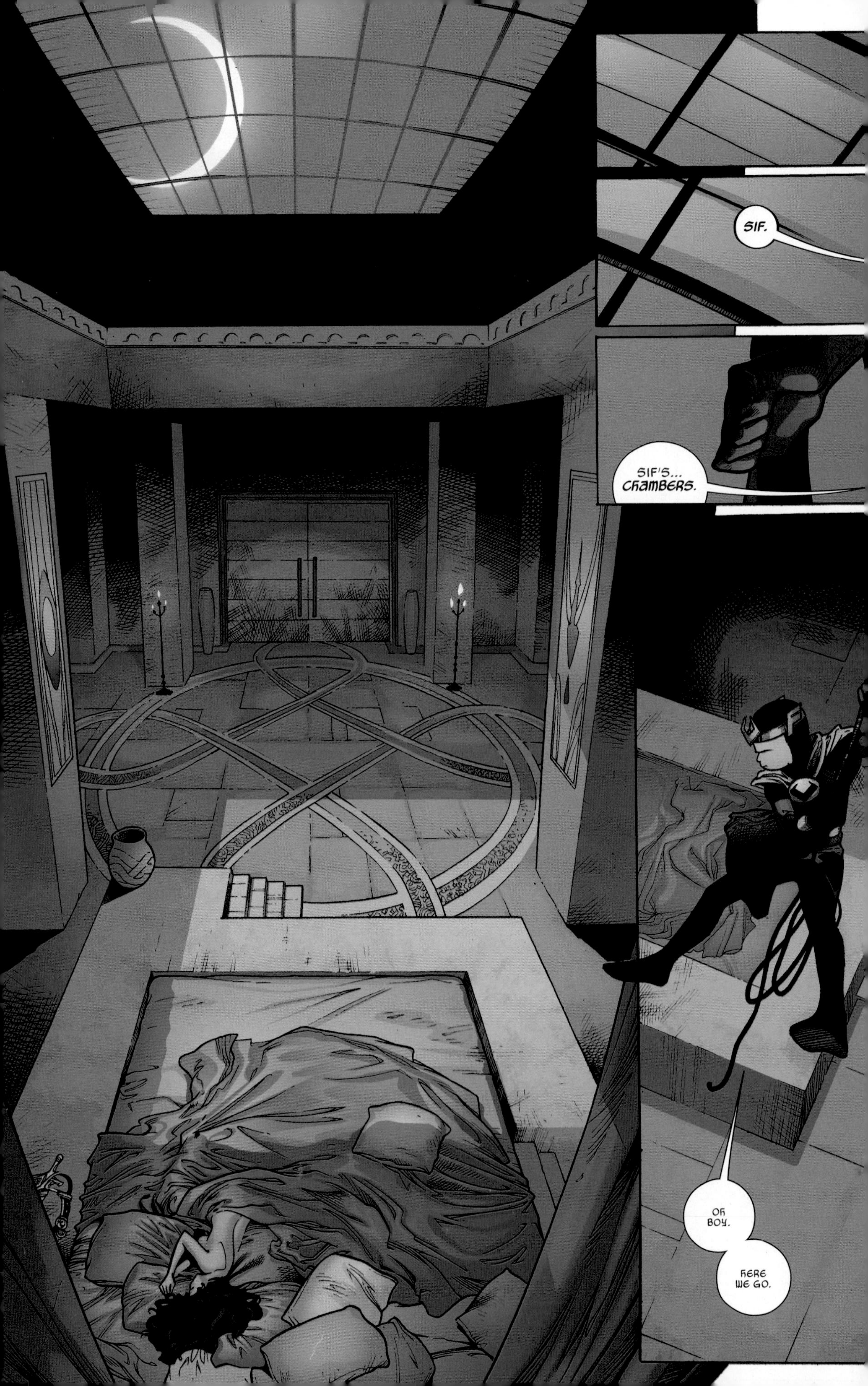
SIF.
SIF'S... CHAMBERS.
OH BOY.
HERE WE GO.

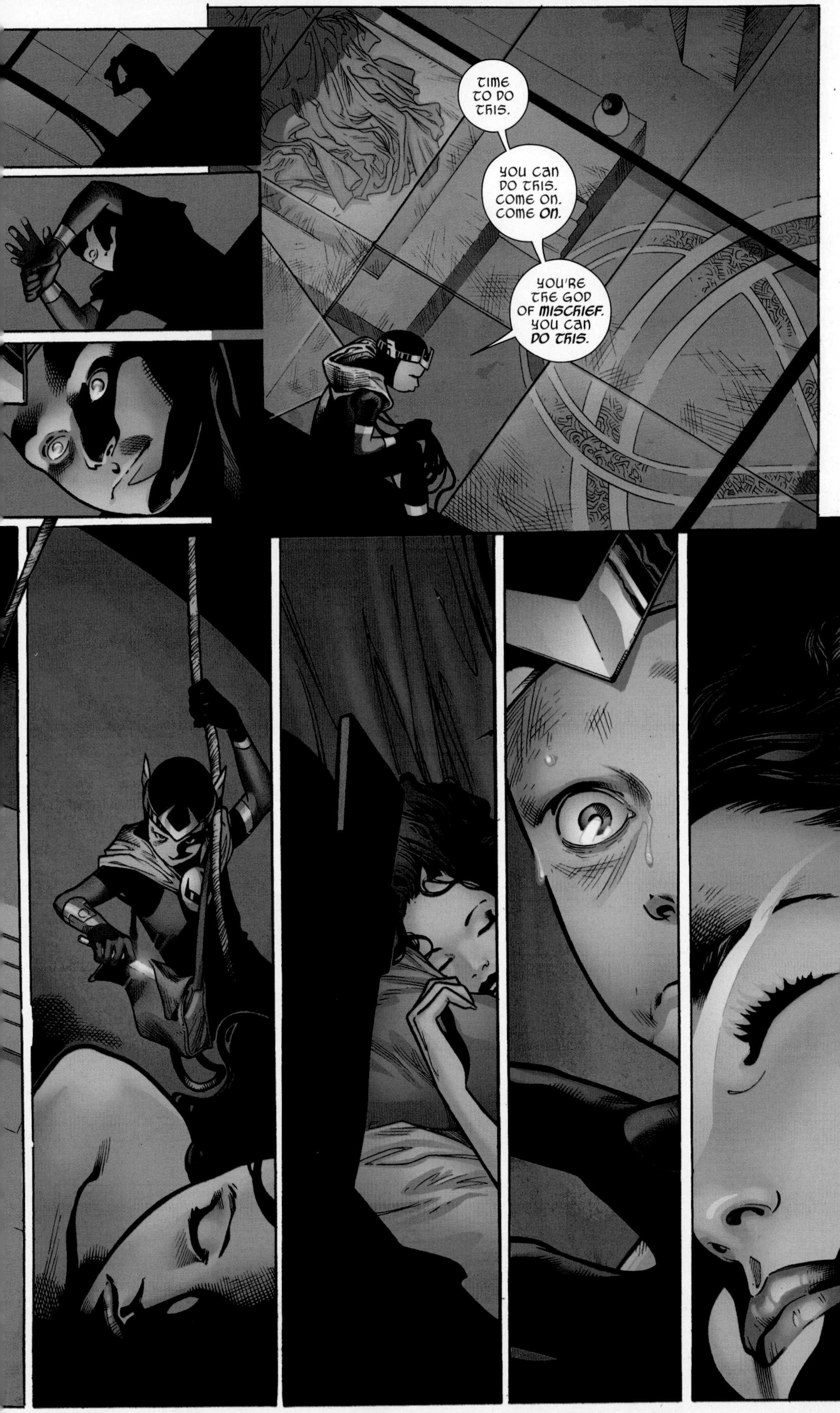
TIME TO DO THIS.
YOU CAN DO THIS. COME ON. COME ON.
YOU'RE THE GOD OF MISCHIEF. YOU CAN DO THIS.

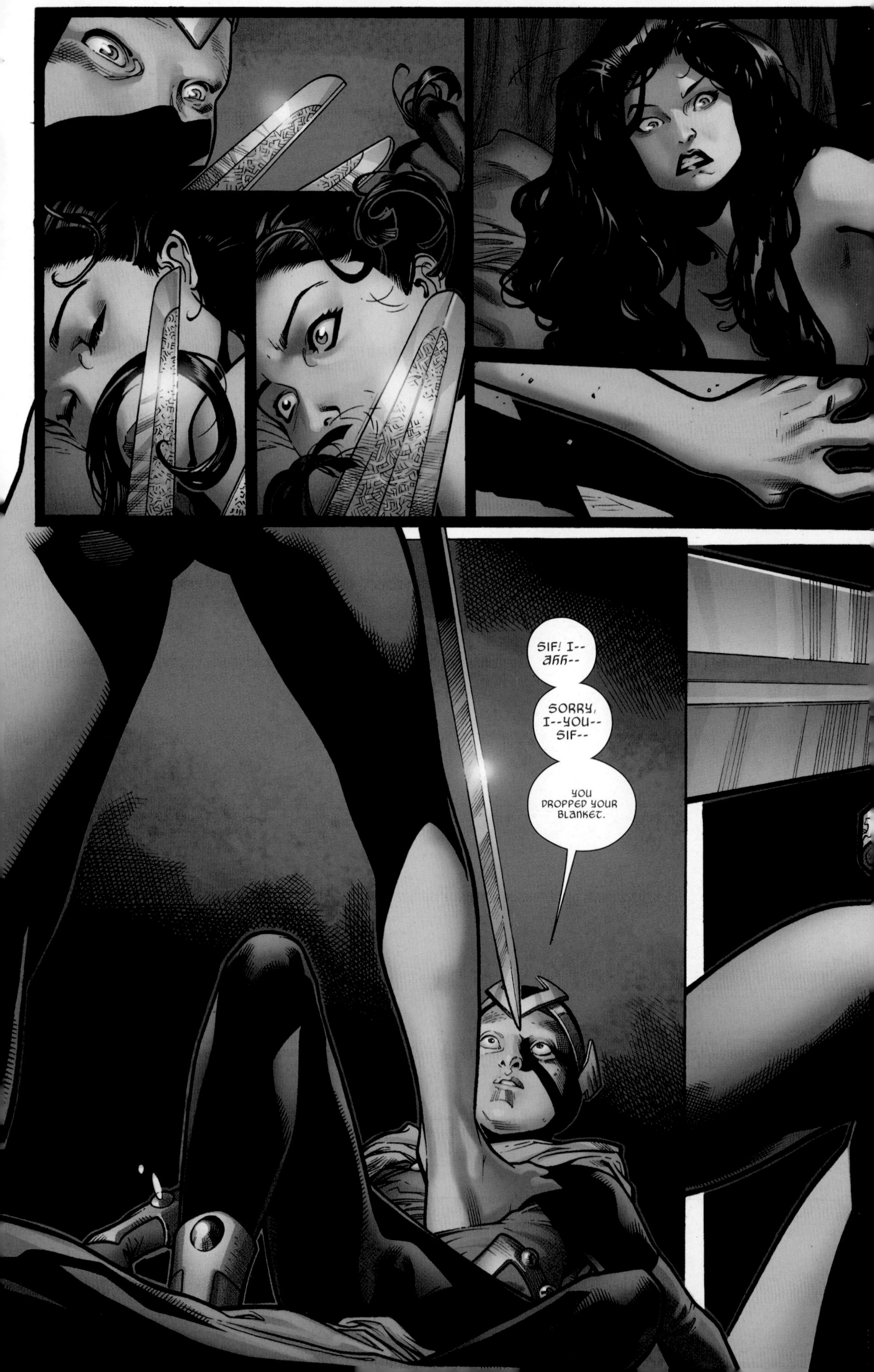
SIF! I-- AHH--
SORRY, I--YOU-- SIF--
YOU DROPPED YOUR BLANKET.

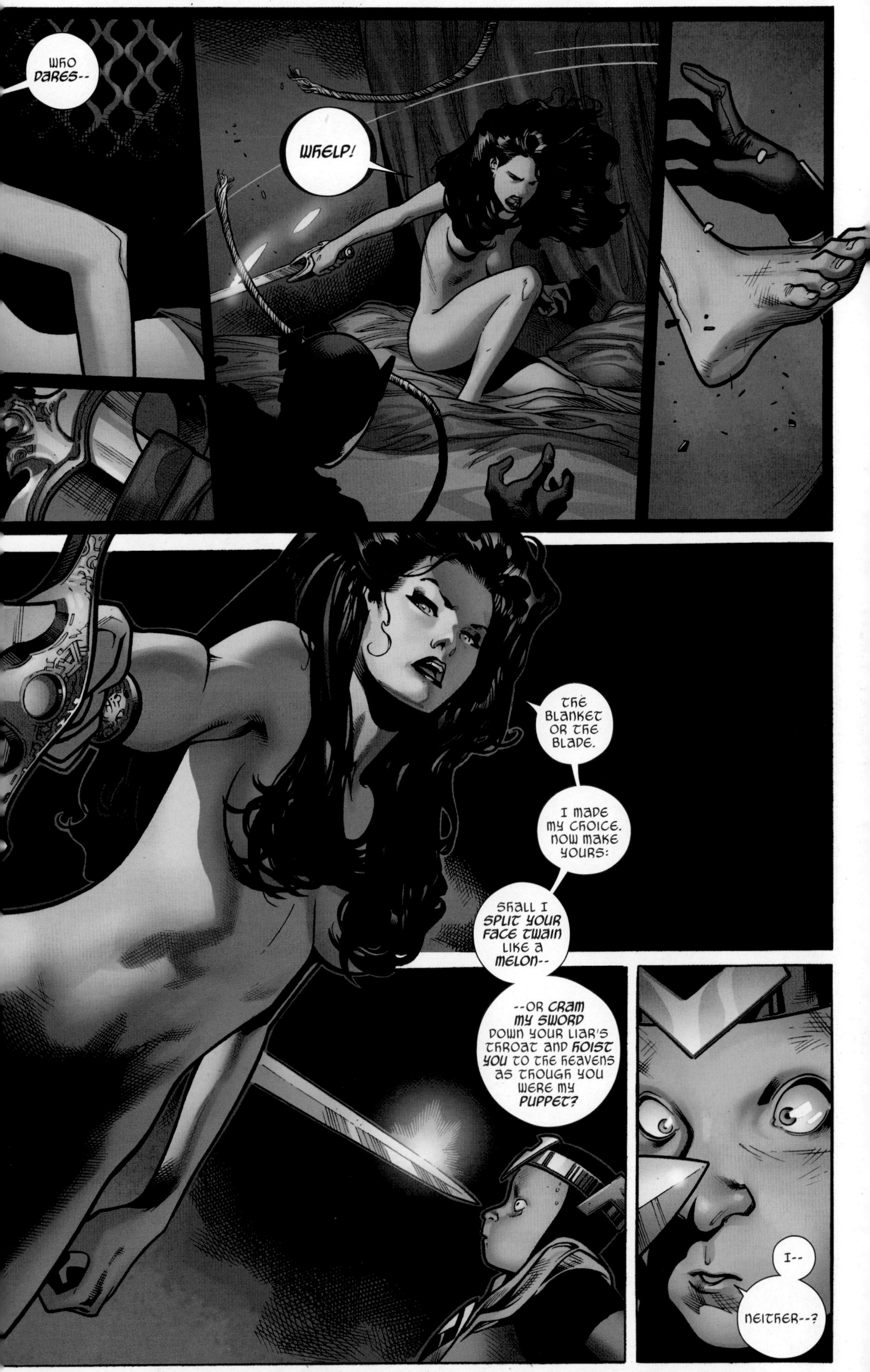
WHO DARES--
WHELP!
THE BLANKET OR THE BLADE.
I MADE MY CHOICE. NOW MAKE YOURS:
SHALL I SPLIT YOUR FACE TWAIN LIKE A MELON--
--OR CRAM MY SWORD DOWN YOUR LIAR'S THROAT AND HOIST YOU TO THE HEAVENS AS THOUGH YOU WERE MY PUPPET?
I--
NEITHER--?

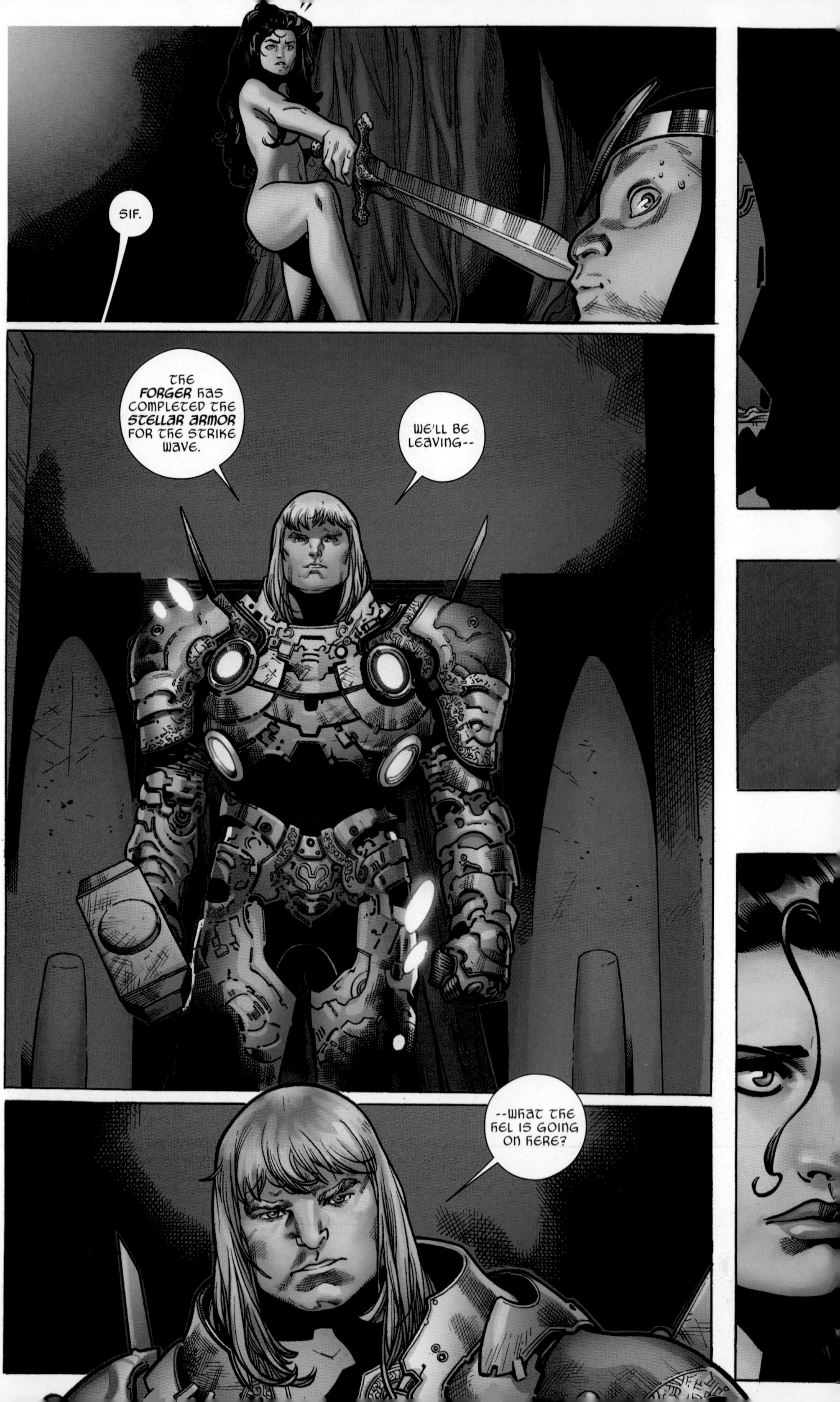
SIF.
THE FORGER HAS COMPLETED THE STELLAR ARMOR FOR THE STRIKE WAVE.
WE'LL BE LEAVING--
--WHAT THE HEL IS GOING ON HERE?

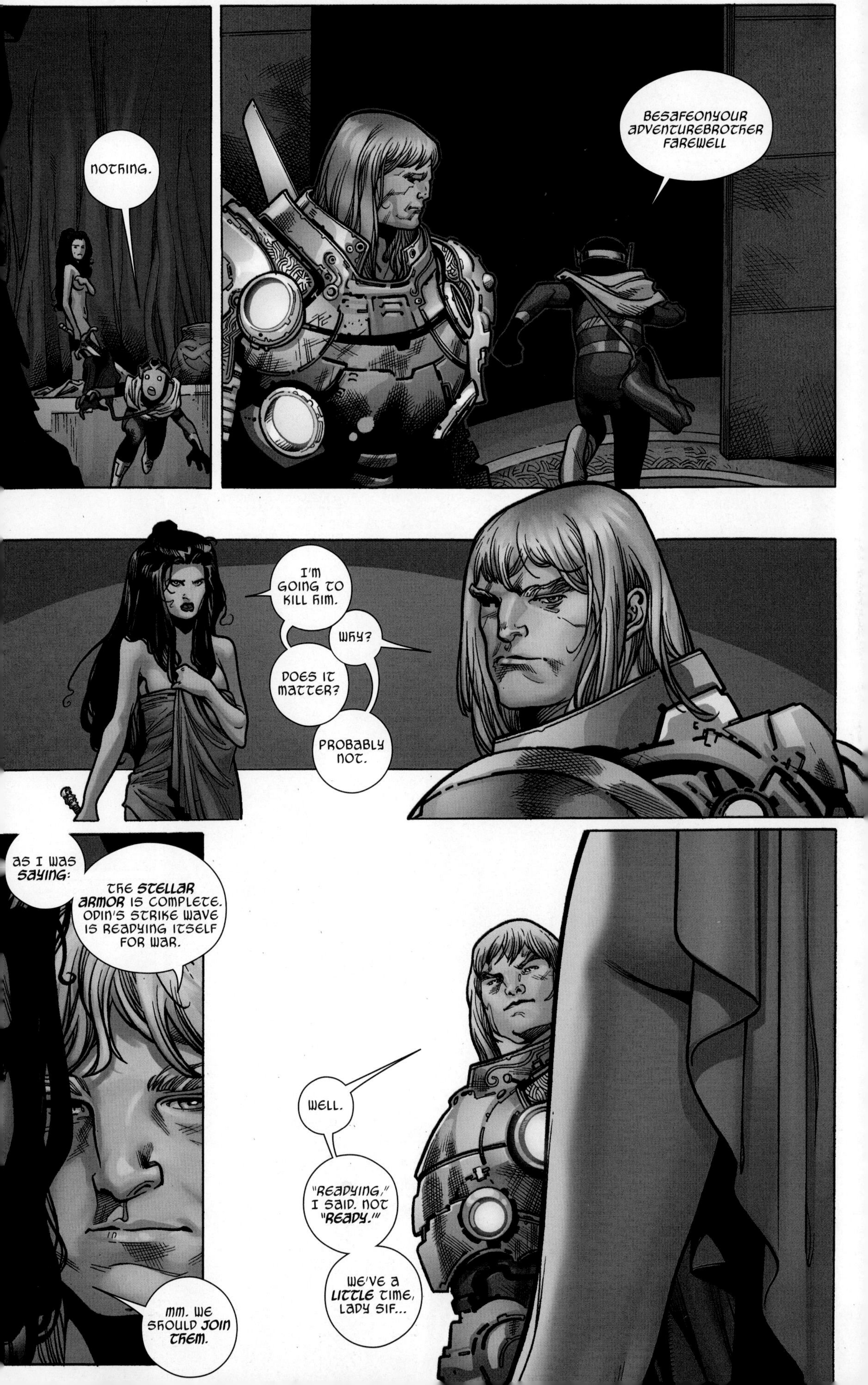
NOTHING.
BESAFEONYOUR ADVENTUREBROTHER FAREWELL
I'M GOING TO KILL HIM.
WHY?
DOES IT MATTER?
PROBABLY NOT.
AS I WAS SAYING:
THE STELLAR ARMOR IS COMPLETE. ODIN'S STRIKE WAVE IS READYING ITSELF FOR WAR.
MM. WE SHOULD JOIN THEM.
WELL.
"READYING," I SAID. NOT "READY."
WE'VE A LITTLE TIME, LADY SIF...

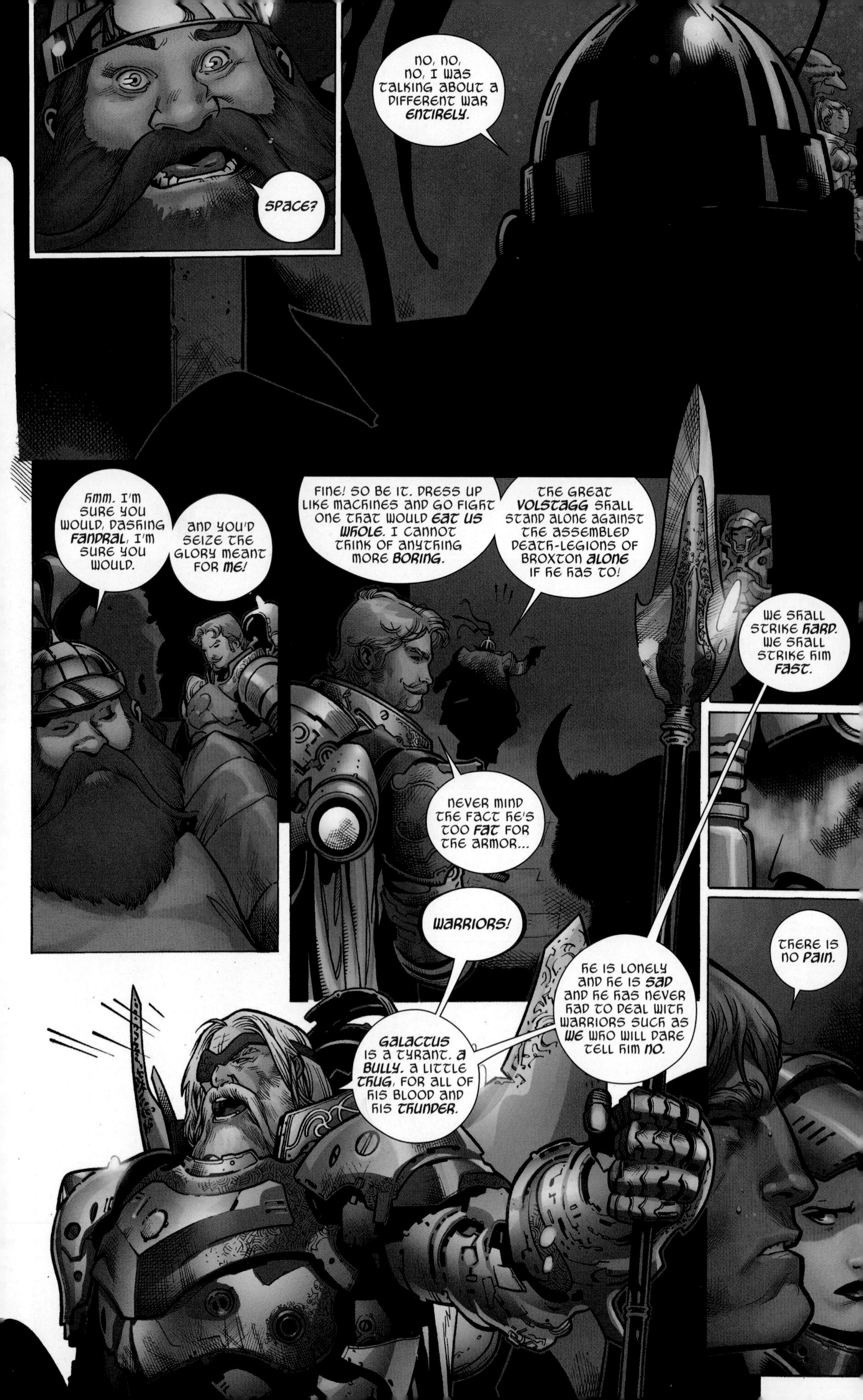

SPACE?
NO, NO, NO, I WAS TALKING ABOUT A DIFFERENT WAR ENTIRELY.
HMM. I'M SURE YOU WOULD, DASHING FANDRAL, I'M SURE YOU WOULD.
AND YOU'D SEIZE THE GLORY MEANT FOR ME!
FINE! SO BE IT. DRESS UP LIKE MACHINES AND GO FIGHT ONE THAT WOULD EAT US WHOLE. I CANNOT THINK OF ANYTHING MORE BORING.
THE GREAT VOLSTAGG SHALL STAND ALONE AGAINST THE ASSEMBLED DEATH-LEGIONS OF BROXTON ALONE IF HE HAS TO!
NEVER MIND THE FACT HE'S TOO FAT FOR THE ARMOR...
WE SHALL STRIKE HARD. WE SHALL STRIKE HIM FAST.
THERE IS NO PAIN.
WARRIORS!
GALACTUS IS A TYRANT. A BULLY. A LITTLE THUG, FOR ALL OF HIS BLOOD AND HIS THUNDER.
HE IS LONELY AND HE IS SAD AND HE HAS NEVER HAD TO DEAL WITH WARRIORS SUCH AS WE WHO WILL DARE TELL HIM NO.

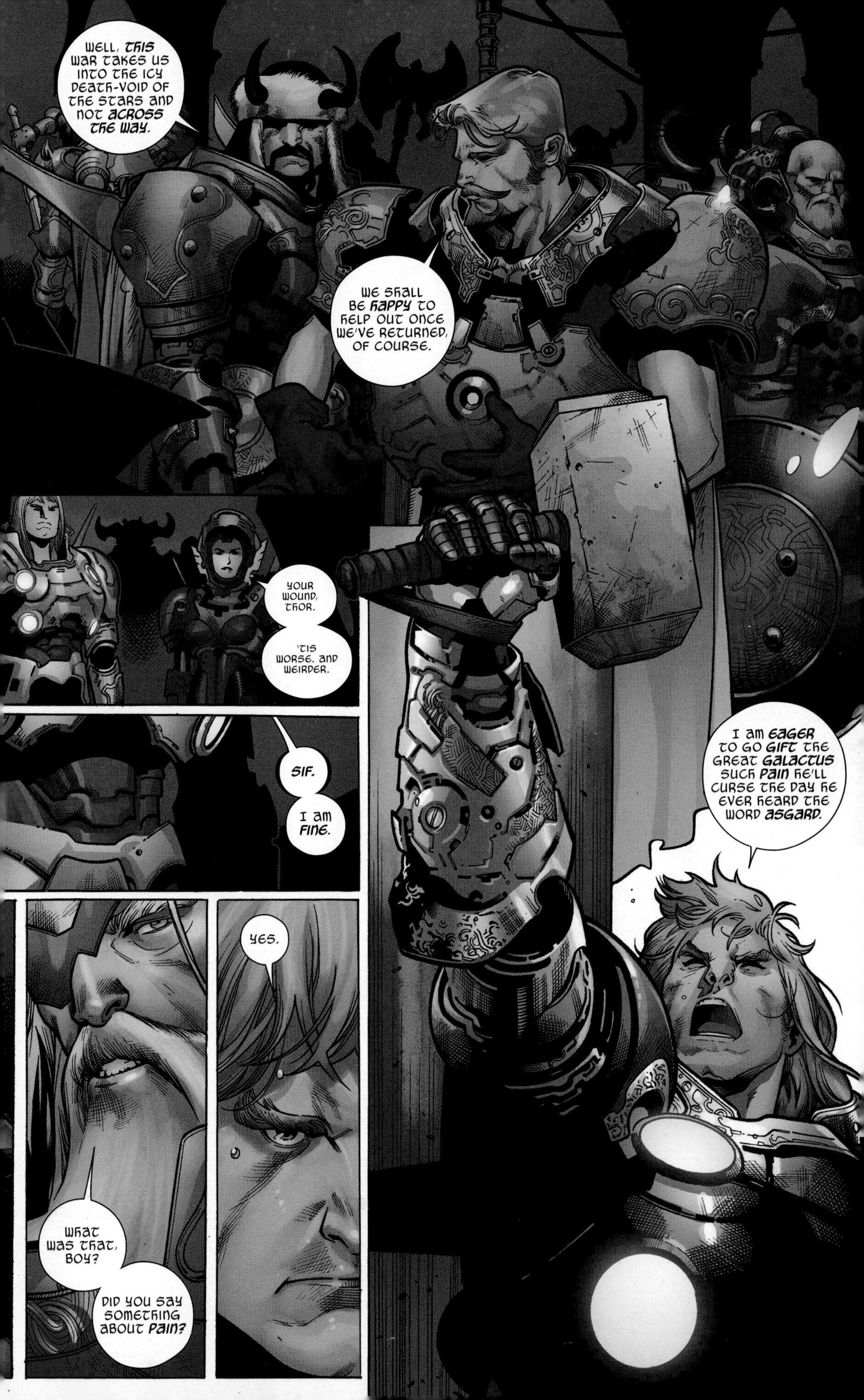
WELL, THIS WAR TAKES US INTO THE ICY DEATH-VOID OF THE STARS AND NOT ACROSS THE WAY.
WE SHALL BE HAPPY TO HELP OUT ONCE WE'VE RETURNED, OF COURSE.
YOUR WOUND, THOR.
'TIS WORSE. AND WEIRDER.
SIF.
I AM FINE.
I AM EAGER TO GO GIFT THE GREAT GALACTUS SUCH PAIN HE'LL CURSE THE DAY HE EVER HEARD THE WORD ASGARD.
YES.
WHAT WAS THAT, BOY?
DID YOU SAY SOMETHING ABOUT PAIN?

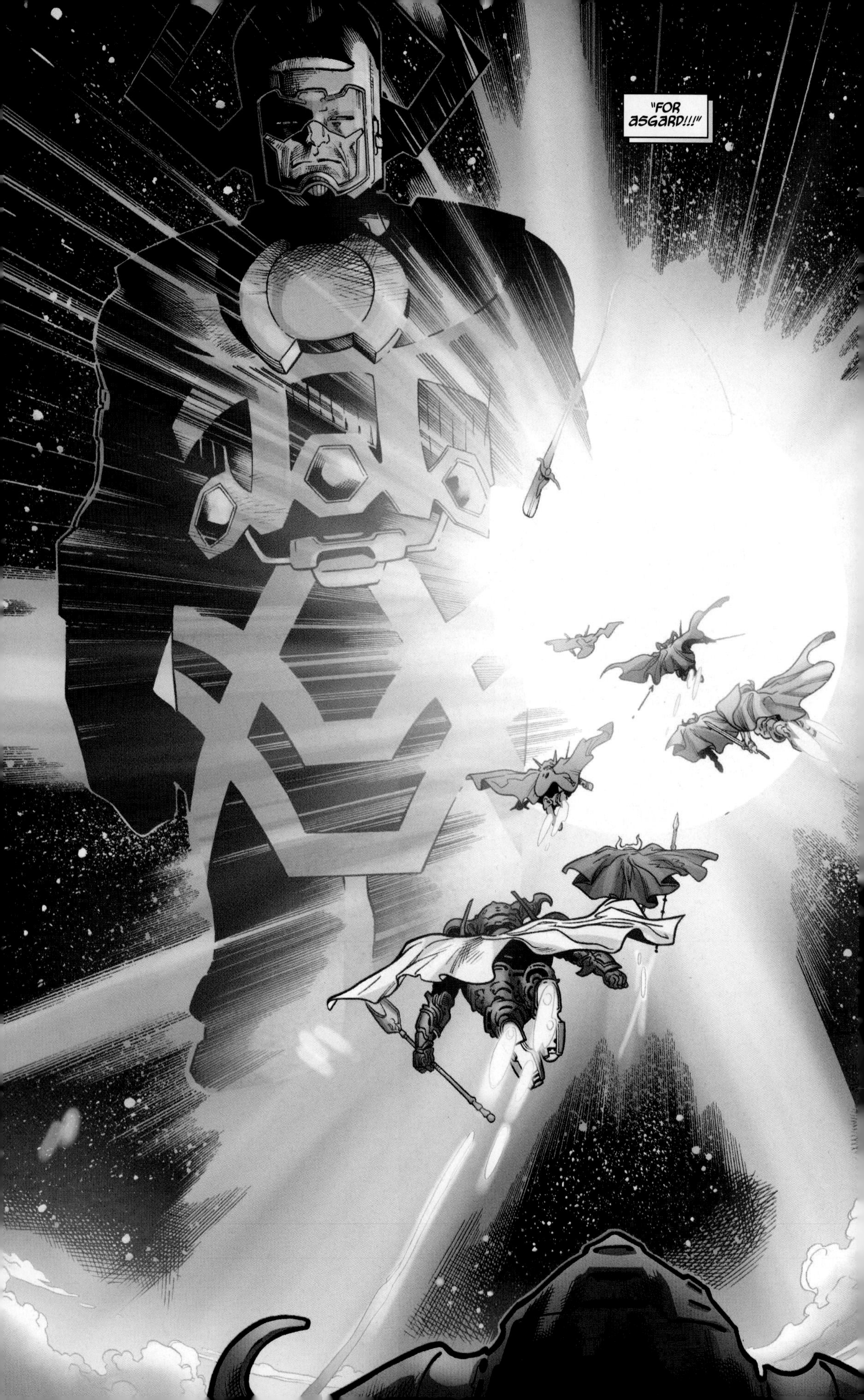
"FOR ASGARD!!!"

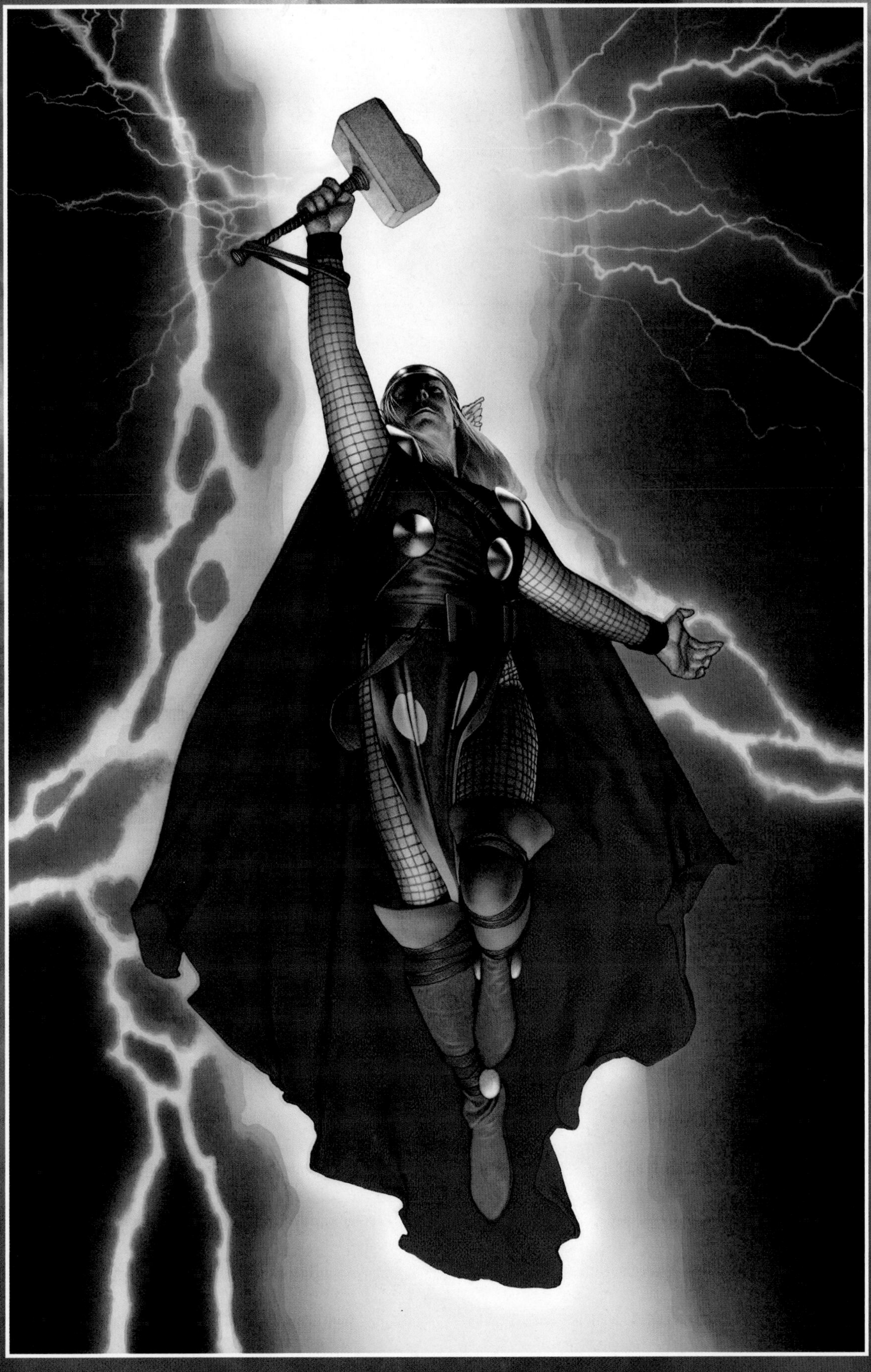

#1 VARIANT BY TRAVIS CHAREST

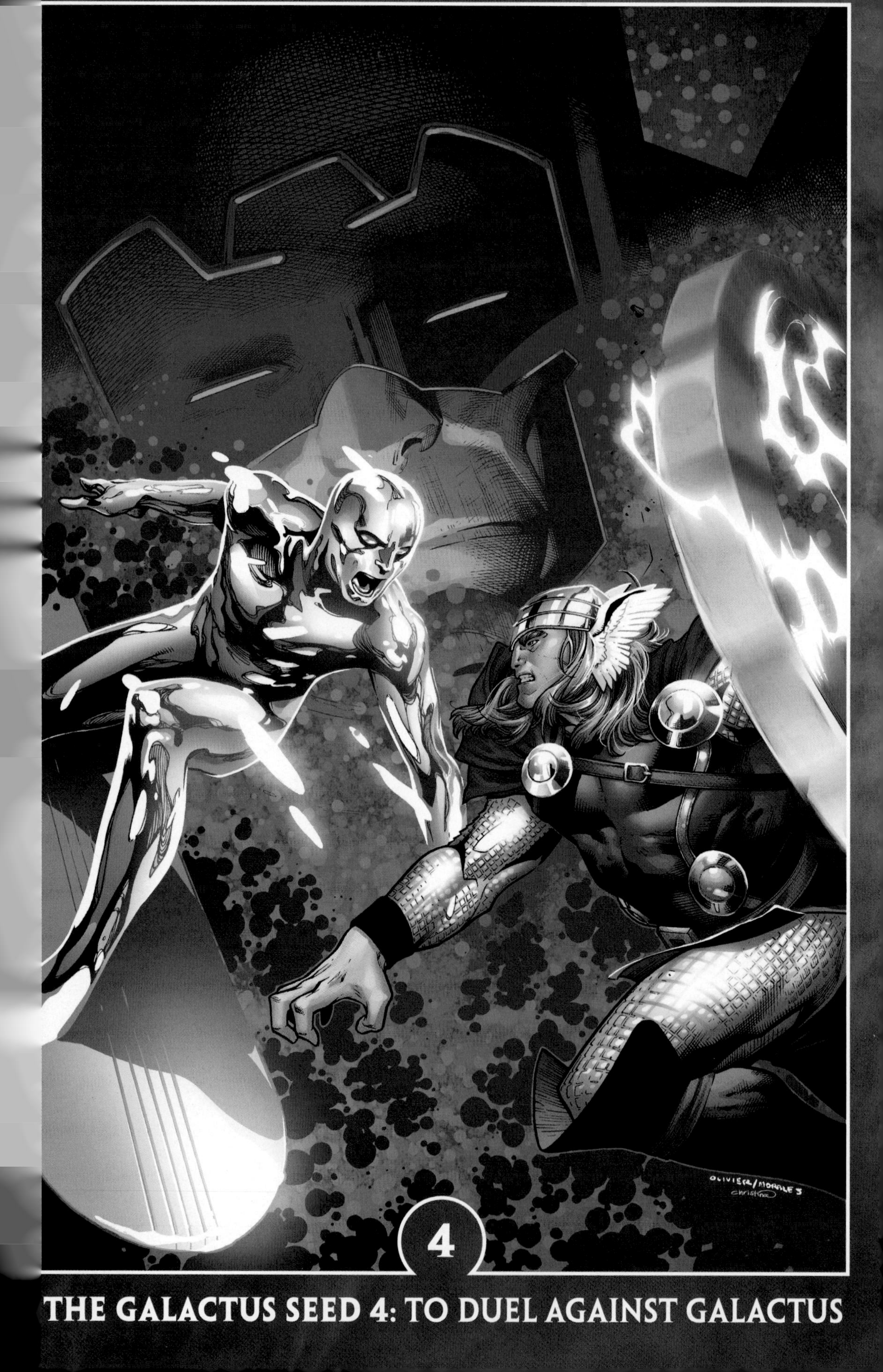
OLIVIER/MORALES
4

THE GALACTUS SEED 4: TO DUEL AGAINST GALACTUS

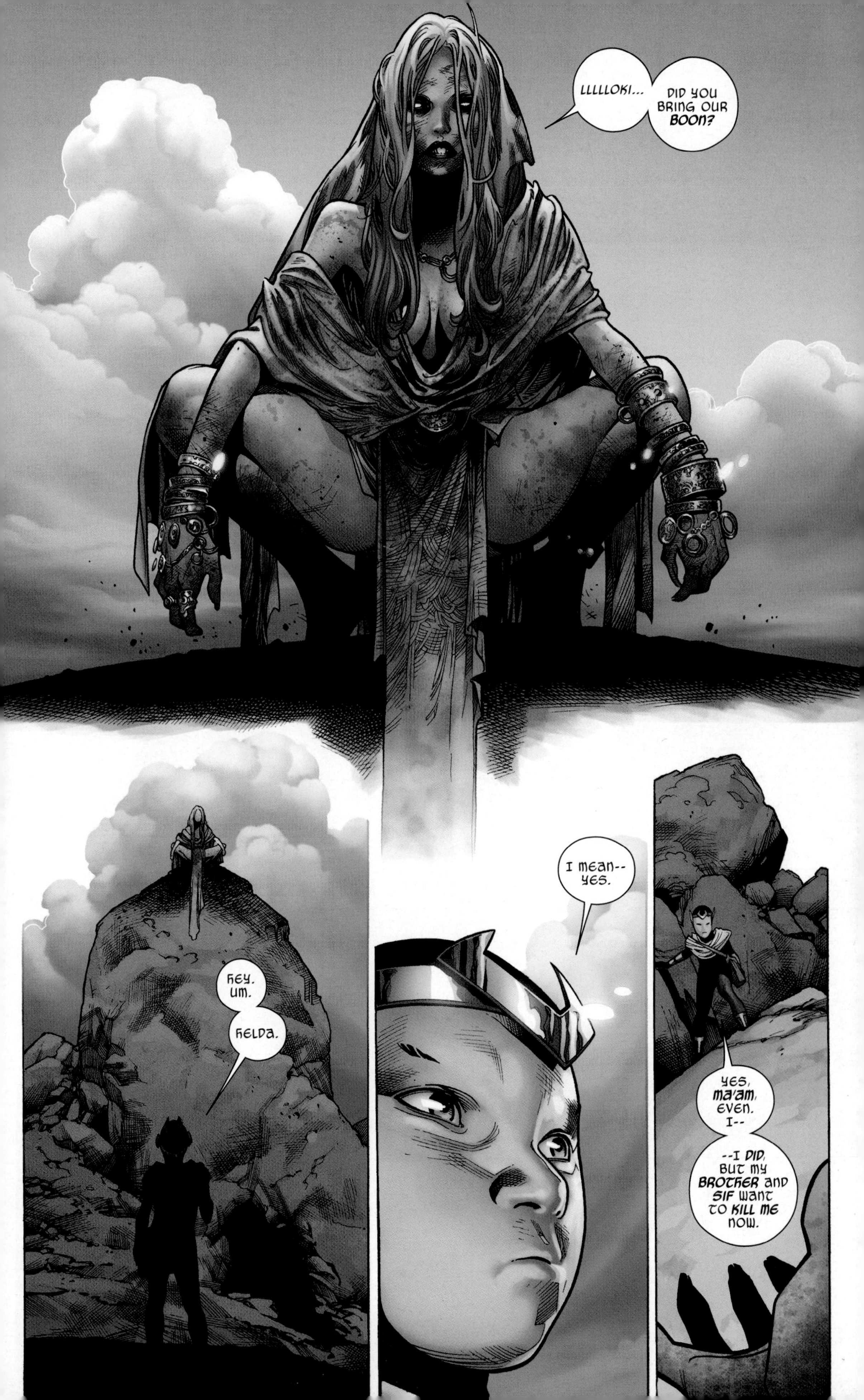
LLLLLOKI...
DID YOU BRING OUR BOON?
HEY. UM.
HELDA.
I MEAN-- YES.
YES, MA'AM, EVEN. I--
--I DID, BUT MY BROTHER AND SIF WANT TO KILL ME NOW.

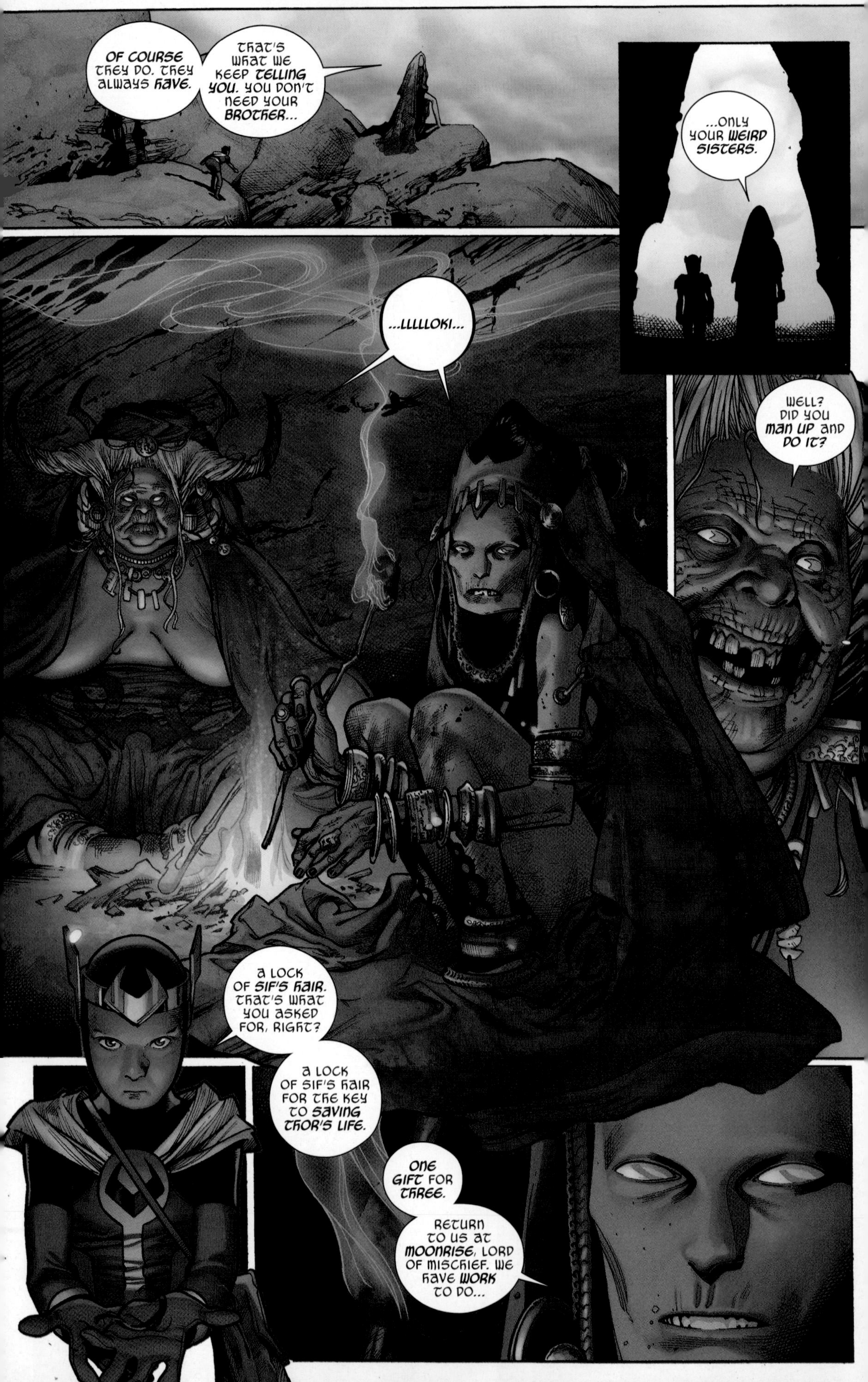
OF COURSE THEY DO. THEY ALWAYS HAVE.
THAT'S WHAT WE KEEP TELLING YOU. YOU DON'T NEED YOUR BROTHER...
...ONLY YOUR WEIRD SISTERS.
...LLLLLOKI...
WELL? DID YOU MAN UP AND DO IT?
A LOCK OF SIF'S HAIR. THAT'S WHAT YOU ASKED FOR, RIGHT?
A LOCK OF SIF'S HAIR FOR THE KEY TO SAVING THOR'S LIFE.
ONE GIFT FOR THREE.
RETURN TO US AT MOONRISE, LORD OF MISCHIEF. WE HAVE WORK TO DO...

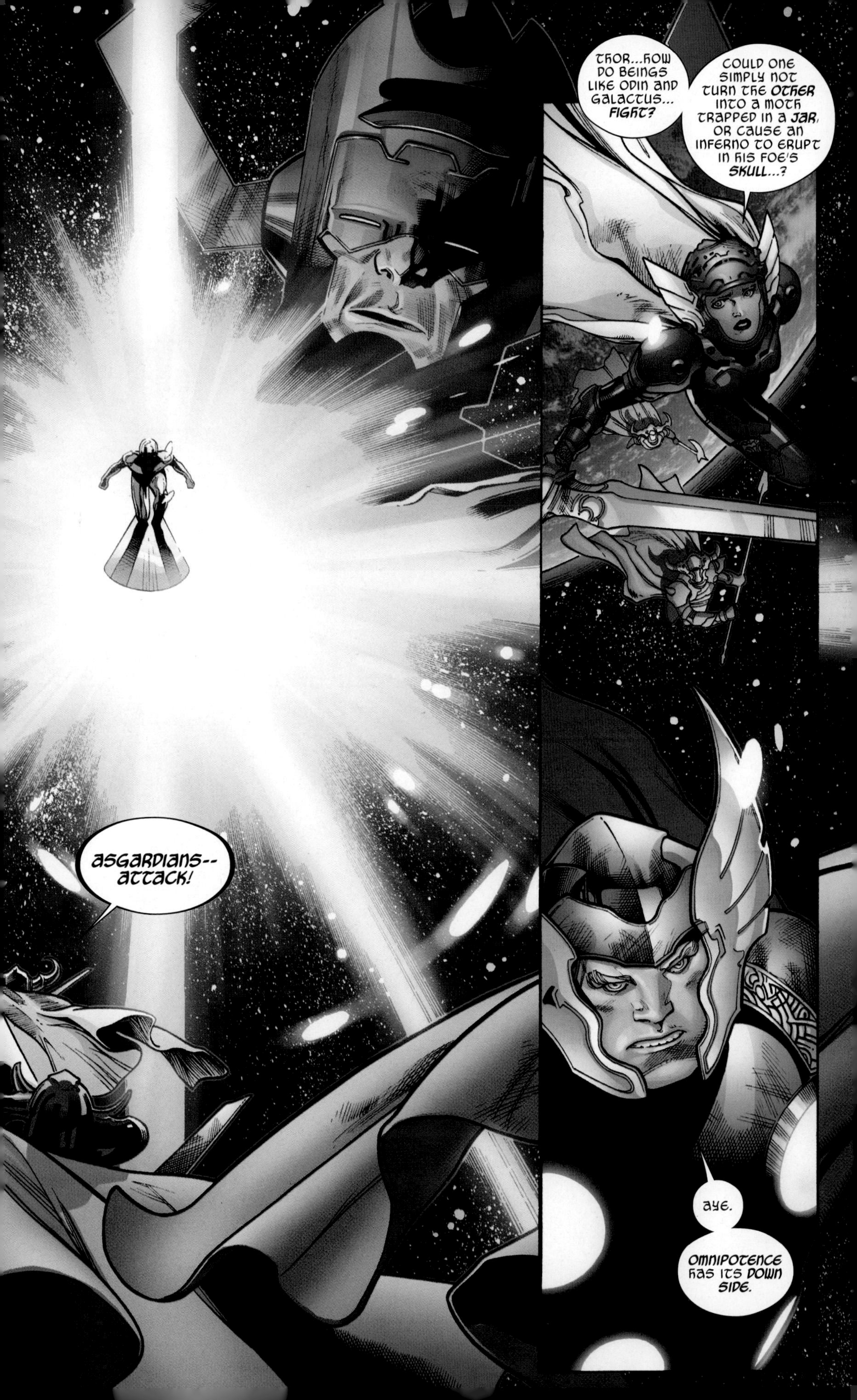
ASGARDIANS--
ATTACK!
THOR...HOW DO BEINGS LIKE ODIN AND GALACTUS... FIGHT?
COULD ONE SIMPLY NOT TURN THE OTHER INTO A MOTH TRAPPED IN A JAR, OR CAUSE AN INFERNO TO ERUPT IN HIS FOE'S SKULL...?
AYE.
OMNIPOTENCE HAS ITS DOWN SIDE.

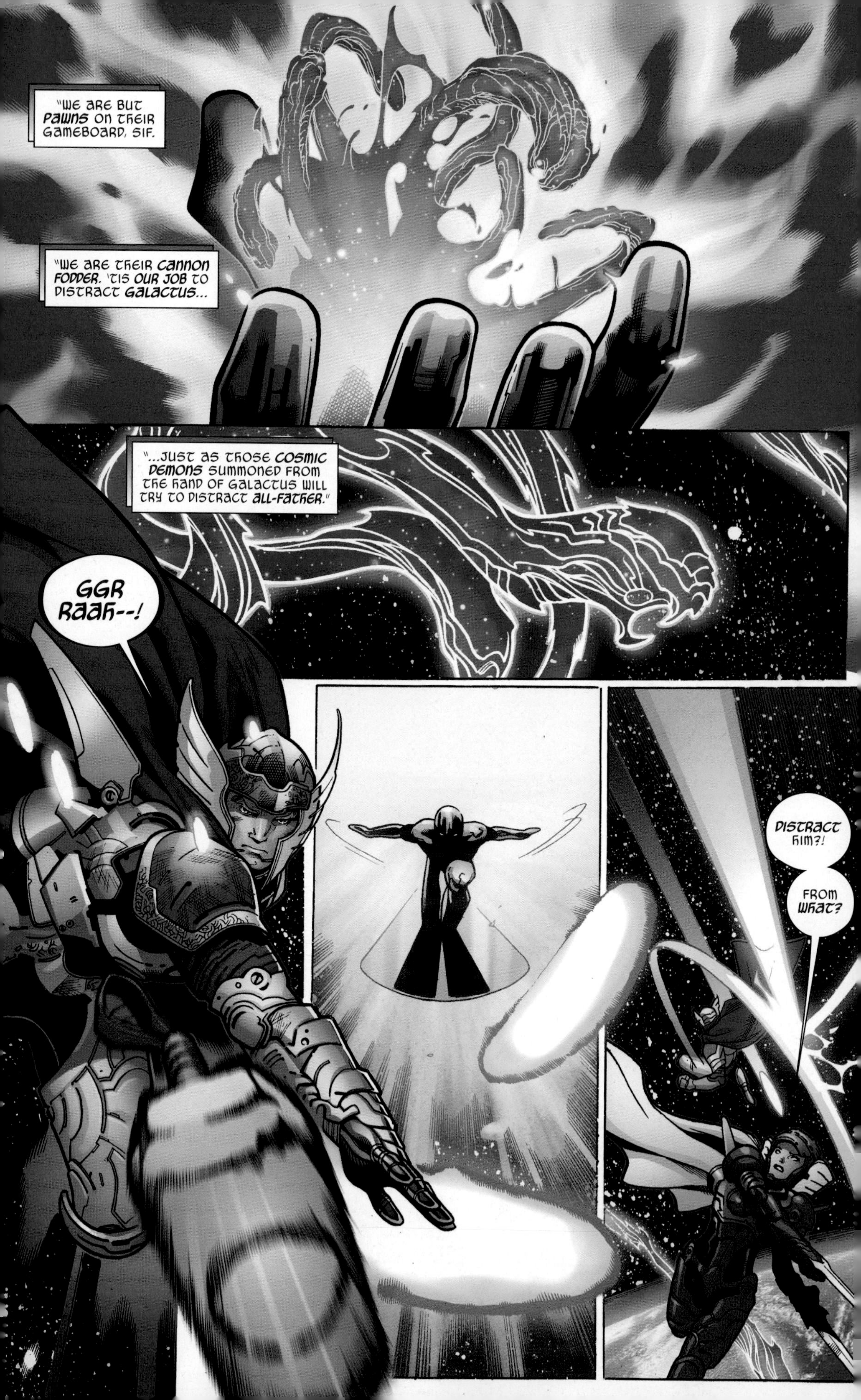
"WE ARE BUT PAWNS ON THEIR GAMEBOARD, SIF.
"WE ARE THEIR CANNON FODDER. 'TIS OUR JOB TO DISTRACT GALACTUS...
"...JUST AS THOSE COSMIC DEMONS SUMMONED FROM THE HAND OF GALACTUS WILL TRY TO DISTRACT ALL-FATHER."
GGR RAAH--!
DISTRACT HIM?!
FROM WHAT?

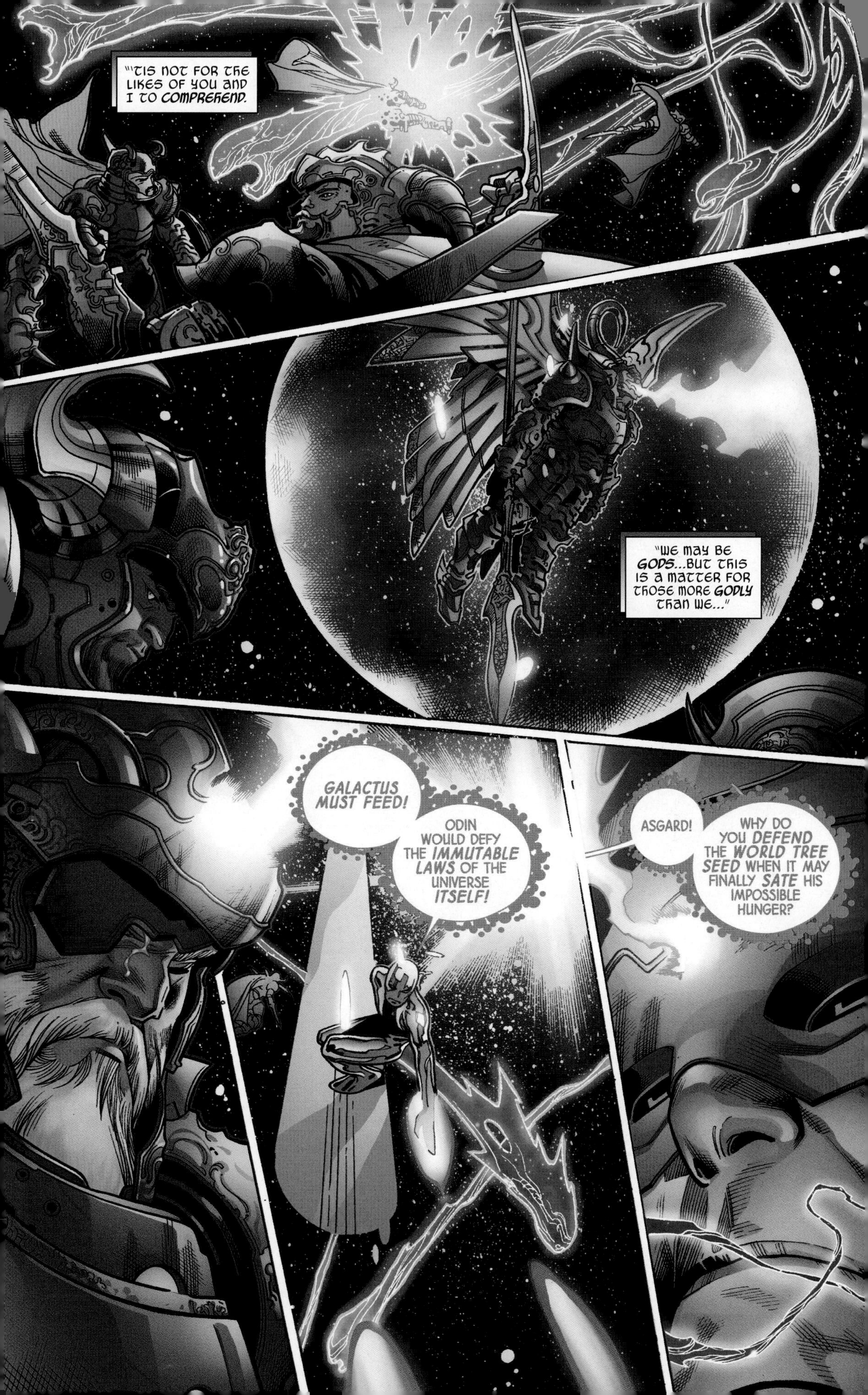

"'TIS NOT FOR THE LIKES OF YOU AND I TO COMPREHEND.
"WE MAY BE GODS...BUT THIS IS A MATTER FOR THOSE MORE GODLY THAN WE..."
GALACTUS MUST FEED!
ODIN WOULD DEFY THE IMMUTABLE LAWS OF THE UNIVERSE ITSELF!
ASGARD!
WHY DO YOU DEFEND THE WORLD TREE SEED WHEN IT MAY FINALLY SATE HIS IMPOSSIBLE HUNGER?

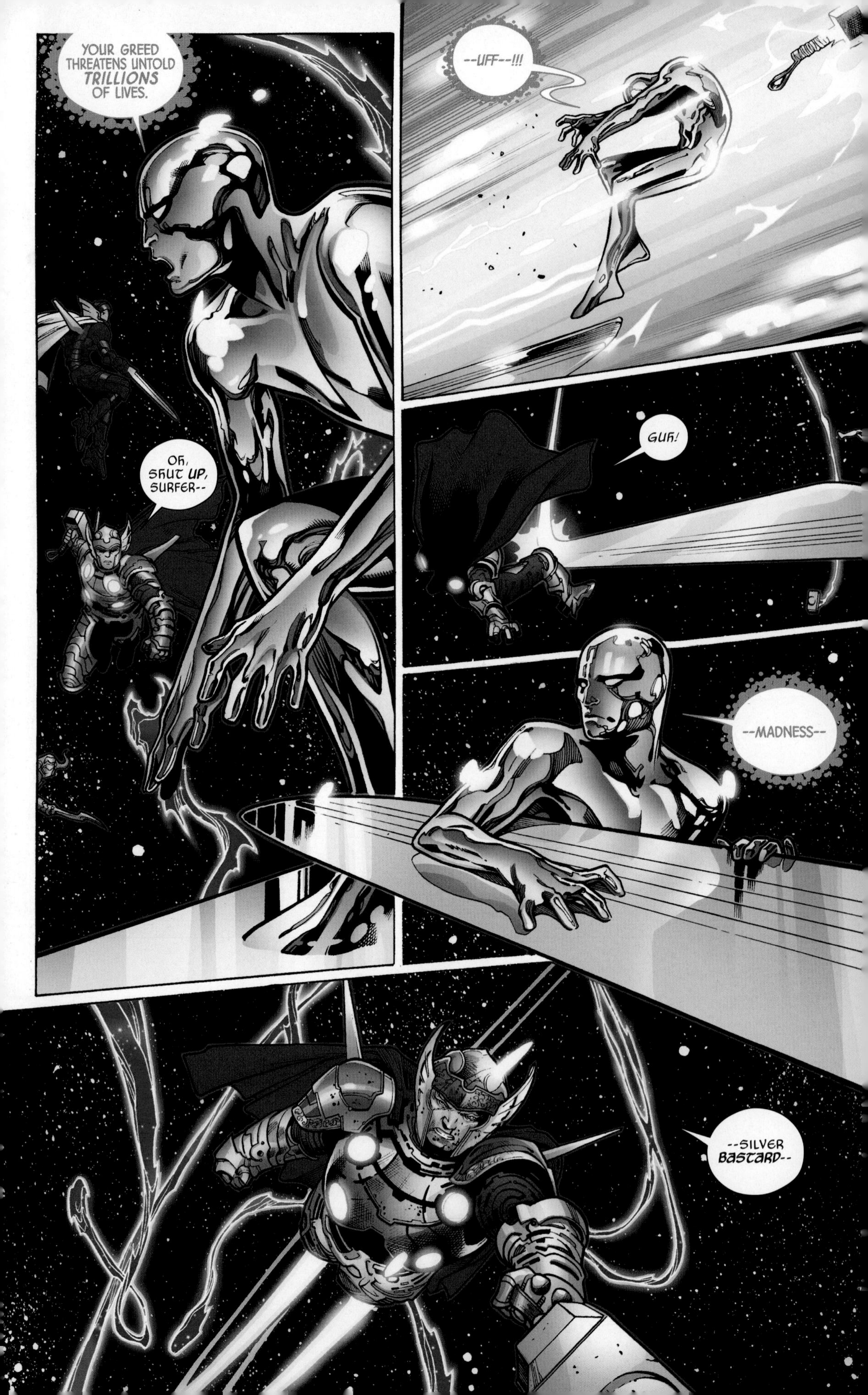
YOUR GREED THREATENS UNTOLD TRILLIONS OF LIVES.
OH, SHUT UP, SURFER--
--UFF--!!!
GUH!
--MADNESS--
--SILVER BASTARD--

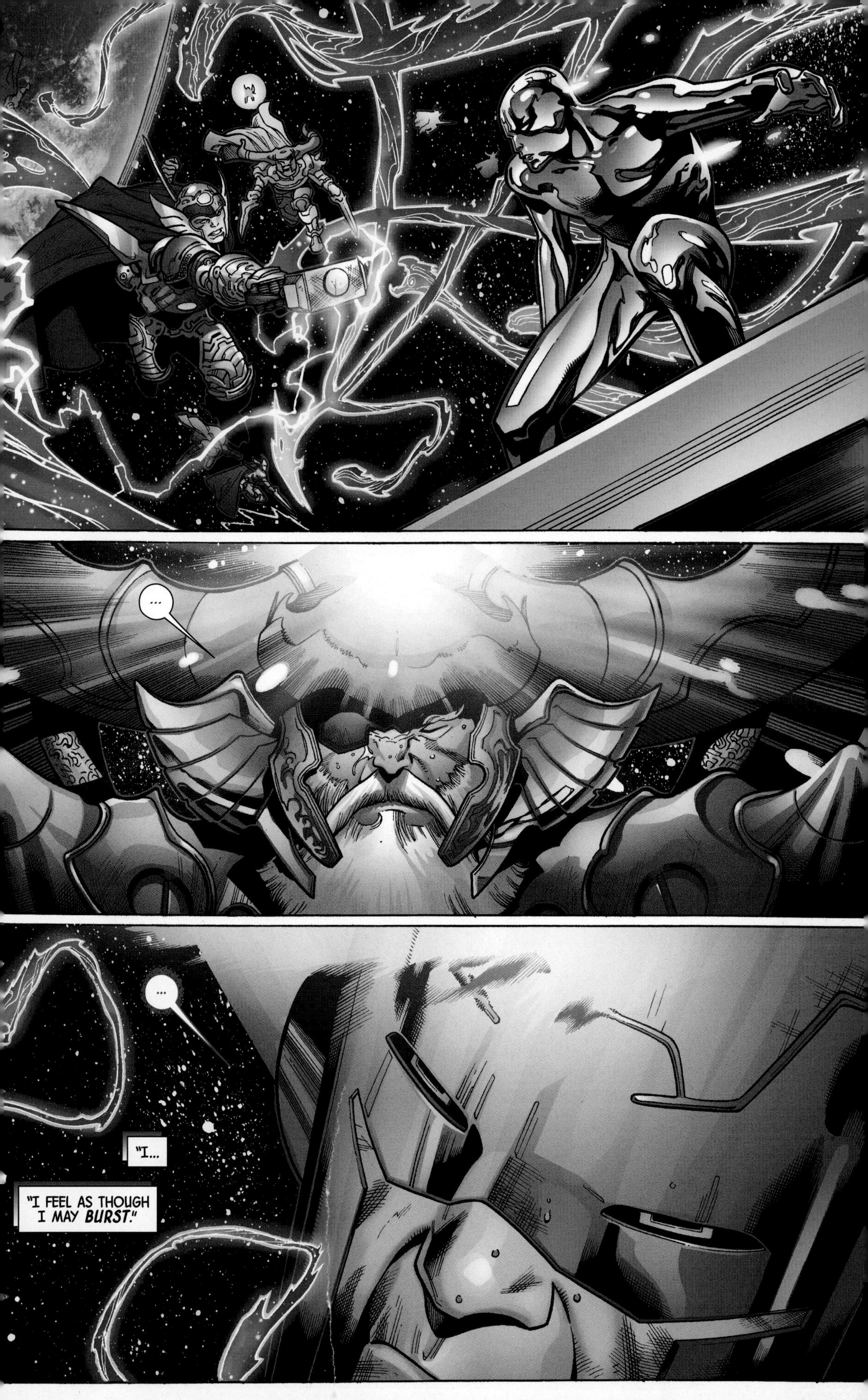
...
...
"I...
"I FEEL AS THOUGH I MAY BURST."

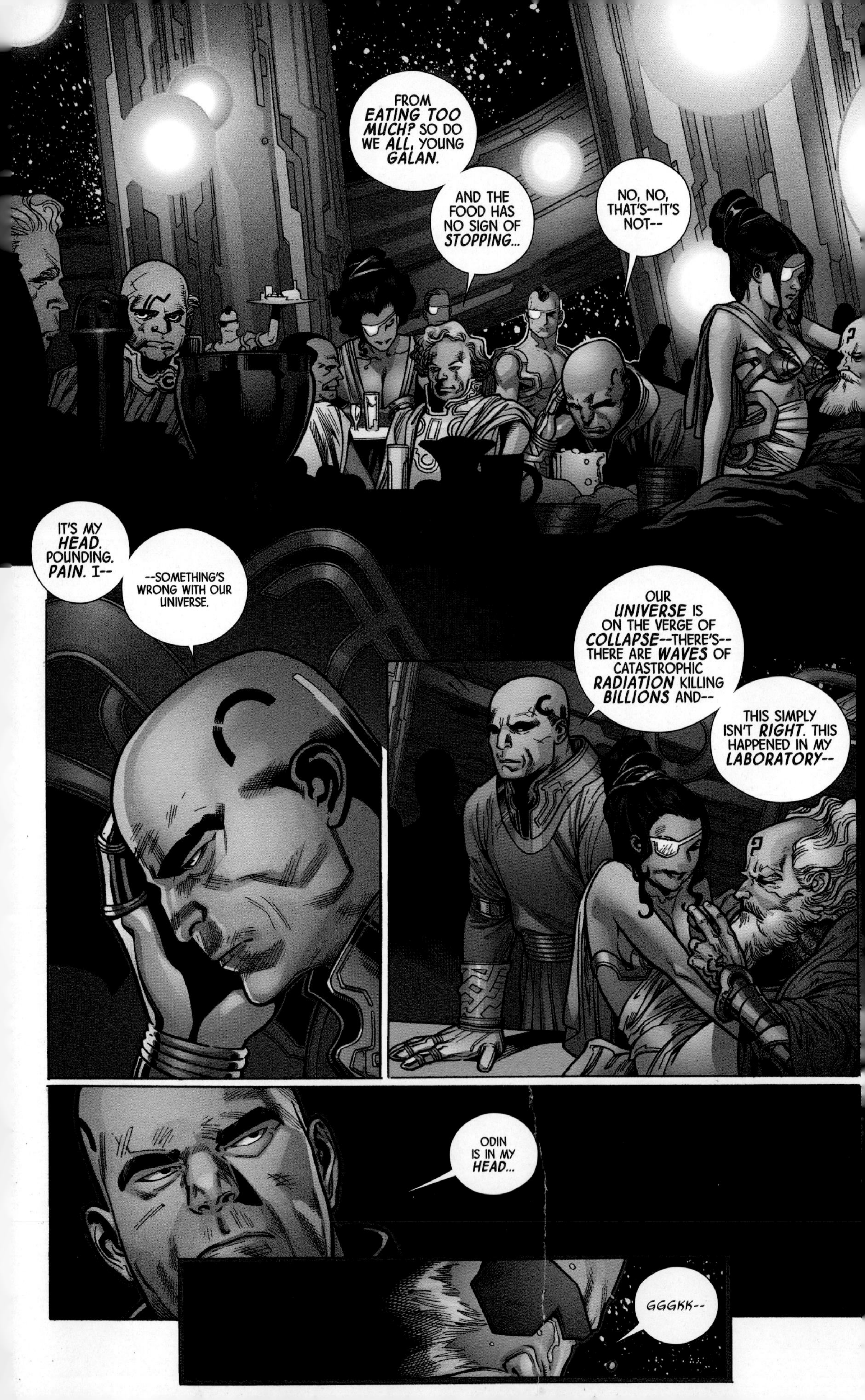
FROM EATING TOO MUCH? SO DO WE ALL, YOUNG GALAN.
AND THE FOOD HAS NO SIGN OF STOPPING...
NO, NO, THAT'S--IT'S NOT--
IT'S MY HEAD. POUNDING. PAIN. I--
--SOMETHING'S WRONG WITH OUR UNIVERSE.
OUR UNIVERSE IS ON THE VERGE OF COLLAPSE--THERE'S--THERE ARE WAVES OF CATASTROPHIC RADIATION KILLING BILLIONS AND--
THIS SIMPLY ISN'T RIGHT. THIS HAPPENED IN MY LABORATORY--
ODIN IS IN MY HEAD...
GGGKK--

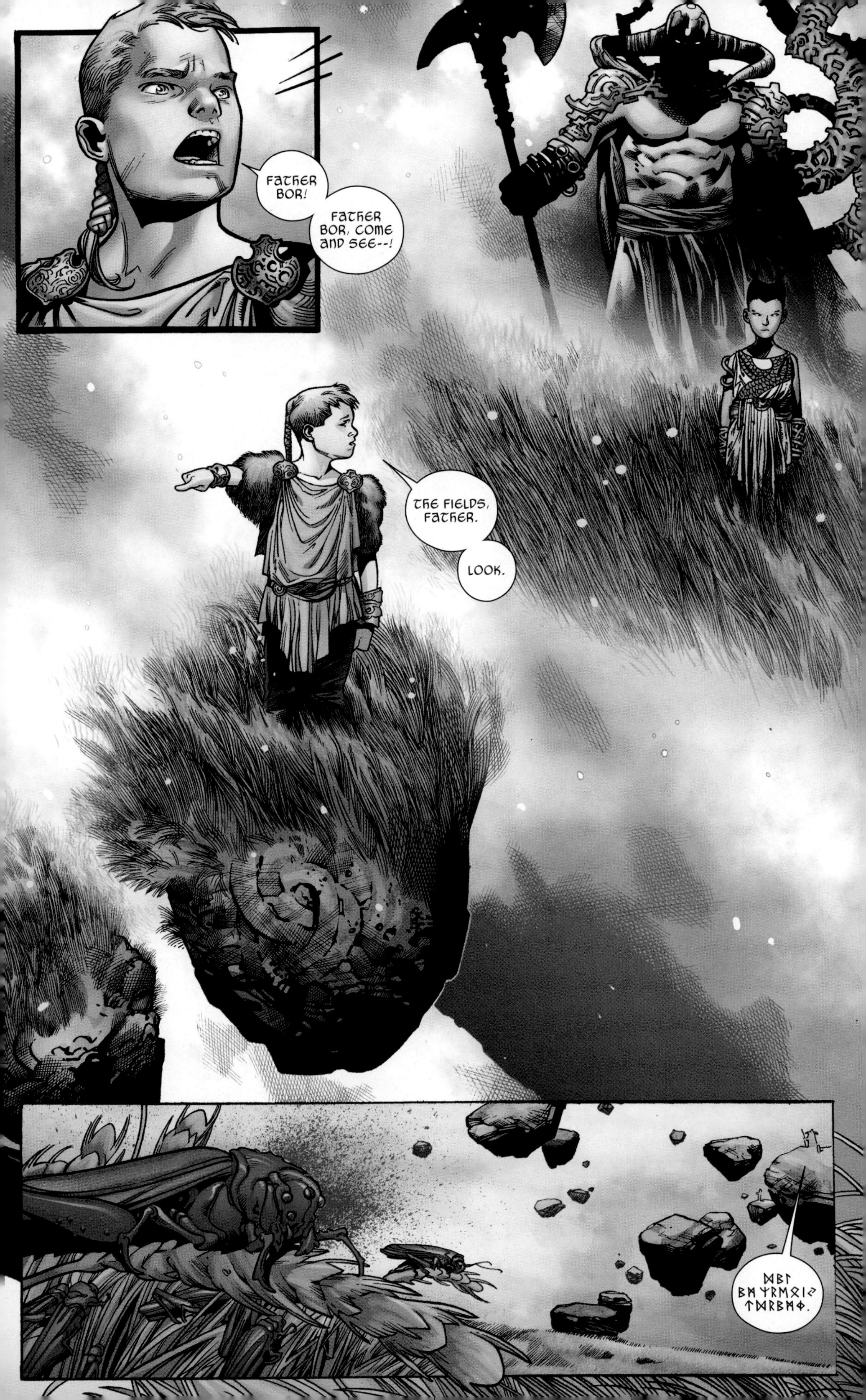
FATHER BOR!
FATHER BOR, COME AND SEE--!
THE FIELDS, FATHER.
LOOK.

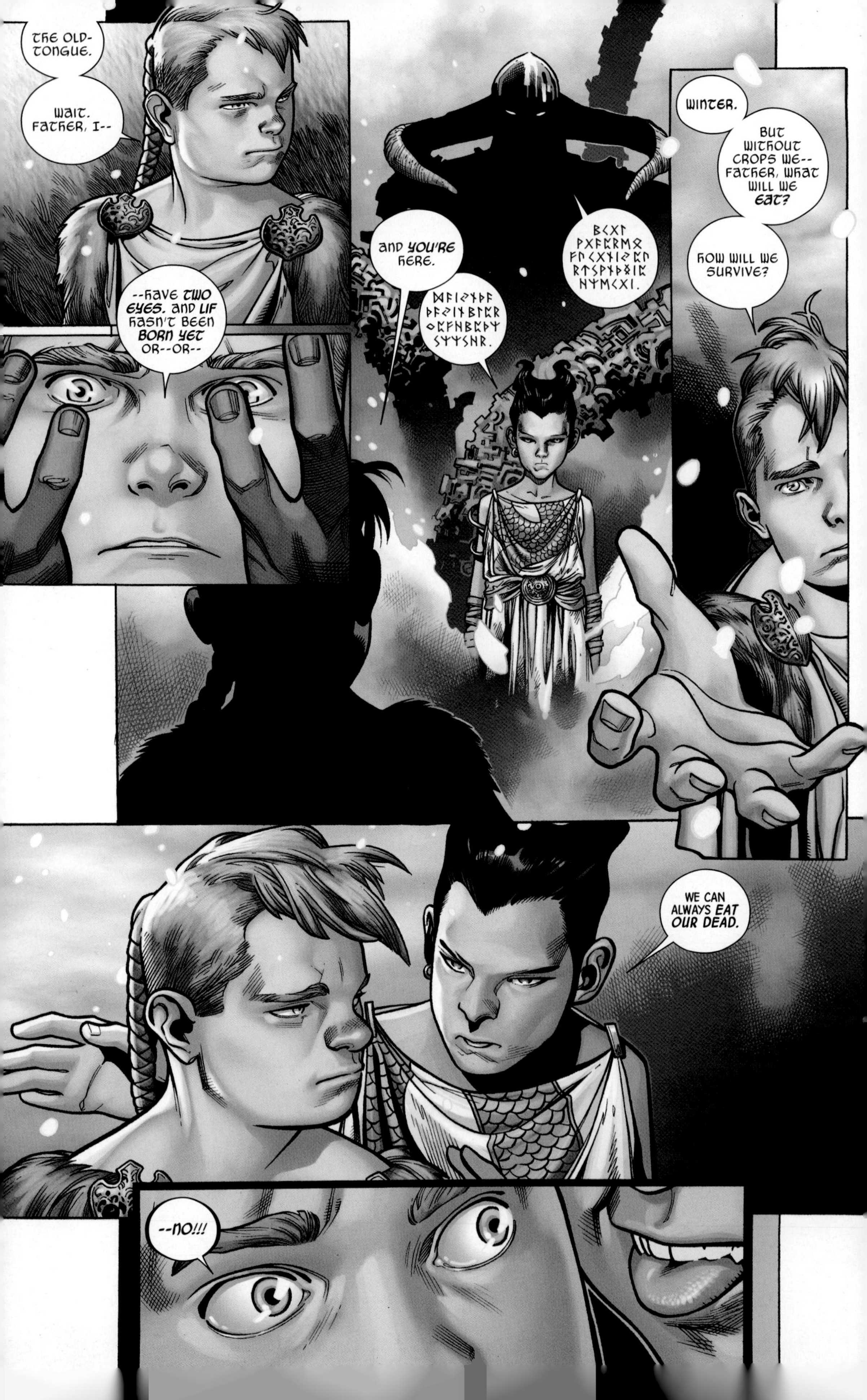

THE OLD-TONGUE.
WAIT. FATHER, I--
--HAVE TWO EYES. AND LIF HASN'T BEEN BORN YET OR--OR--
AND YOU'RE HERE.
WINTER.
BUT WITHOUT CROPS WE-- FATHER, WHAT WILL WE EAT?
HOW WILL WE SURVIVE?
WE CAN ALWAYS EAT OUR DEAD.
--NO!!!

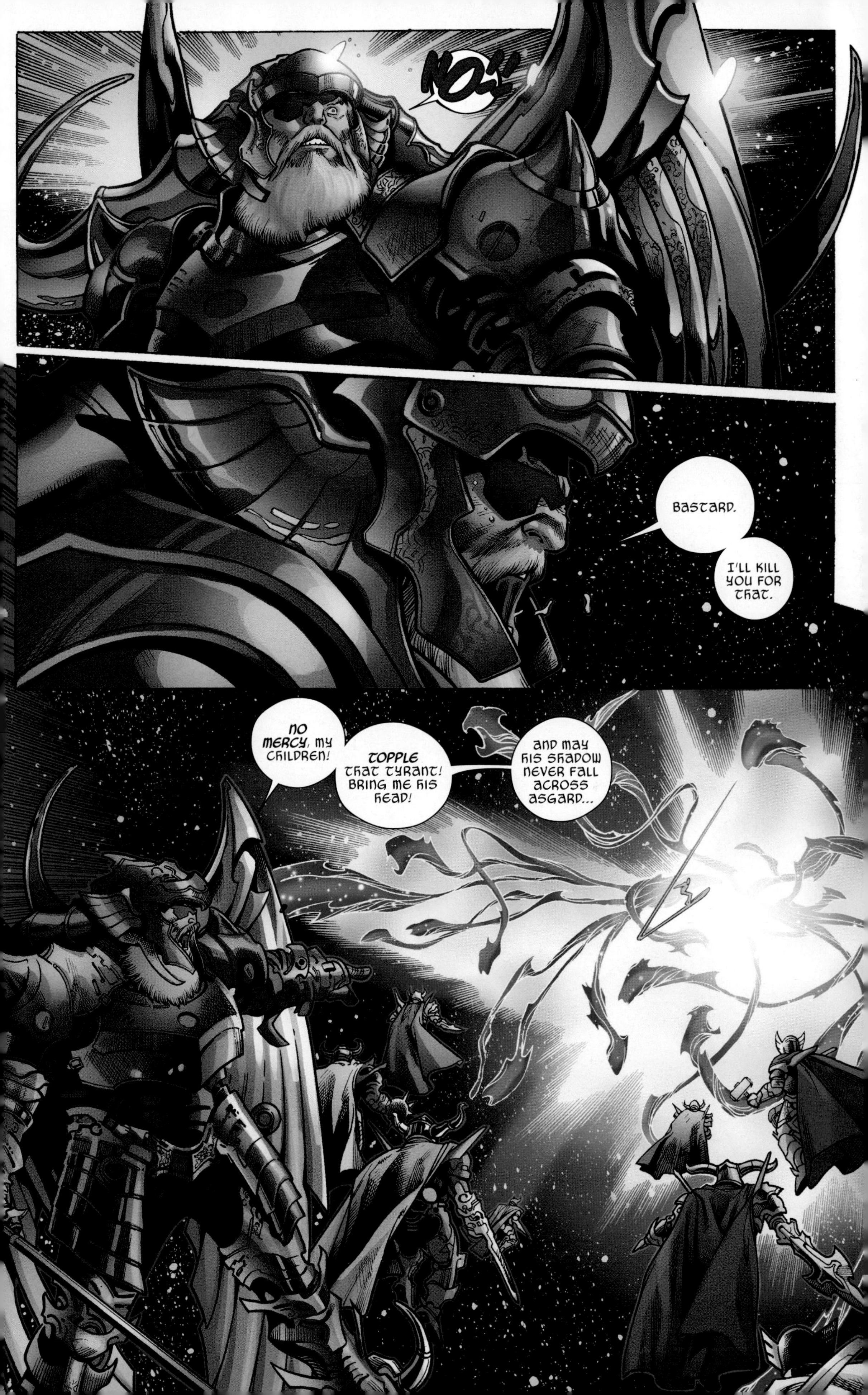
NO!!
BASTARD.
I'LL KILL YOU FOR THAT.
NO MERCY, MY CHILDREN!
TOPPLE THAT TYRANT! BRING ME HIS HEAD!
AND MAY HIS SHADOW NEVER FALL ACROSS ASGARD...

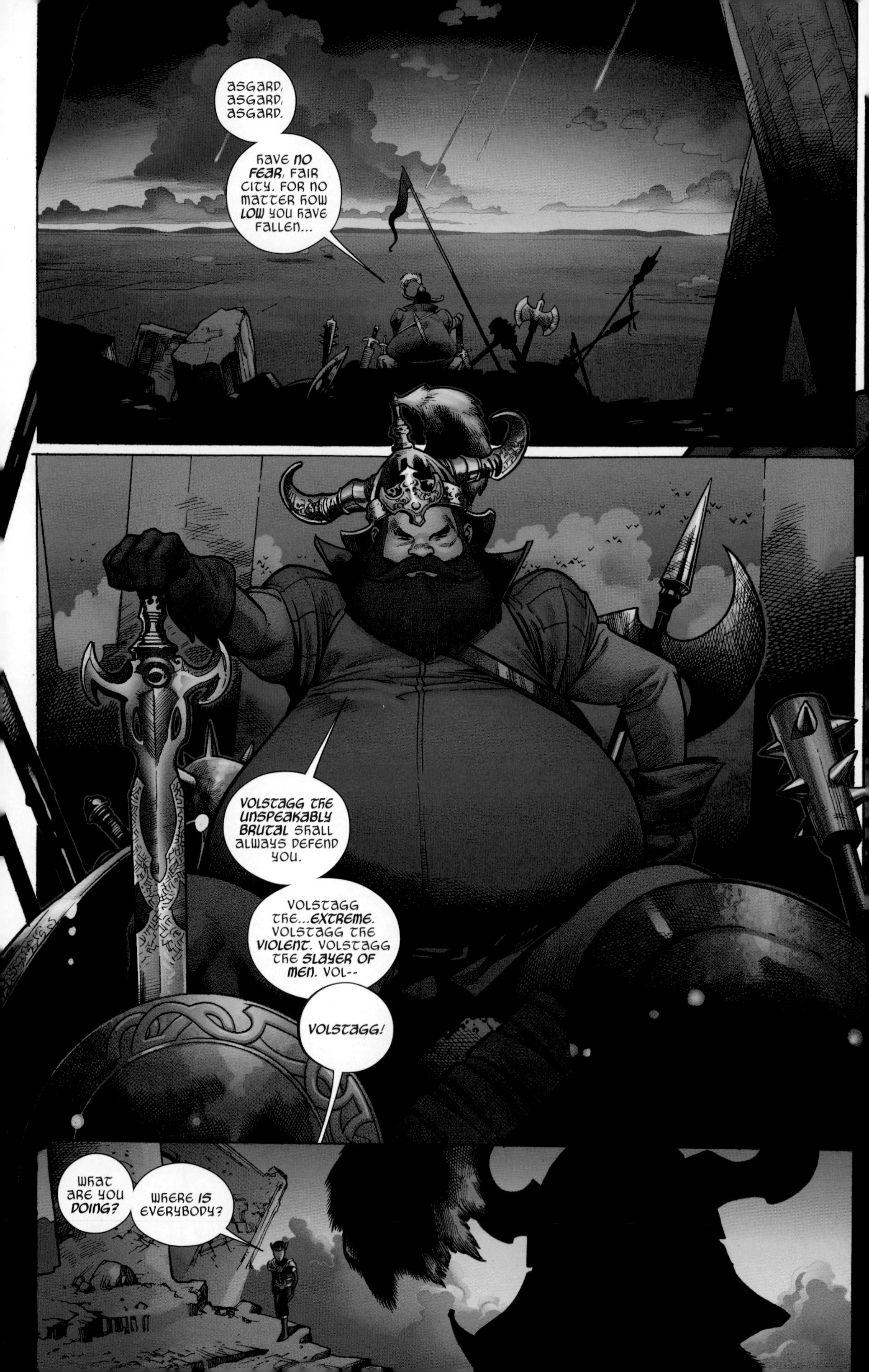
ASGARD, ASGARD, ASGARD.
HAVE NO FEAR, FAIR CITY. FOR NO MATTER HOW LOW YOU HAVE FALLEN...
VOLSTAGG THE UNSPEAKABLY BRUTAL SHALL ALWAYS DEFEND YOU.
VOLSTAGG THE...EXTREME. VOLSTAGG THE VIOLENT. VOLSTAGG THE SLAYER OF MEN. VOL--
VOLSTAGG!
WHAT ARE YOU DOING?
WHERE IS EVERYBODY?

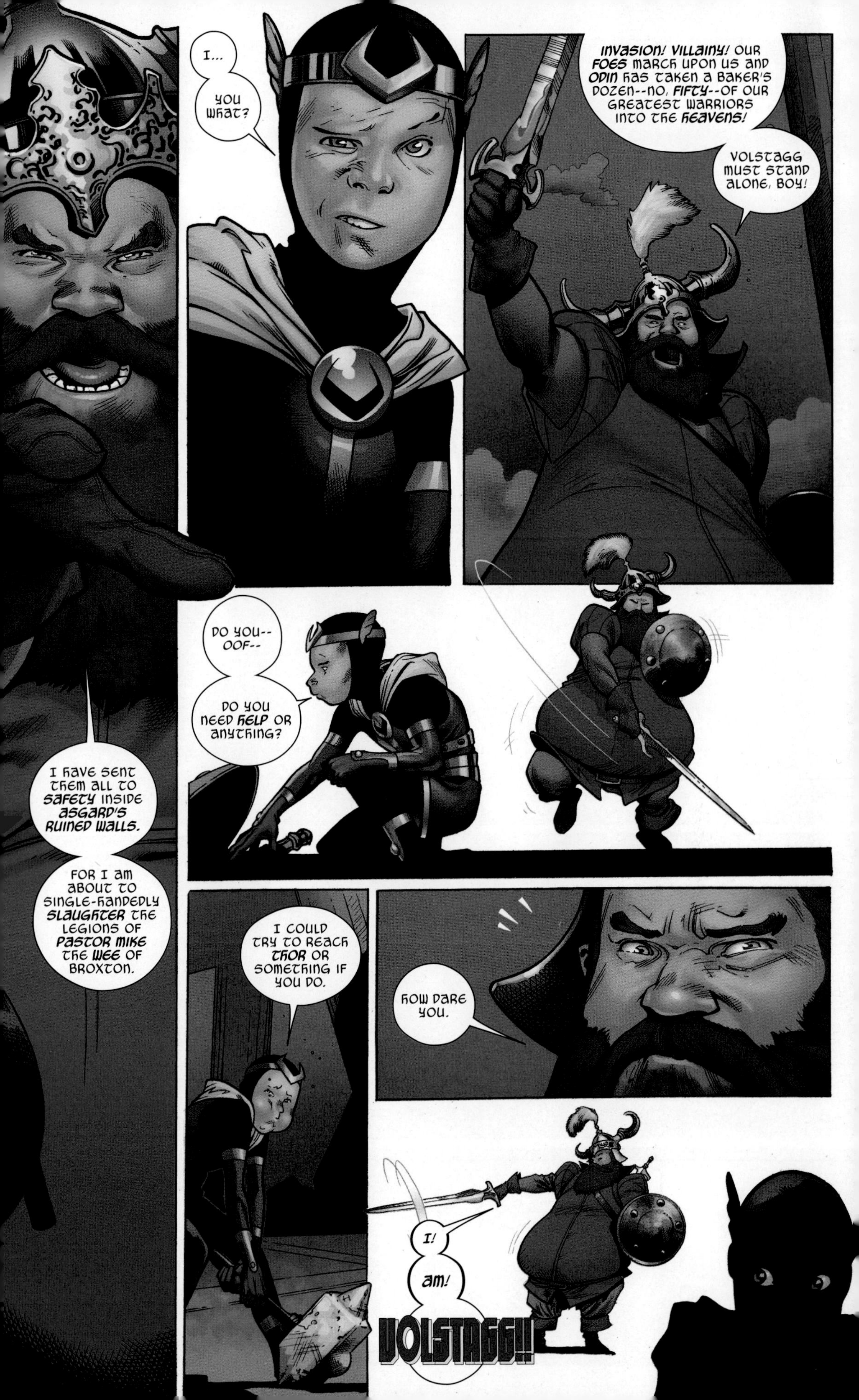
I...
YOU WHAT?
INVASION! VILLAINY! OUR FOES MARCH UPON US AND ODIN HAS TAKEN A BAKER'S DOZEN--NO, FIFTY--OF OUR GREATEST WARRIORS INTO THE HEAVENS!
VOLSTAGG MUST STAND ALONE, BOY!
DO YOU-- OOF--
DO YOU NEED HELP OR ANYTHING?
I HAVE SENT THEM ALL TO SAFETY INSIDE ASGARD'S RUINED WALLS.
FOR I AM ABOUT TO SINGLE-HANDEDLY SLAUGHTER THE LEGIONS OF PASTOR MIKE THE WEE OF BROXTON.
I COULD TRY TO REACH THOR OR SOMETHING IF YOU DO.
HOW DARE YOU.
I!
AM!
VOLSTAGG!!

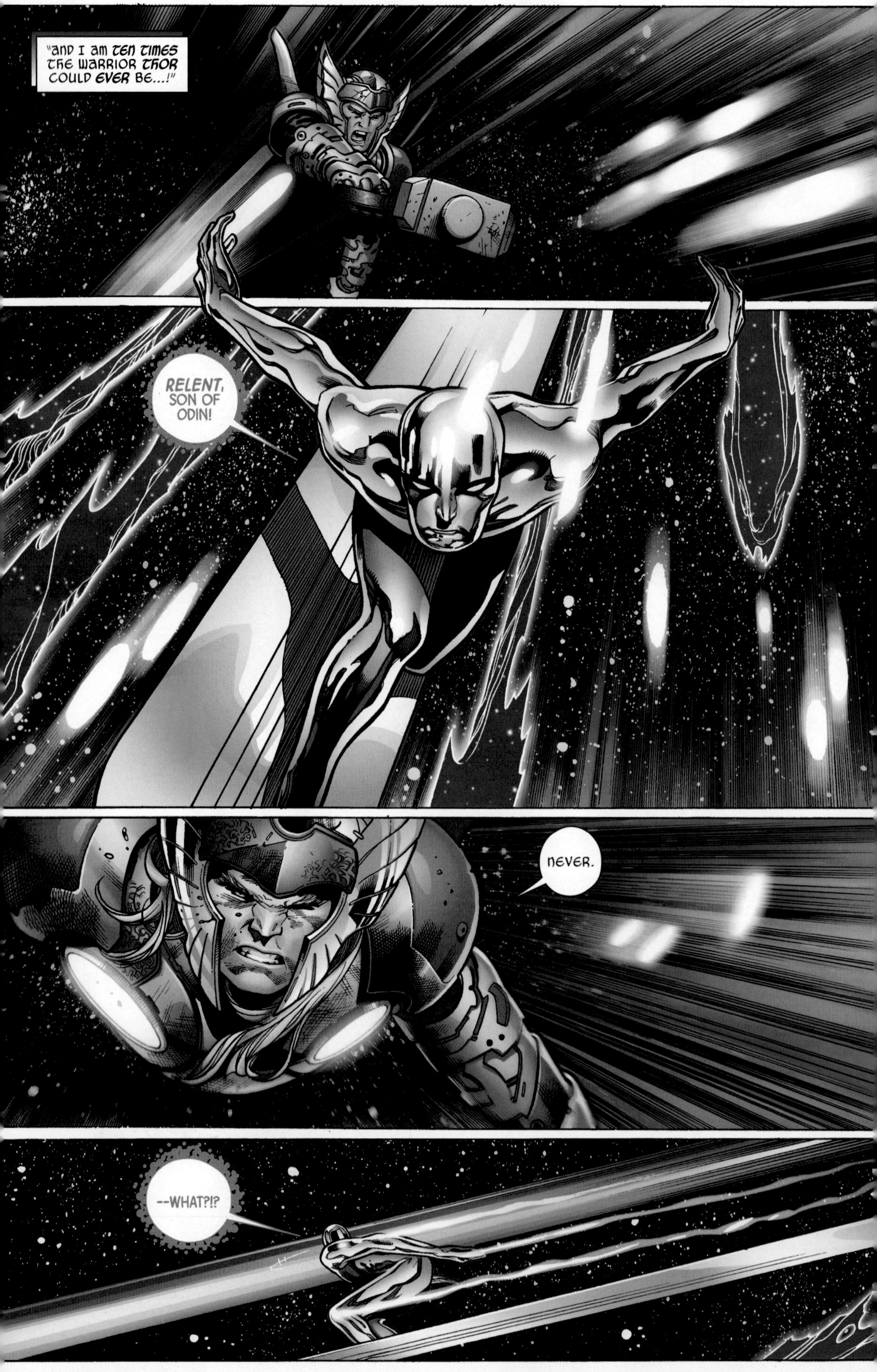
"AND I AM TEN TIMES THE WARRIOR THOR COULD EVER BE...!"
RELENT, SON OF ODIN!
NEVER.
--WHAT?!?

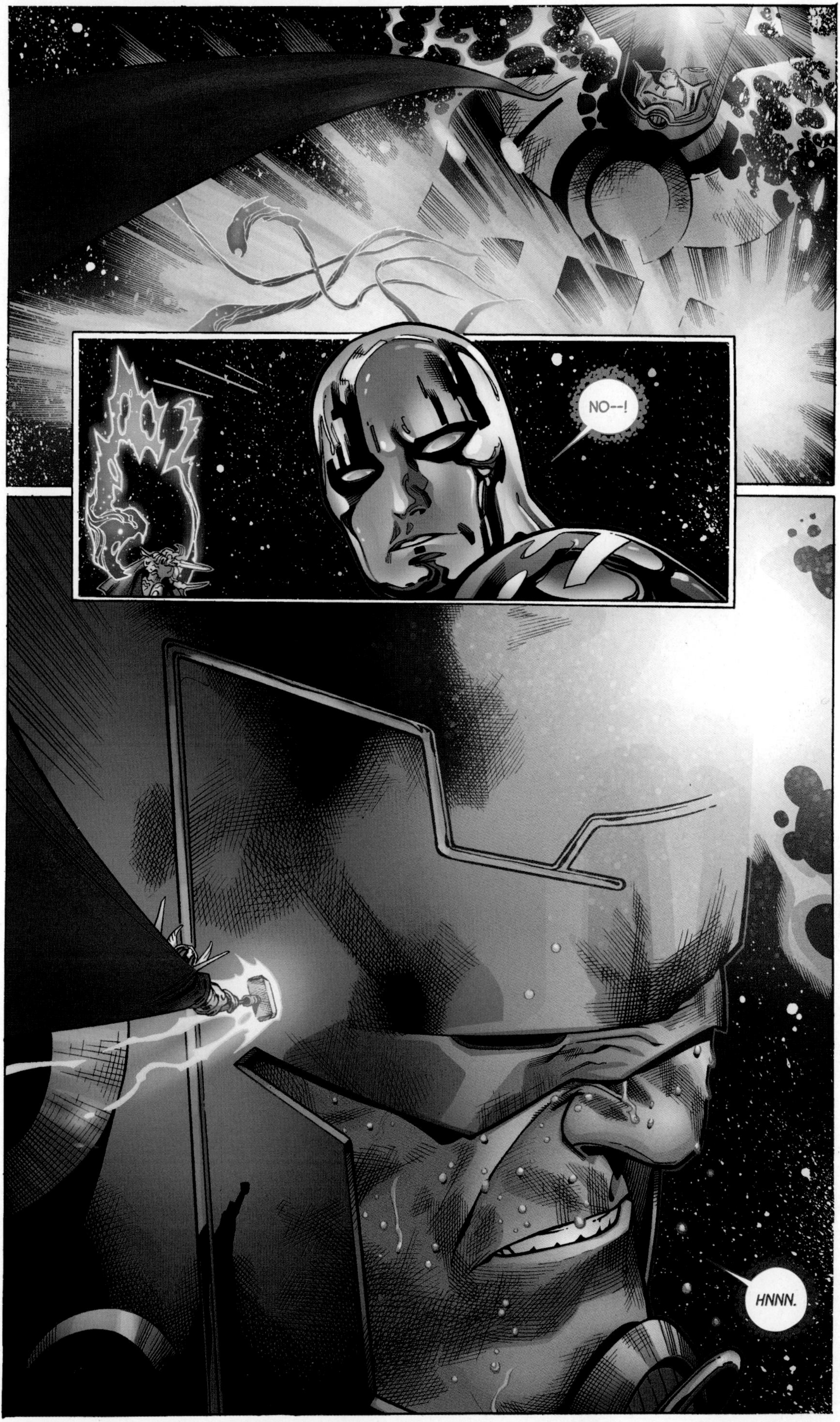
NO--!
HNNN.

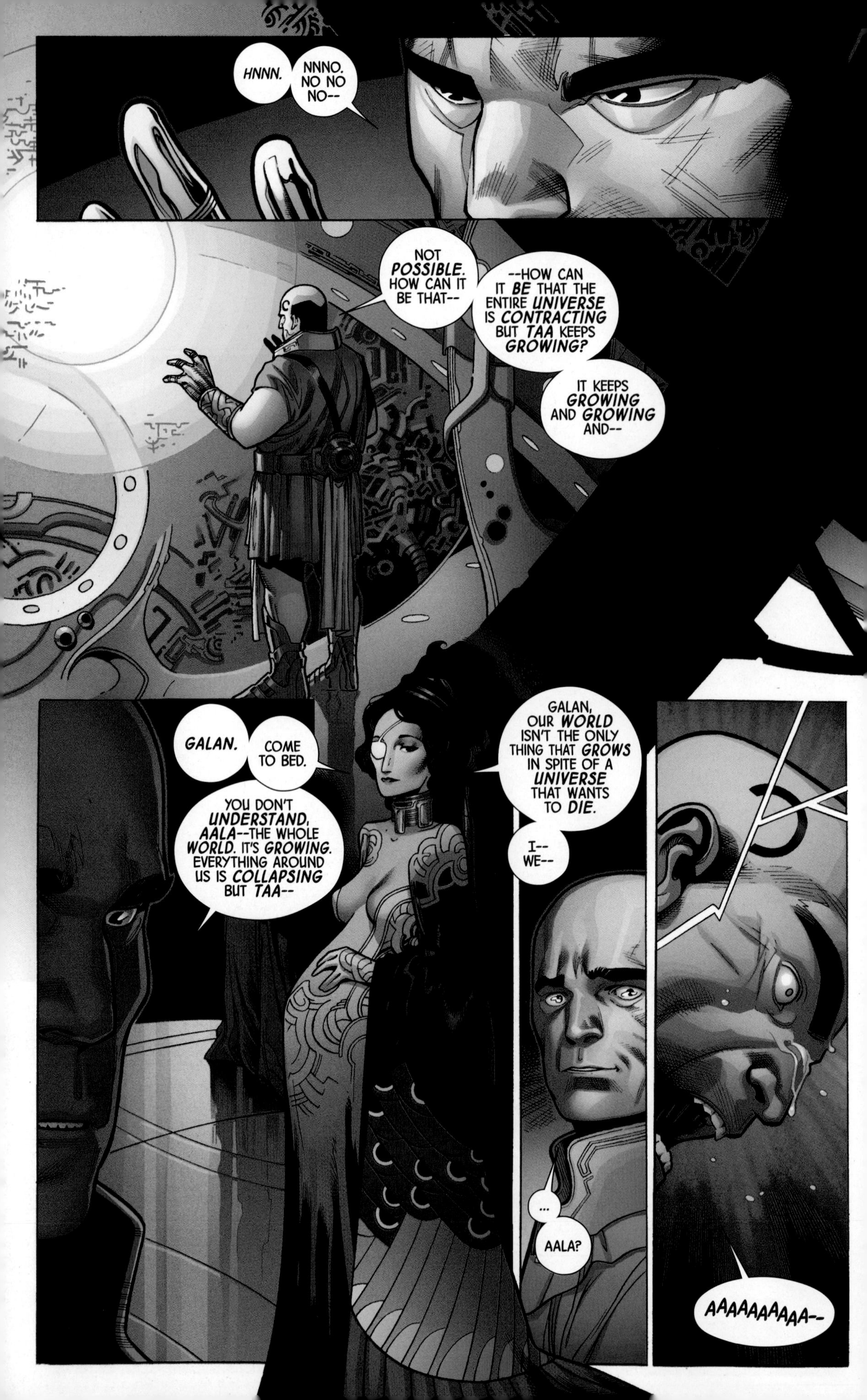
HNNN.
NNNO. NO NO NO--
NOT POSSIBLE. HOW CAN IT BE THAT--
--HOW CAN IT BE THAT THE ENTIRE UNIVERSE IS CONTRACTING BUT TAA KEEPS GROWING?
IT KEEPS GROWING AND GROWING AND--
GALAN.
COME TO BED.
YOU DON'T UNDERSTAND, AALA--THE WHOLE WORLD. IT'S GROWING. EVERYTHING AROUND US IS COLLAPSING BUT TAA--
GALAN, OUR WORLD ISN'T THE ONLY THING THAT GROWS IN SPITE OF A UNIVERSE THAT WANTS TO DIE.
I-- WE--
...
AALA?
AAAAAAAAAA--

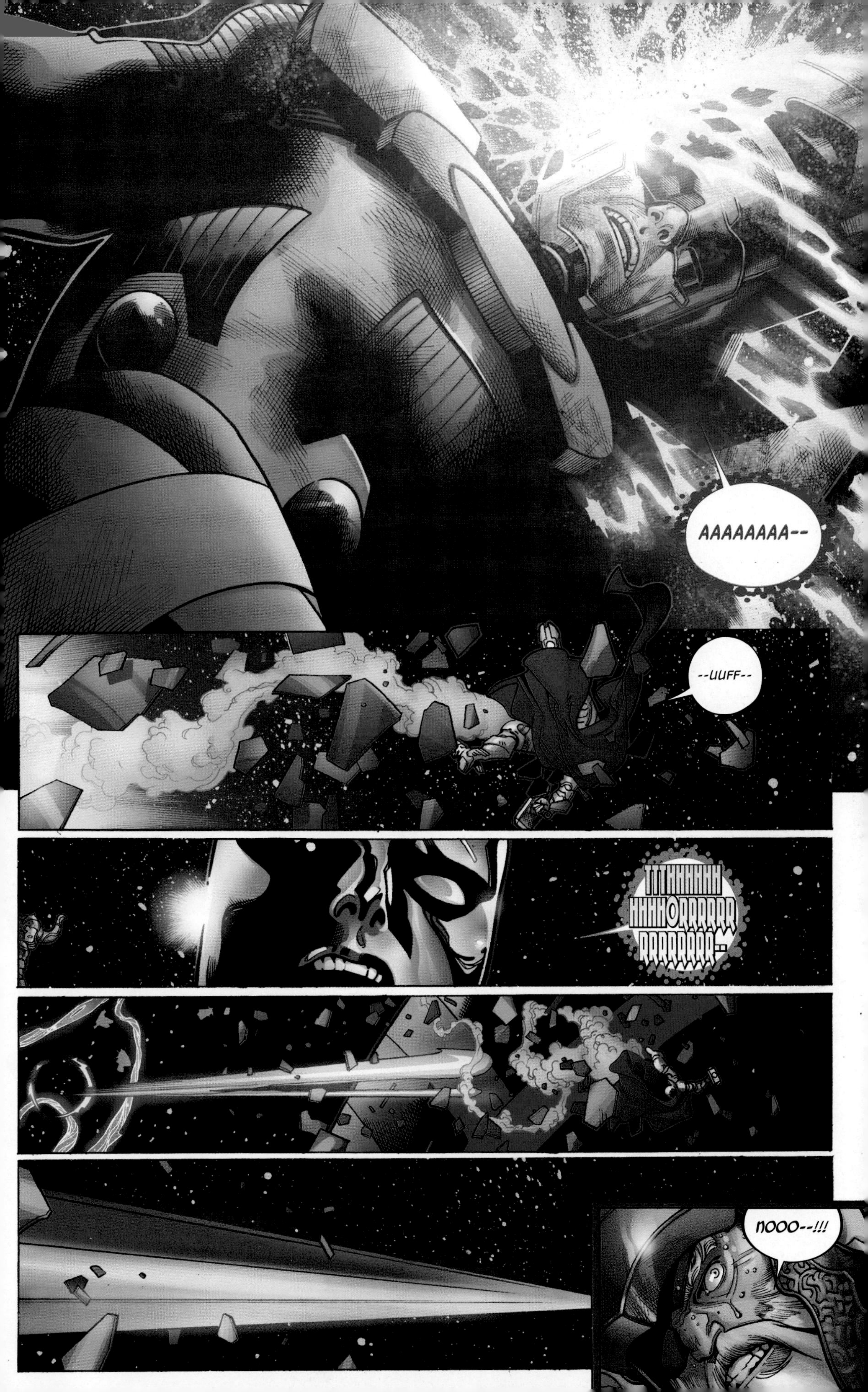
AAAAAAAA--
--UUFF--
TTTHHHHHH HHHHORRRRRR RRRRRRRR--
NOOO--!!!

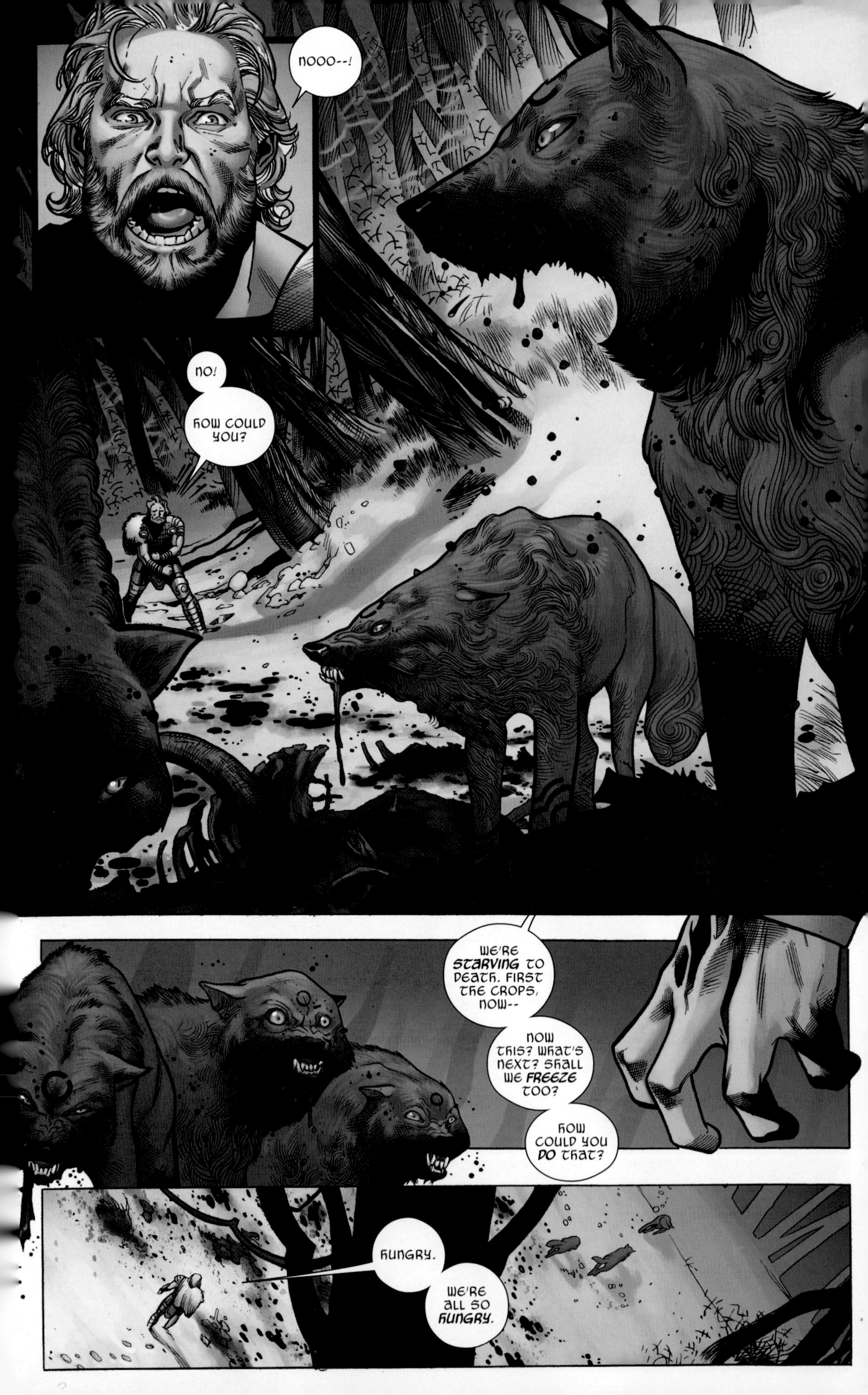
NOOO--!
NO!
HOW COULD YOU?
WE'RE STARVING TO DEATH. FIRST THE CROPS, NOW--
NOW THIS? WHAT'S NEXT? SHALL WE FREEZE TOO?
HOW COULD YOU DO THAT?
HUNGRY.
WE'RE ALL SO HUNGRY.

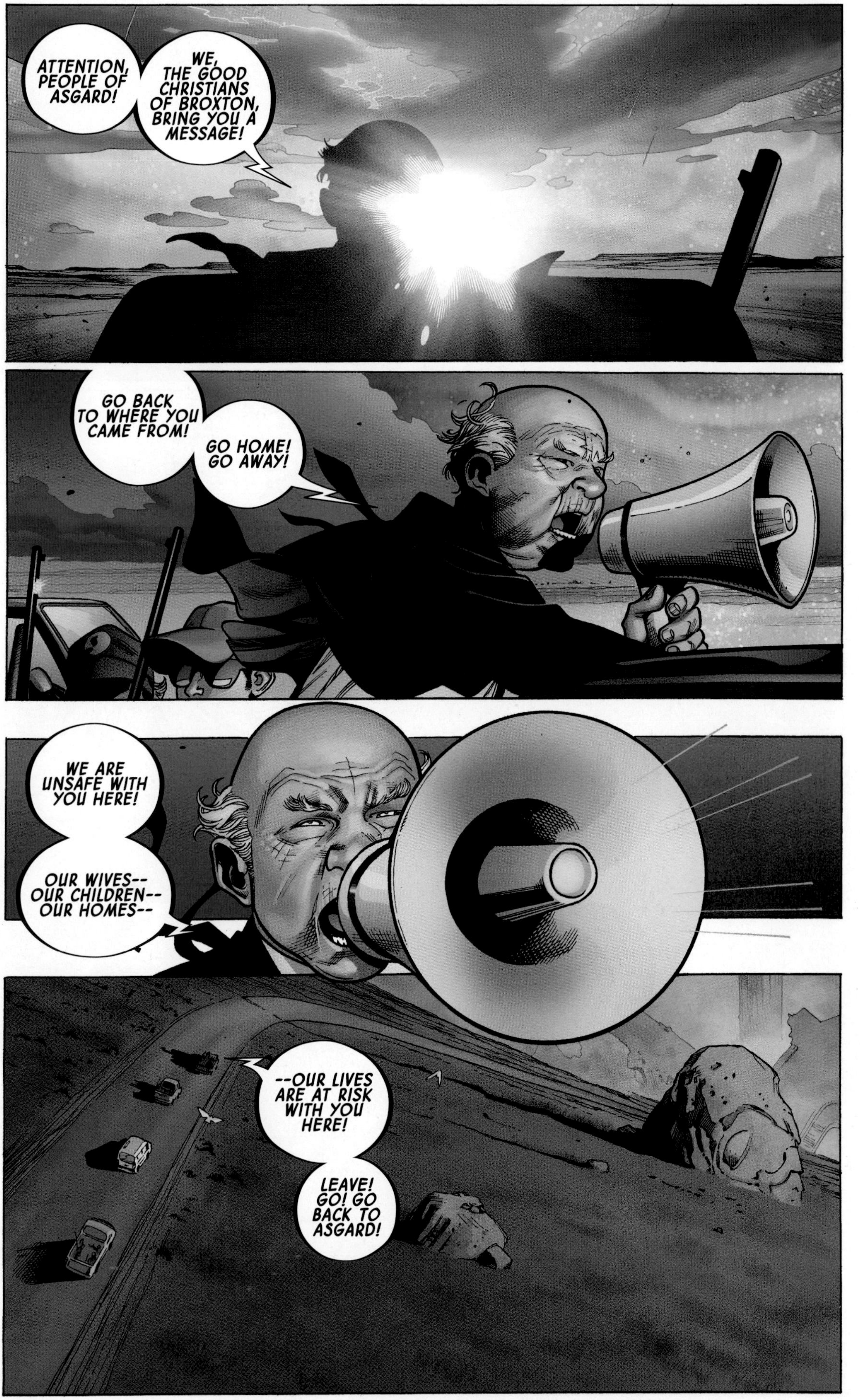

ATTENTION, PEOPLE OF ASGARD!
WE, THE GOOD CHRISTIANS OF BROXTON, BRING YOU A MESSAGE!
GO BACK TO WHERE YOU CAME FROM!
GO HOME! GO AWAY!
WE ARE UNSAFE WITH YOU HERE!
OUR WIVES-- OUR CHILDREN-- OUR HOMES--
--OUR LIVES ARE AT RISK WITH YOU HERE!
LEAVE! GO! GO BACK TO ASGARD!

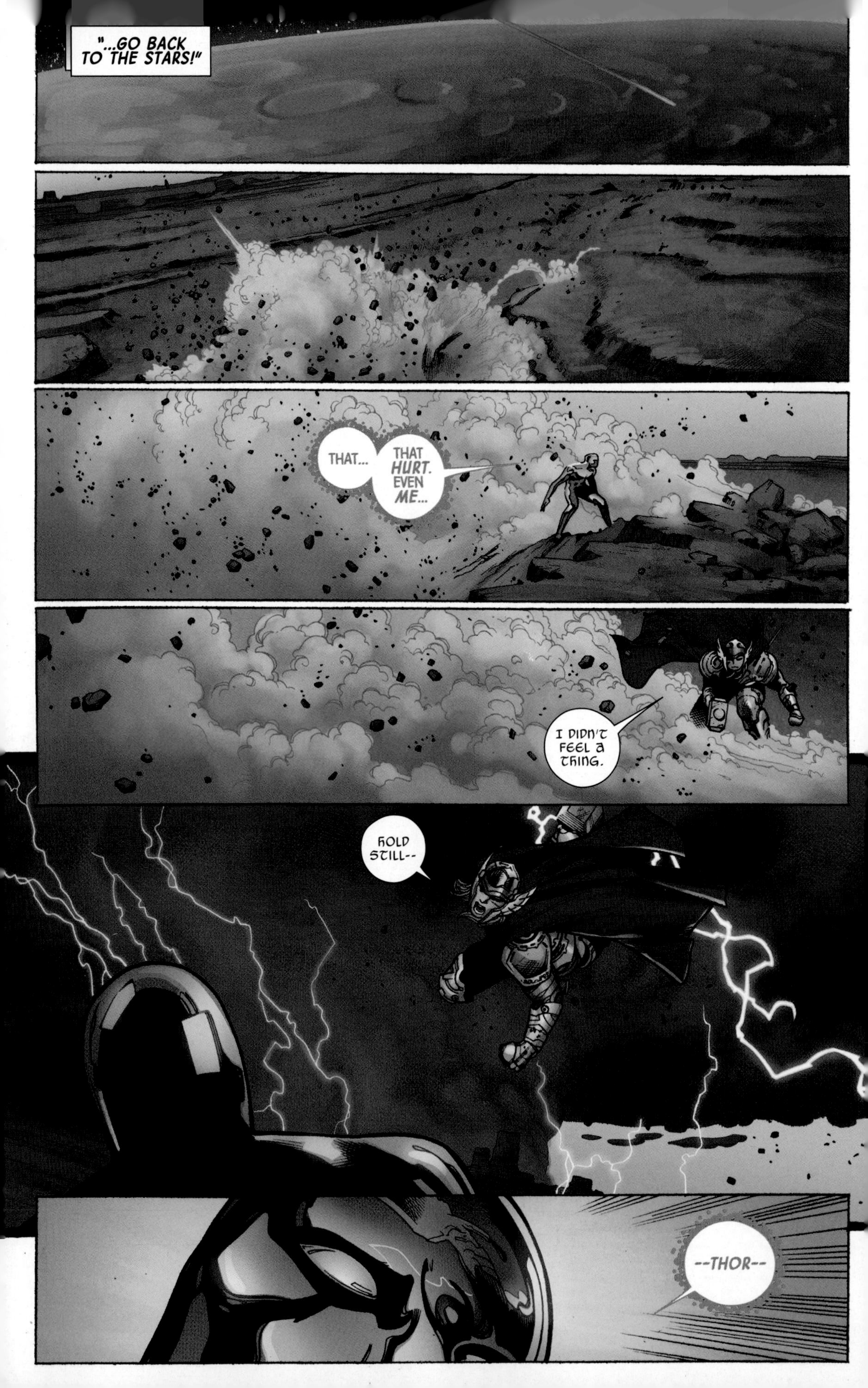
"...GO BACK TO THE STARS!"
THAT...
THAT HURT. EVEN ME...
I DIDN'T FEEL A THING.
HOLD STILL--
--THOR--

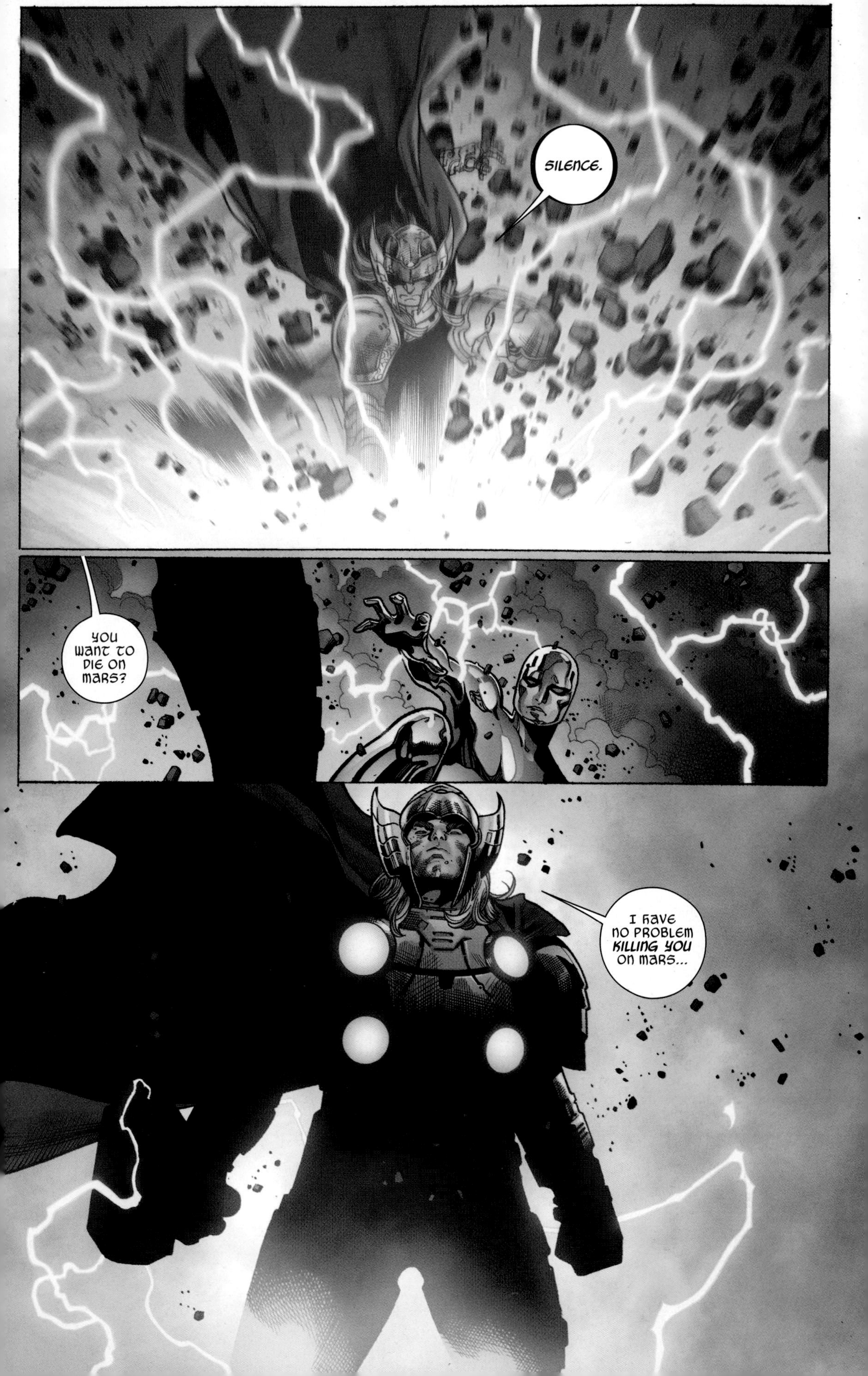
SILENCE.
YOU WANT TO DIE ON MARS?
I HAVE NO PROBLEM **KILLING YOU** ON MARS...

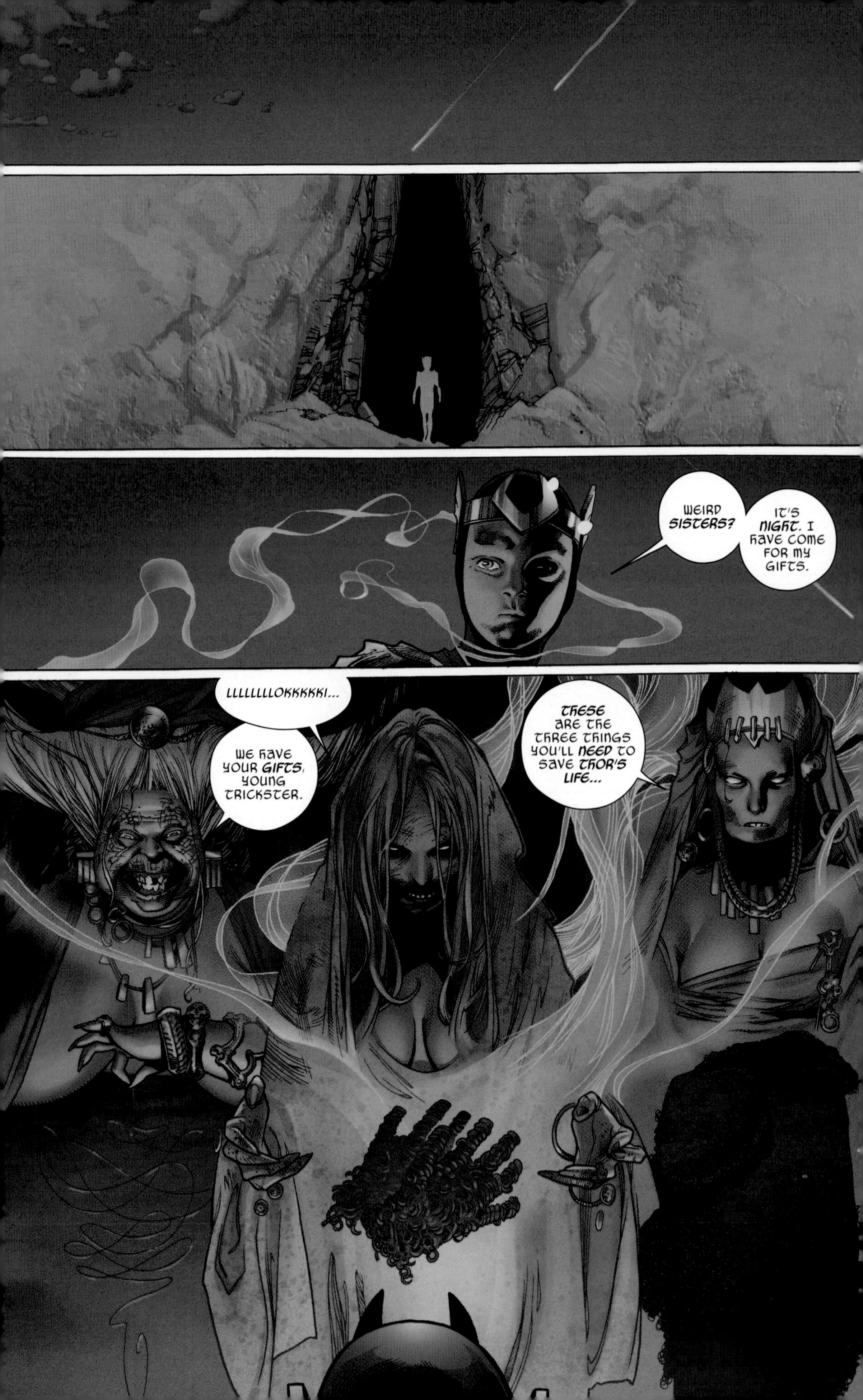
WEIRD SISTERS?
IT'S NIGHT. I HAVE COME FOR MY GIFTS.
LLLLLLLLOKKKKKI...
WE HAVE YOUR GIFTS, YOUNG TRICKSTER.
THESE ARE THE THREE THINGS YOU'LL NEED TO SAVE THOR'S LIFE...

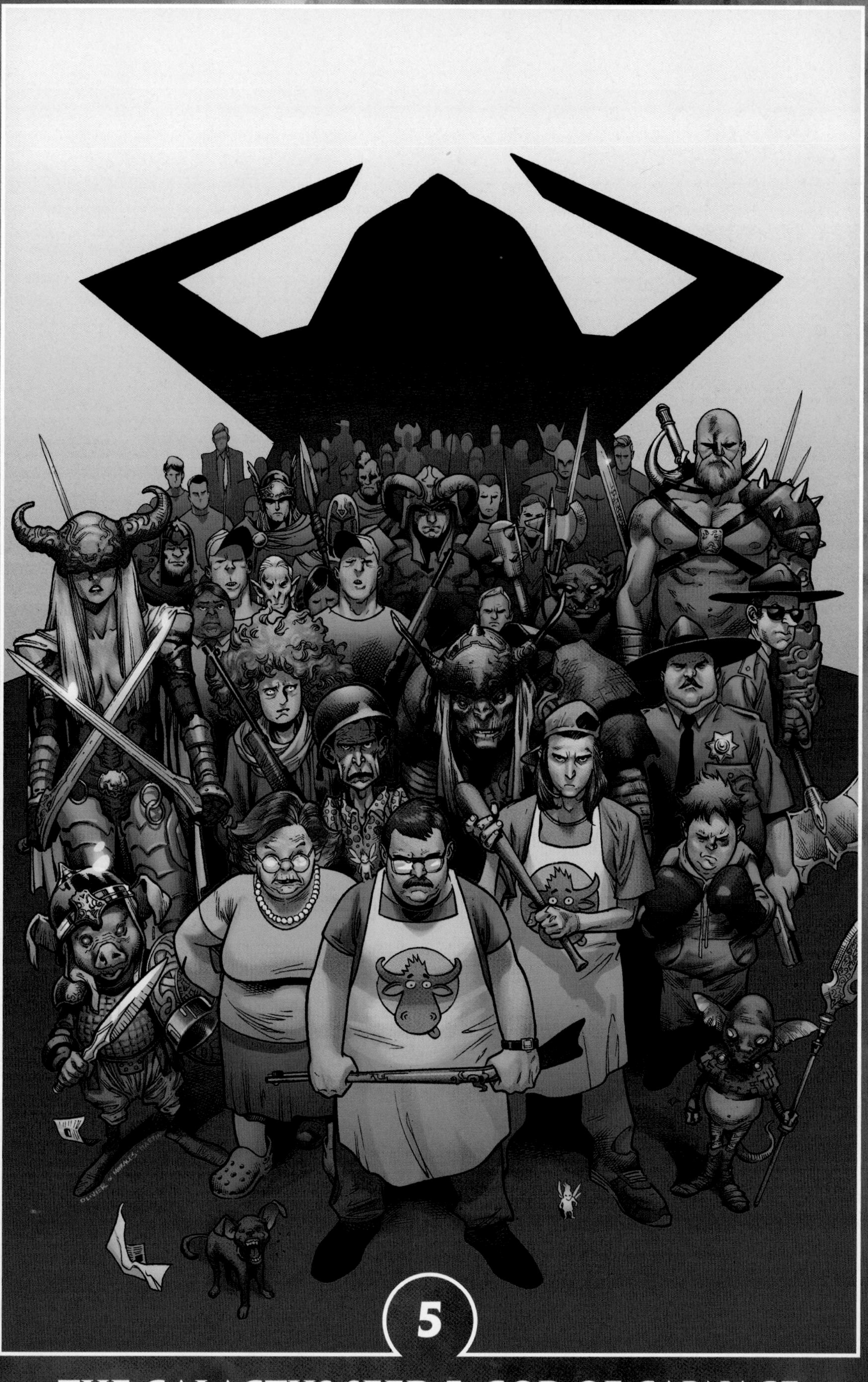
5

THE GALACTUS SEED 5: GOD OF CARNAGE

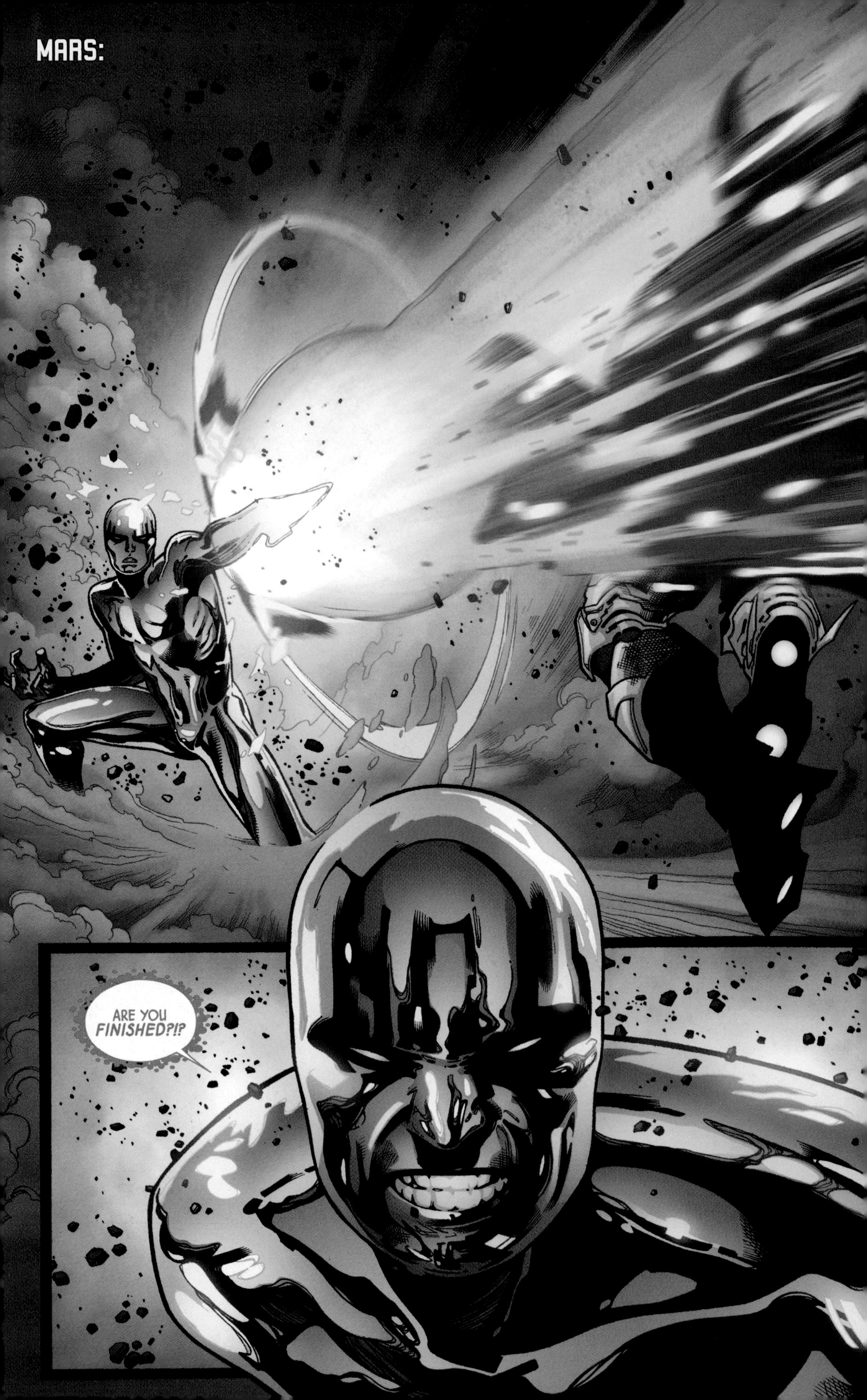
MARS:
ARE YOU FINISHED?!?

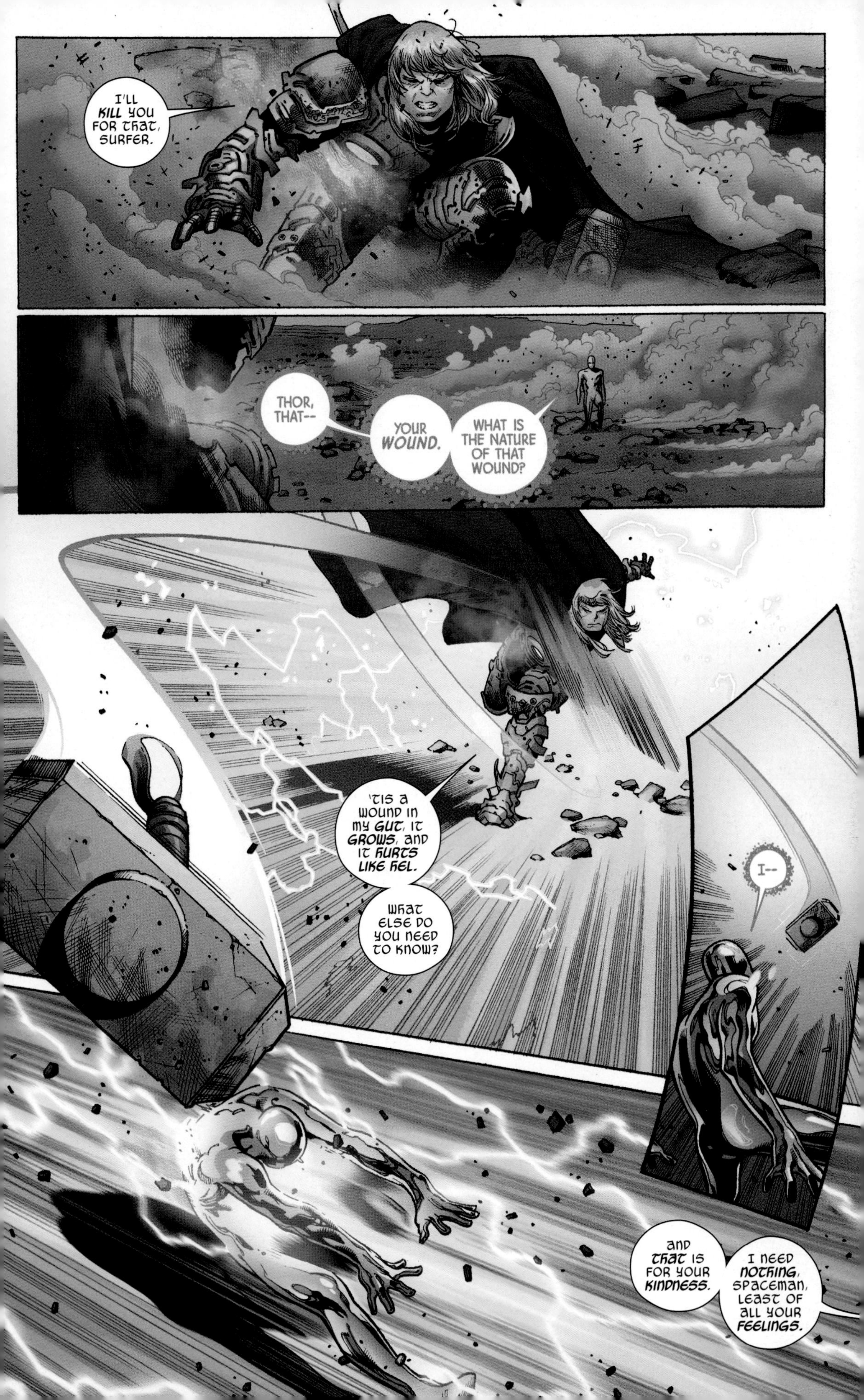
I'LL KILL YOU FOR THAT, SURFER.
THOR, THAT--
YOUR WOUND.
WHAT IS THE NATURE OF THAT WOUND?
'TIS A WOUND IN MY GUT, IT GROWS, AND IT HURTS LIKE HEL.
WHAT ELSE DO YOU NEED TO KNOW?
I--
I NEED NOTHING, SPACEMAN, LEAST OF ALL YOUR FEELINGS.
AND THAT IS FOR YOUR KINDNESS.

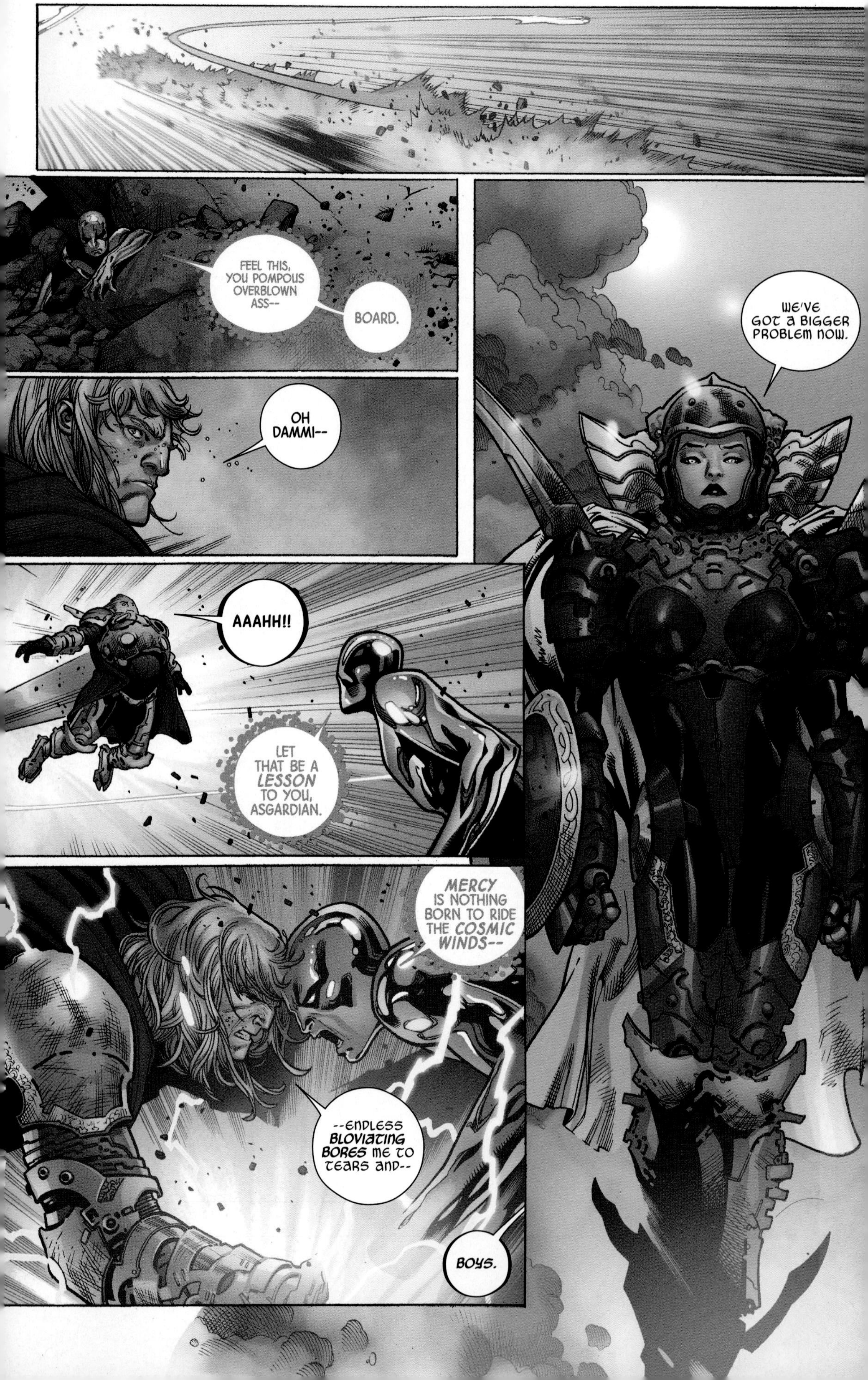
FEEL THIS, YOU POMPOUS OVERBLOWN ASS--
BOARD.
OH DAMMI--
AAAHH!!
LET THAT BE A *LESSON* TO YOU, ASGARDIAN.
MERCY IS NOTHING BORN TO RIDE THE *COSMIC WINDS*--
--ENDLESS *BLOVIATING BORES* ME TO TEARS AND--
WE'VE GOT A BIGGER PROBLEM NOW.
BOYS.

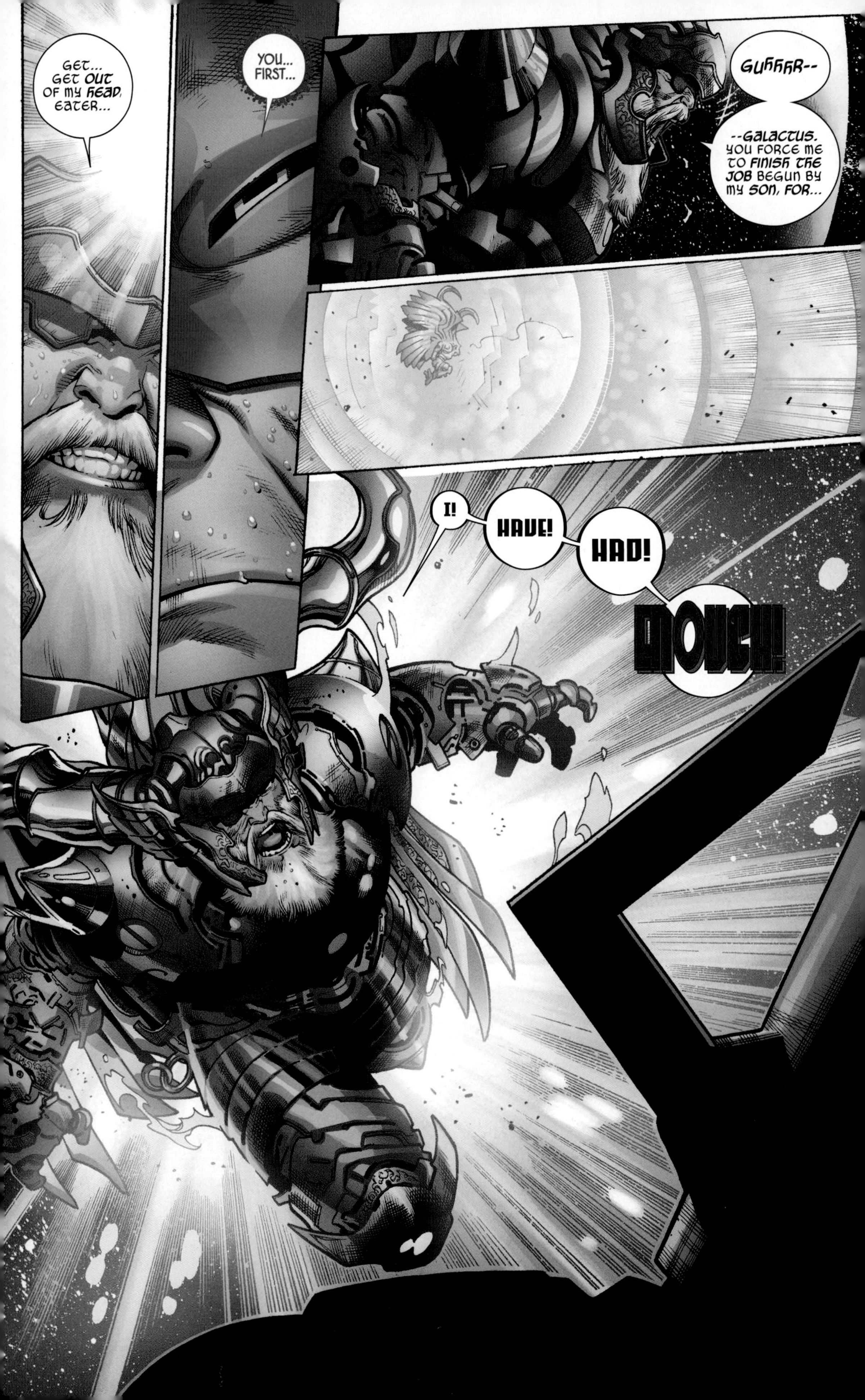
GET... GET OUT OF MY HEAD, EATER...
YOU... FIRST...
GUHHHR--
--GALACTUS. YOU FORCE ME TO FINISH THE JOB BEGUN BY MY SON, FOR...
I!
HAVE!
HAD!
ENOUGH!

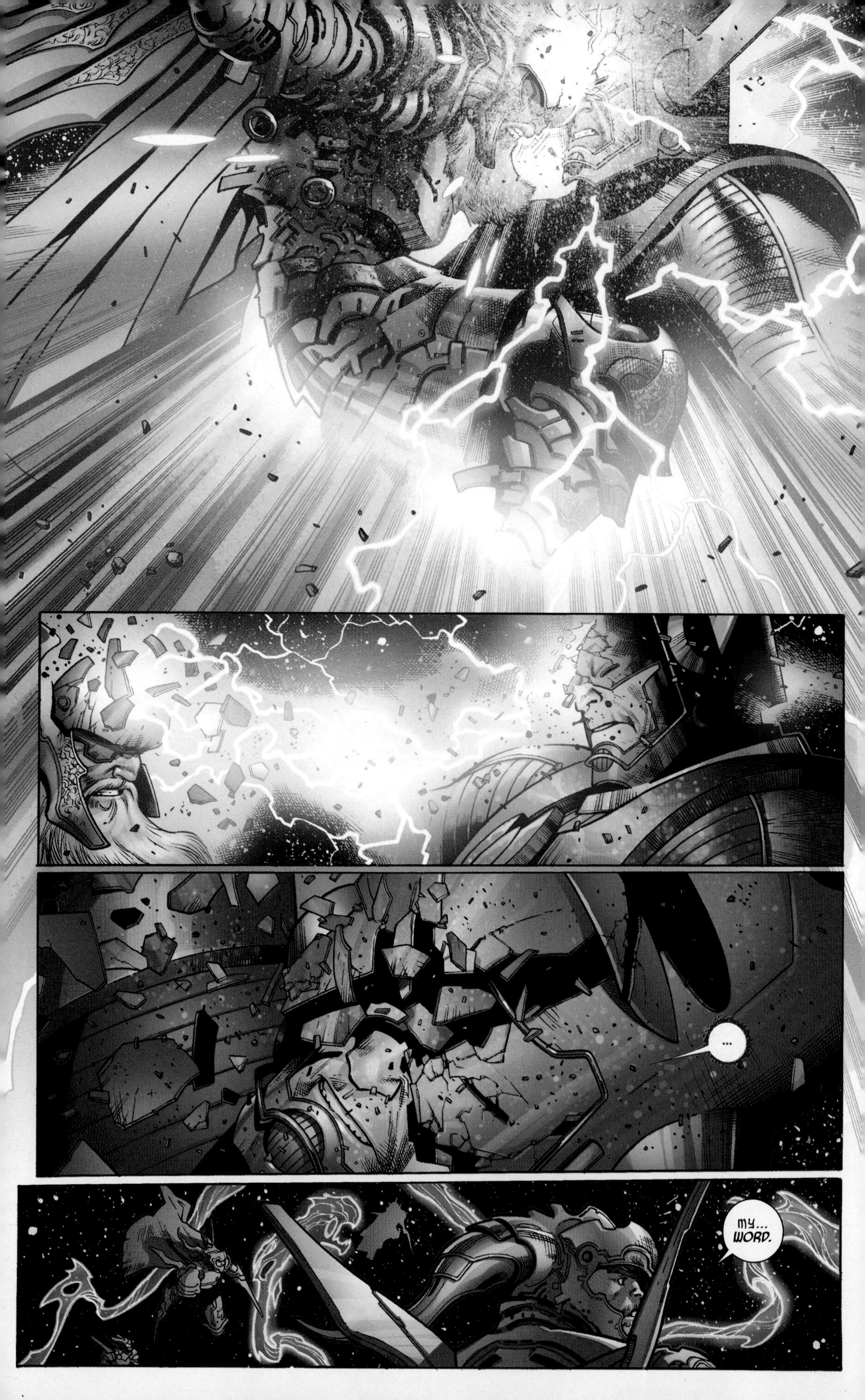
...
MY... WORD.

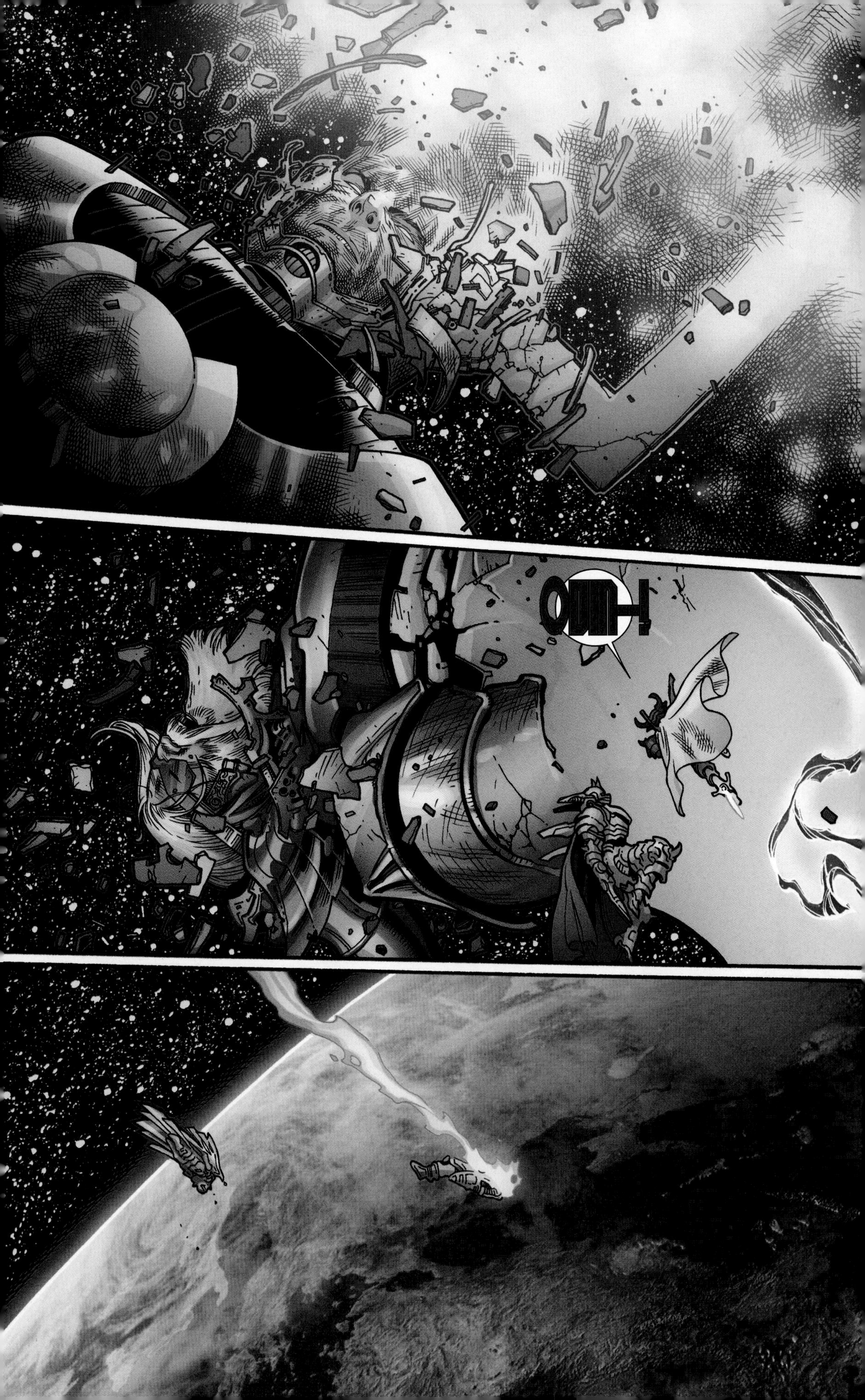
ODIN—!

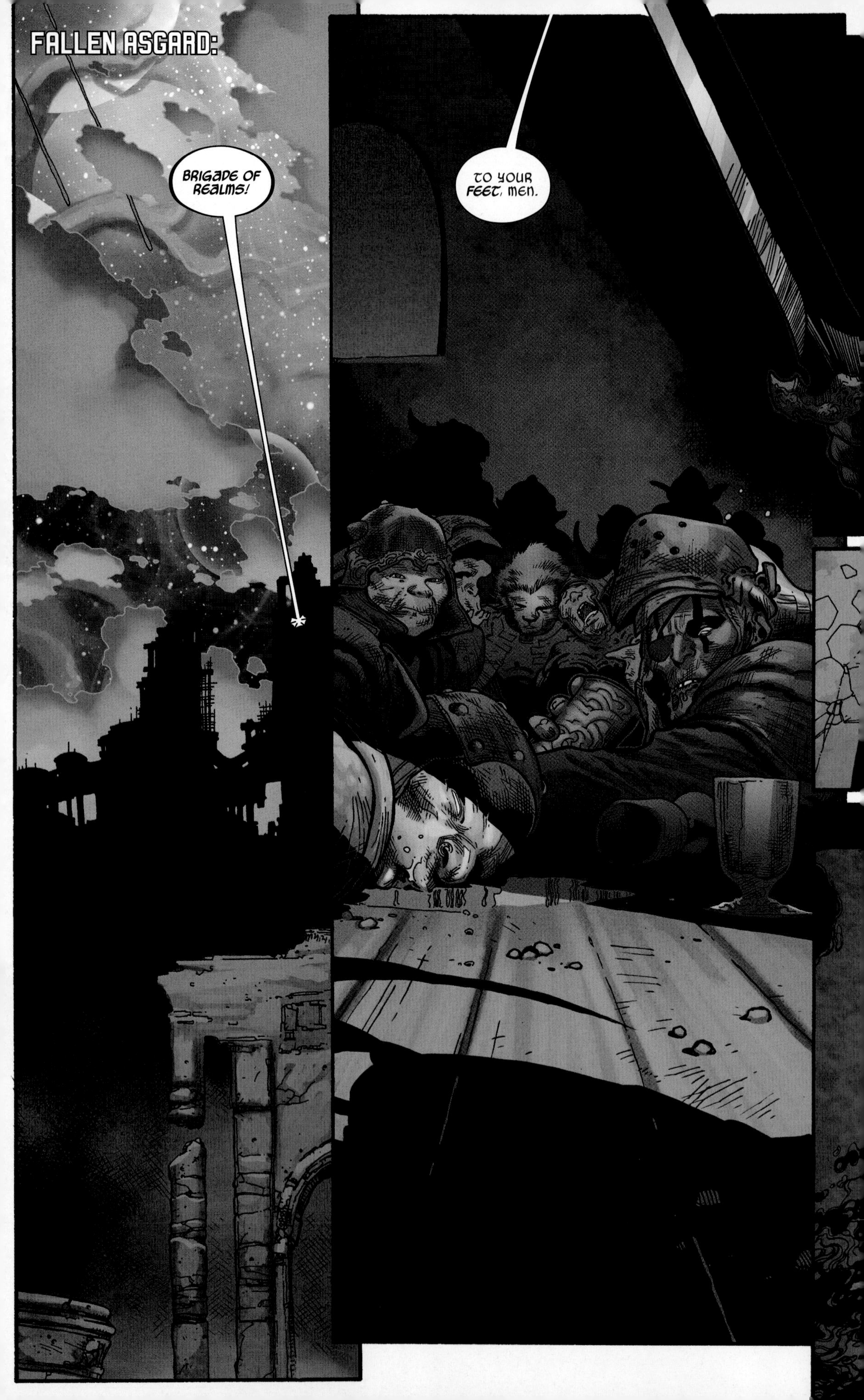
FALLEN ASGARD:
BRIGADE OF REALMS!
TO YOUR FEET, MEN.

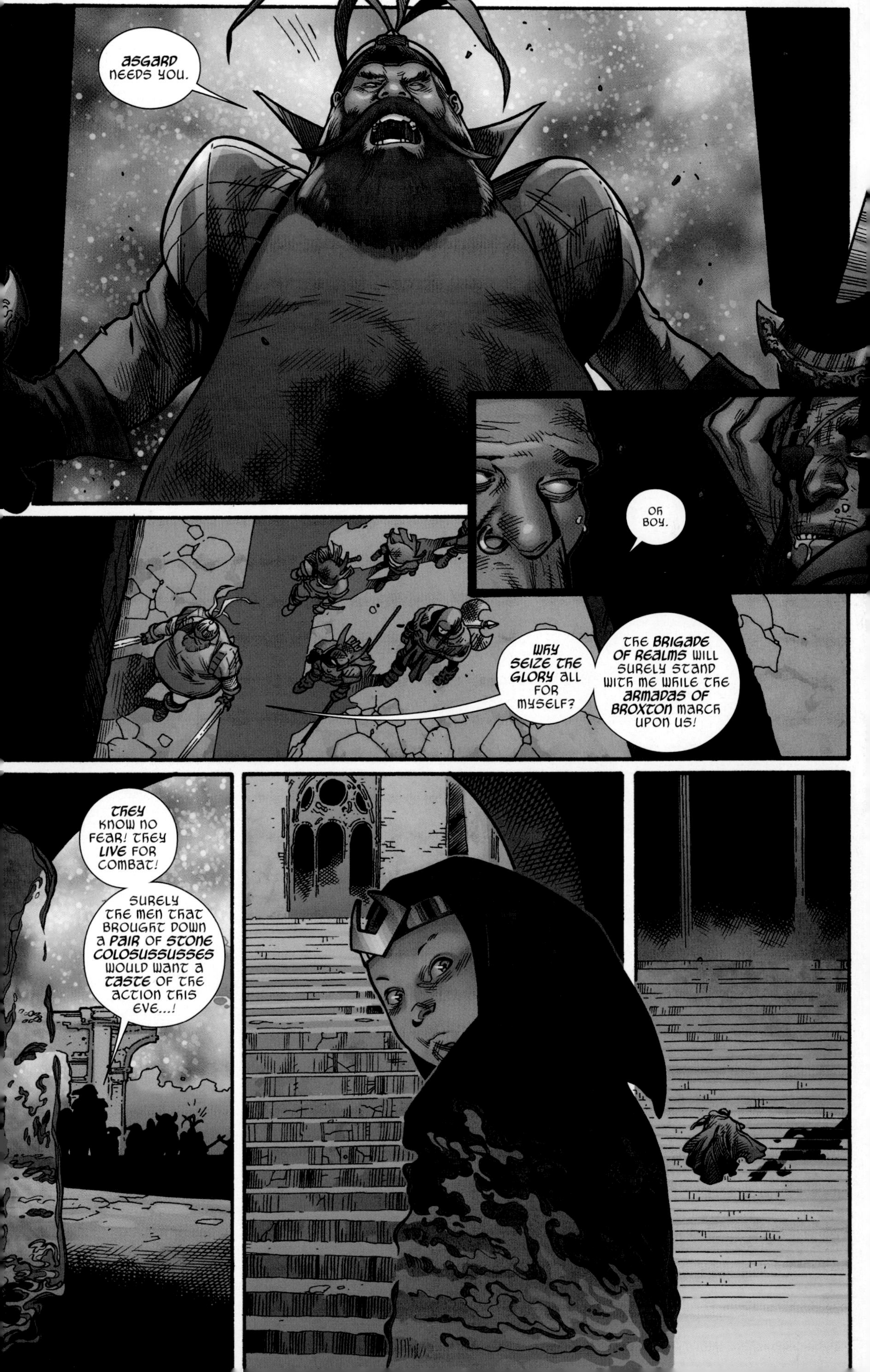
ASGARD NEEDS YOU.
OH BOY.
WHY SEIZE THE GLORY ALL FOR MYSELF?
THE BRIGADE OF REALMS WILL SURELY STAND WITH ME WHILE THE ARMADAS OF BROXTON MARCH UPON US!
THEY KNOW NO FEAR! THEY LIVE FOR COMBAT!
SURELY THE MEN THAT BROUGHT DOWN A PAIR OF STONE COLOSUSSUSSES WOULD WANT A TASTE OF THE ACTION THIS EVE...!

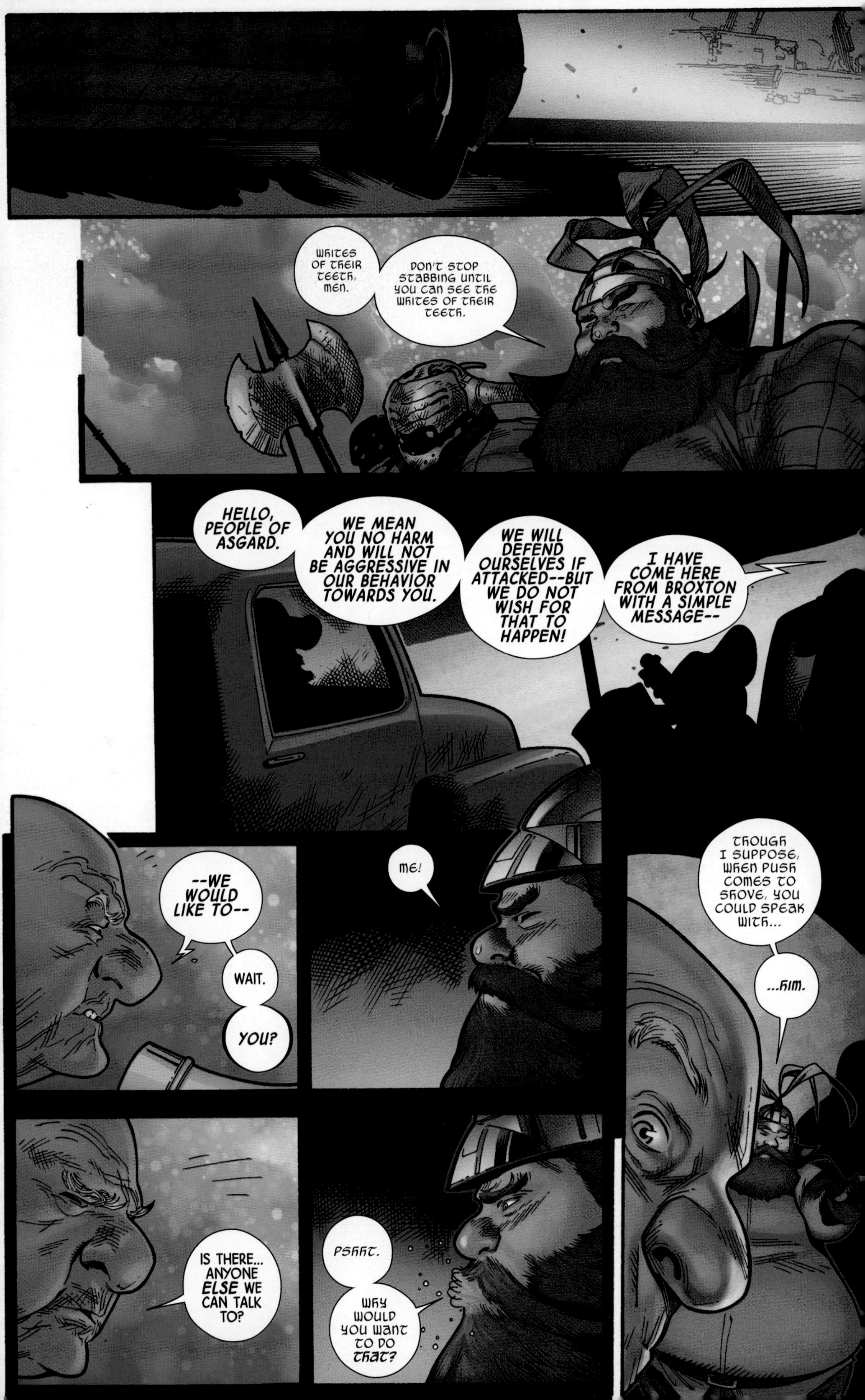
WHITES OF THEIR TEETH, MEN.
DON'T STOP STABBING UNTIL YOU CAN SEE THE WHITES OF THEIR TEETH.
HELLO, PEOPLE OF ASGARD.
WE MEAN YOU NO HARM AND WILL NOT BE AGGRESSIVE IN OUR BEHAVIOR TOWARDS YOU.
WE WILL DEFEND OURSELVES IF ATTACKED--BUT WE DO NOT WISH FOR THAT TO HAPPEN!
I HAVE COME HERE FROM BROXTON WITH A SIMPLE MESSAGE--
--WE WOULD LIKE TO--
WAIT.
YOU?
ME!
THOUGH I SUPPOSE, WHEN PUSH COMES TO SHOVE, YOU COULD SPEAK WITH...
...HIM.
IS THERE... ANYONE ELSE WE CAN TALK TO?
PSHHT.
WHY WOULD YOU WANT TO DO THAT?

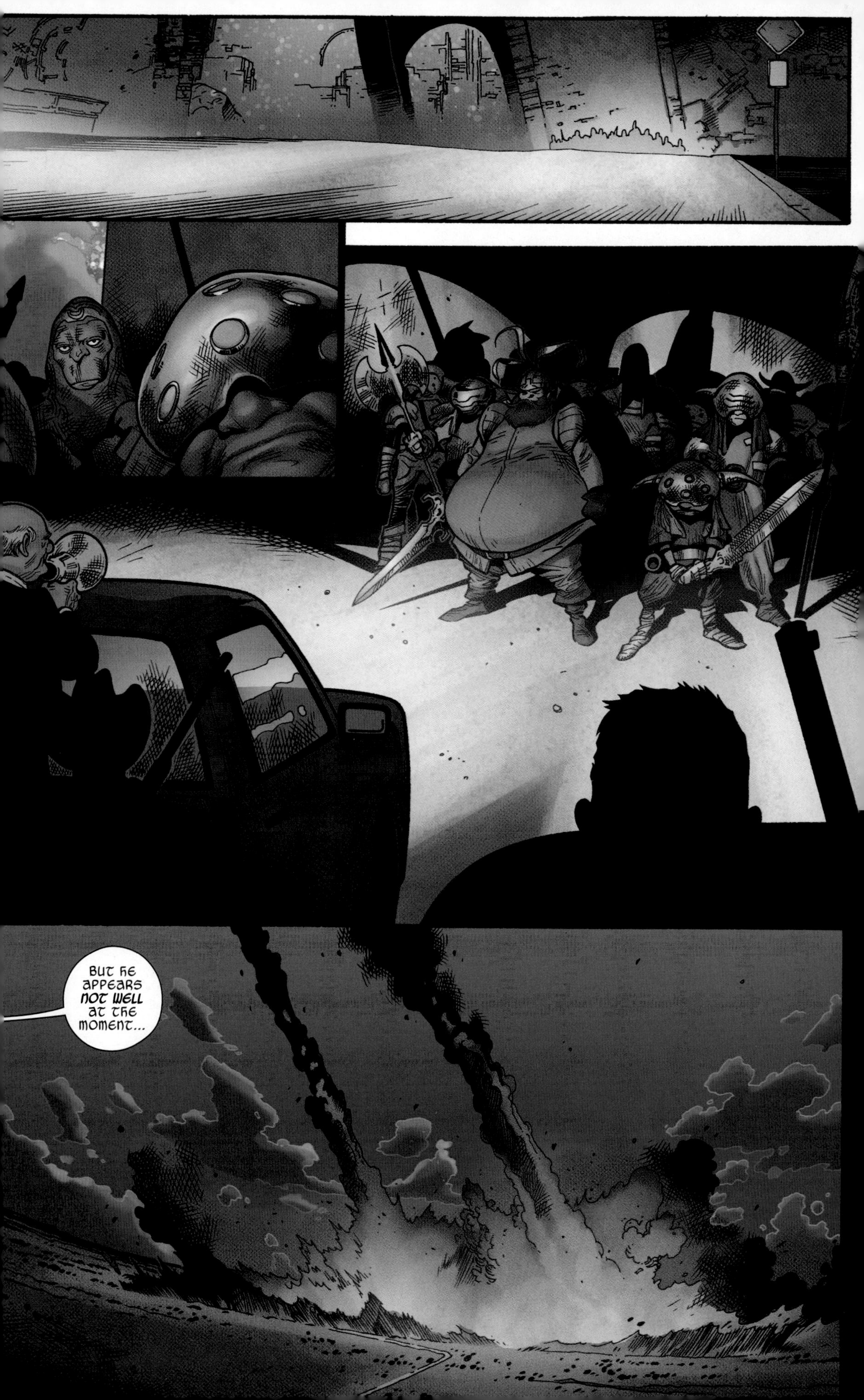
BUT HE APPEARS NOT WELL AT THE MOMENT...

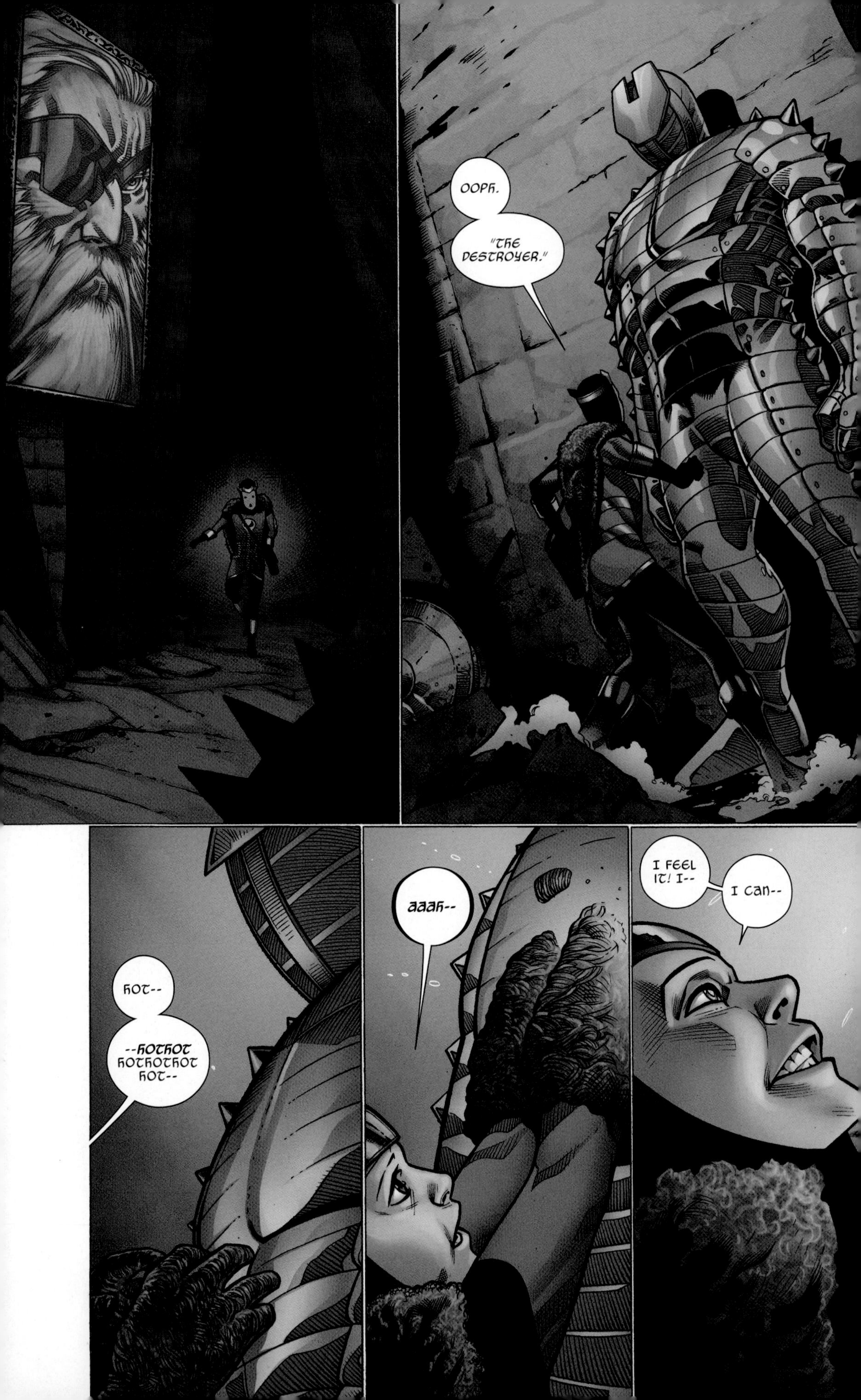
OOPH.
"THE DESTROYER."
HOT--
--HOTHOT HOTHOTHOT HOT--
AAAH--
I FEEL IT! I--
I CAN--

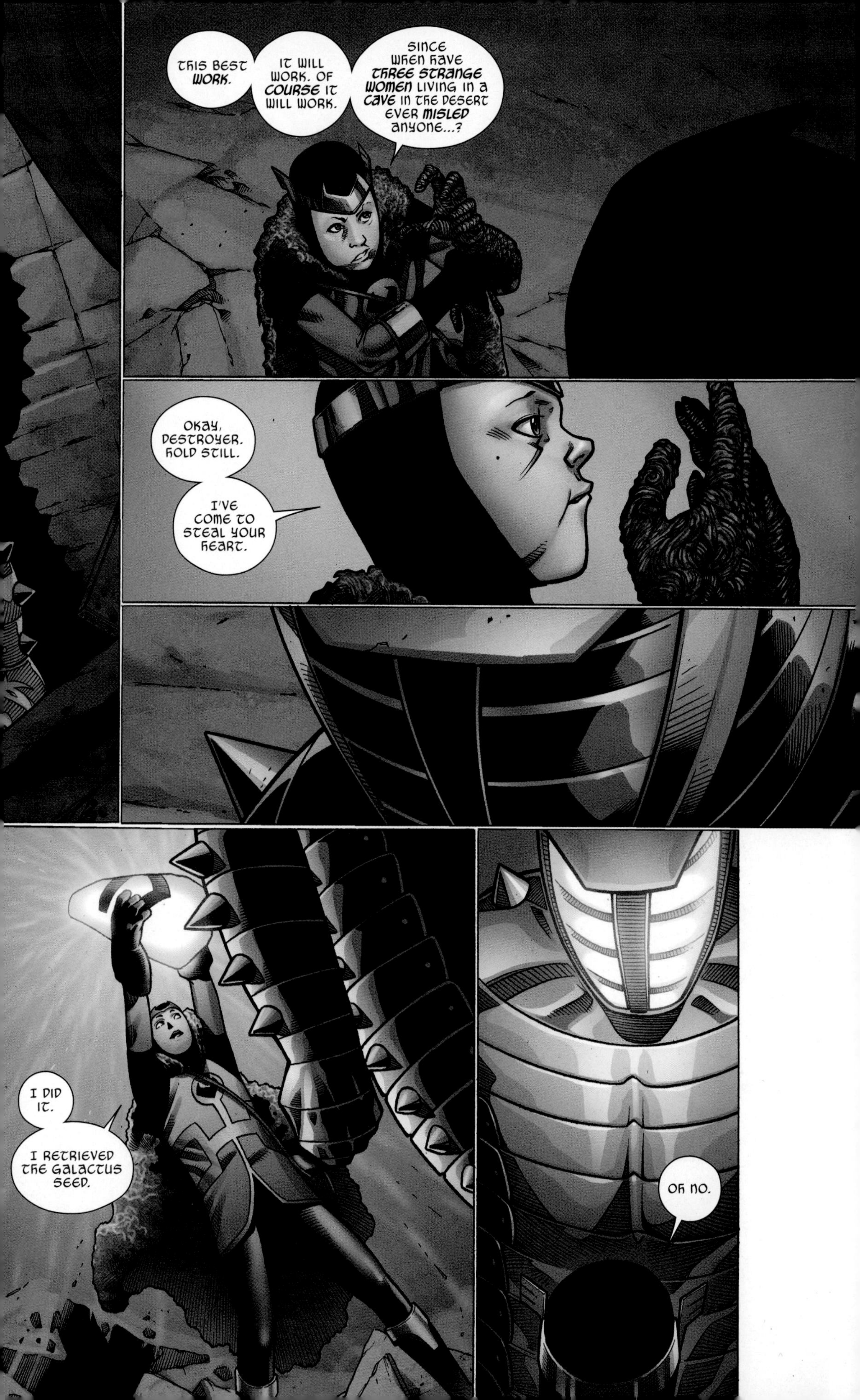

THIS BEST WORK.
IT WILL WORK. OF COURSE IT WILL WORK.
SINCE WHEN HAVE THREE STRANGE WOMEN LIVING IN A CAVE IN THE DESERT EVER MISLED ANYONE...?
OKAY, DESTROYER. HOLD STILL.
I'VE COME TO STEAL YOUR HEART.
I DID IT.
I RETRIEVED THE GALACTUS SEED.
OH NO.

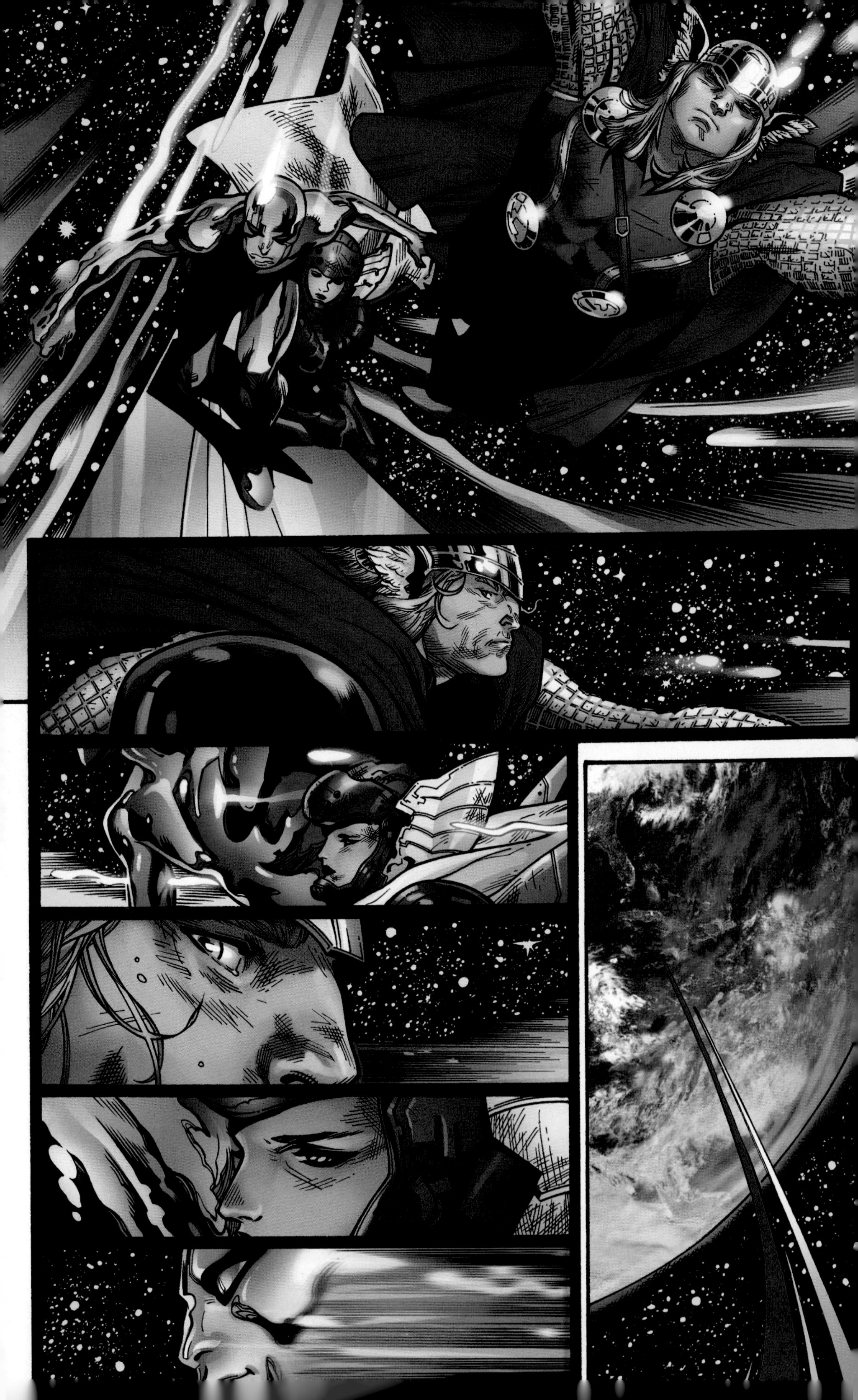

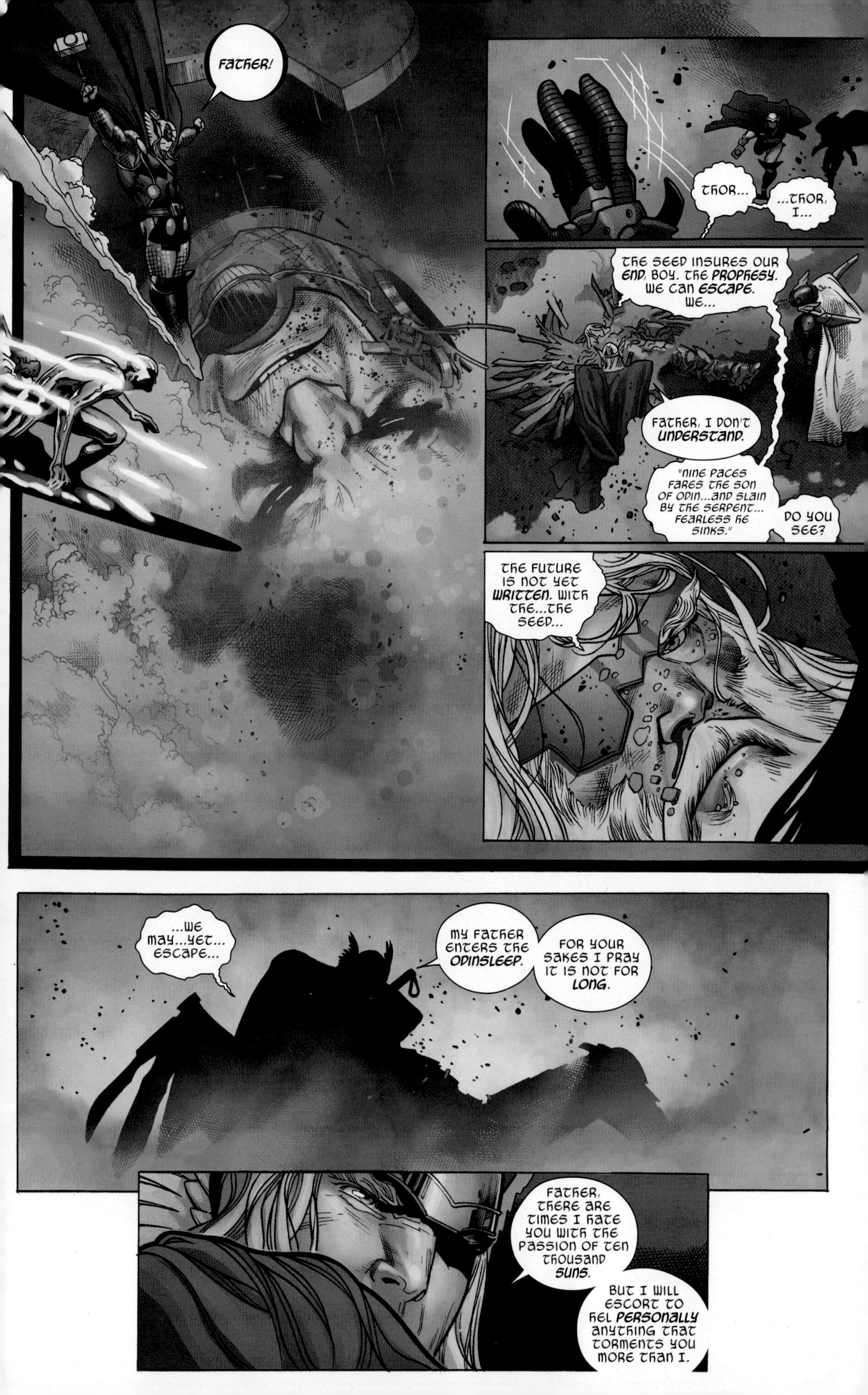

FATHER!
THOR...
...THOR, I...
THE SEED INSURES OUR END, BOY. THE PROPHESY. WE CAN ESCAPE. WE...
FATHER, I DON'T UNDERSTAND.
"NINE PACES FARES THE SON OF ODIN...AND SLAIN BY THE SERPENT... FEARLESS HE SINKS."
DO YOU SEE?
THE FUTURE IS NOT YET WRITTEN. WITH THE...THE SEED...
...WE MAY...YET... ESCAPE...
MY FATHER ENTERS THE ODINSLEEP.
FOR YOUR SAKES I PRAY IT IS NOT FOR LONG.
FATHER, THERE ARE TIMES I HATE YOU WITH THE PASSION OF TEN THOUSAND SUNS.
BUT I WILL ESCORT TO HEL PERSONALLY ANYTHING THAT TORMENTS YOU MORE THAN I.

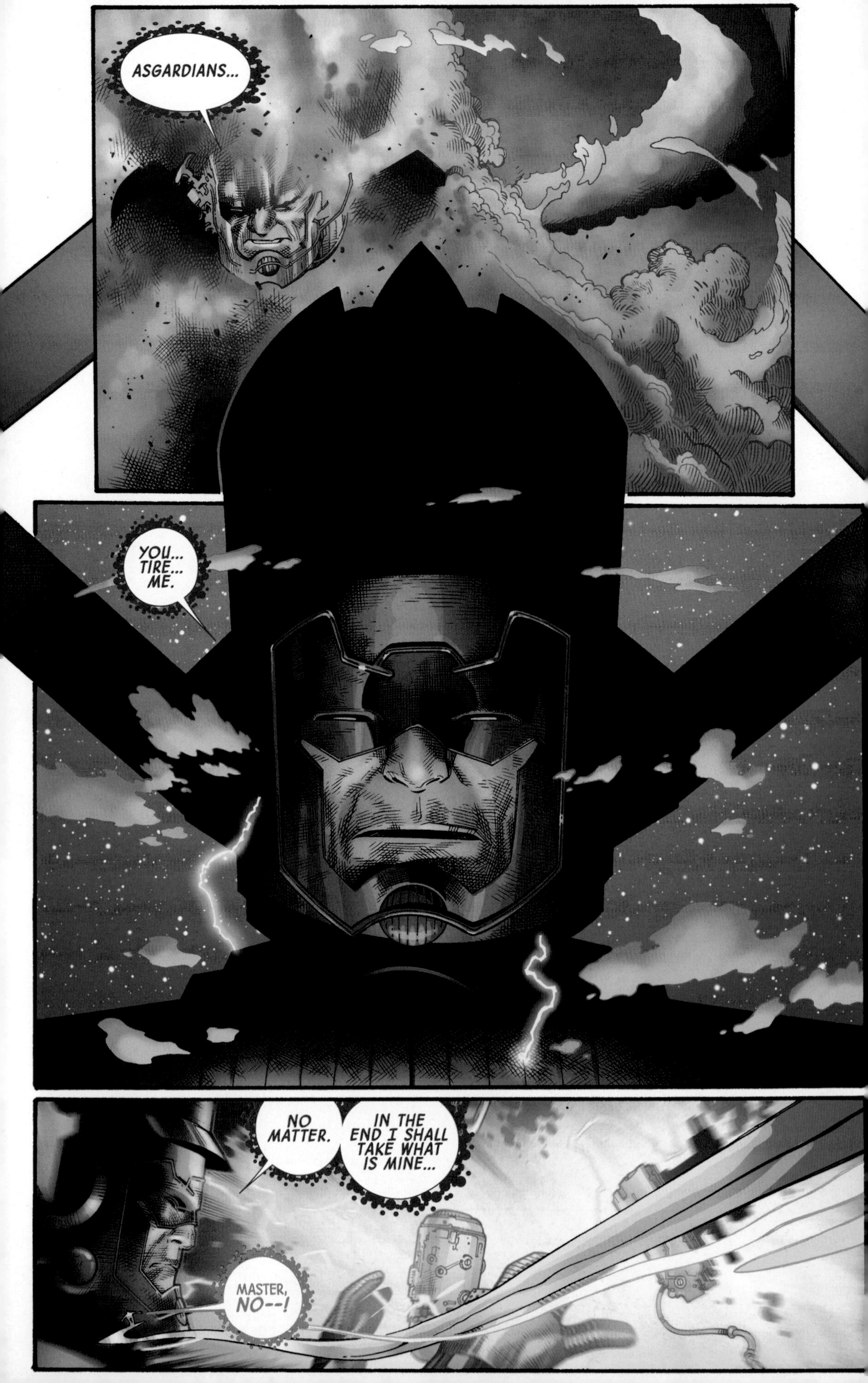
ASGARDIANS...
YOU... TIRE... ME.
NO MATTER.
IN THE END I SHALL TAKE WHAT IS MINE...
MASTER, NO--!

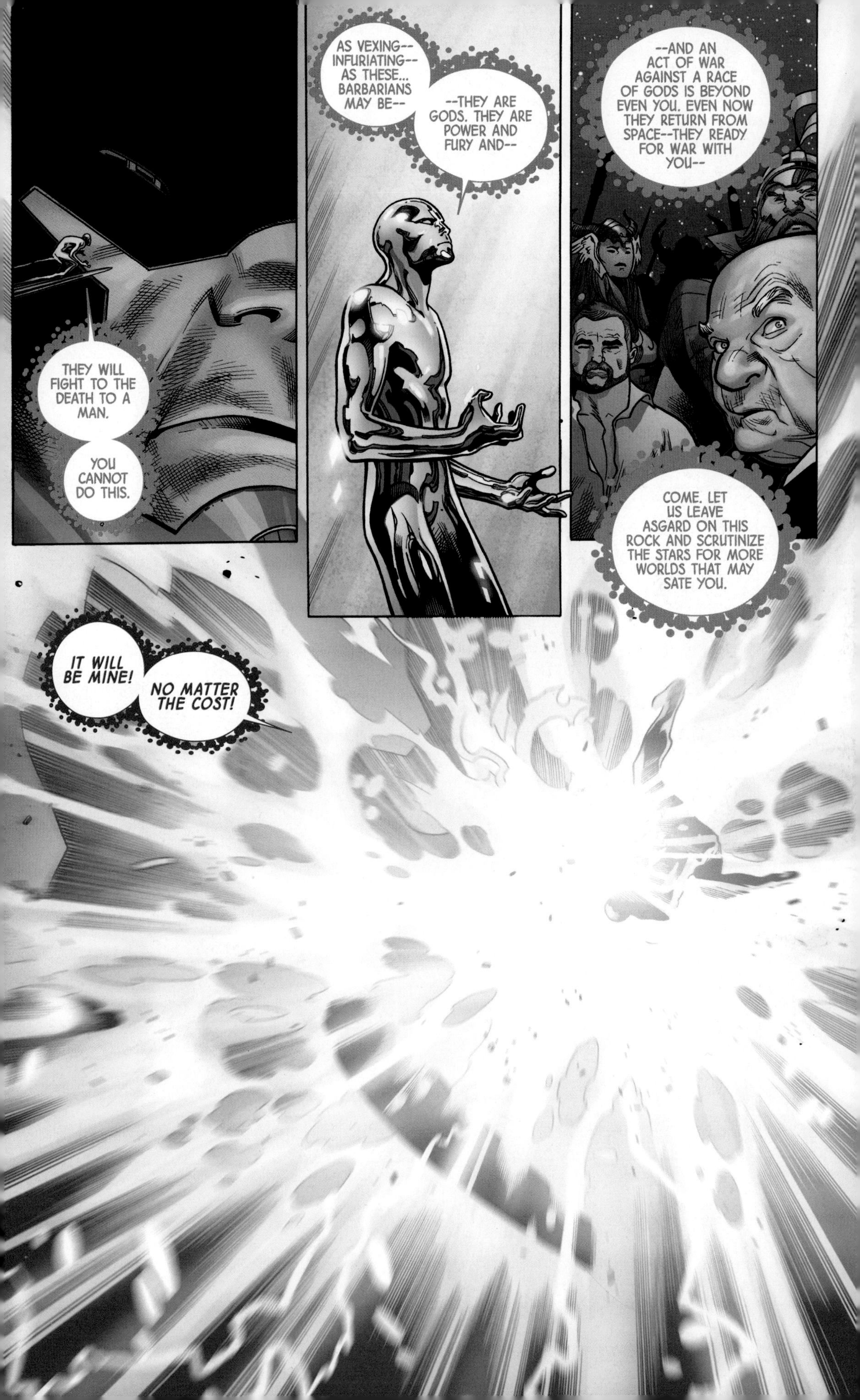
THEY WILL FIGHT TO THE DEATH TO A MAN.
YOU CANNOT DO THIS.
AS VEXING-- INFURIATING-- AS THESE... BARBARIANS MAY BE--
--THEY ARE GODS. THEY ARE POWER AND FURY AND--
--AND AN ACT OF WAR AGAINST A RACE OF GODS IS BEYOND EVEN YOU. EVEN NOW THEY RETURN FROM SPACE--THEY READY FOR WAR WITH YOU--
COME. LET US LEAVE ASGARD ON THIS ROCK AND SCRUTINIZE THE STARS FOR MORE WORLDS THAT MAY SATE YOU.
IT WILL BE MINE!
NO MATTER THE COST!

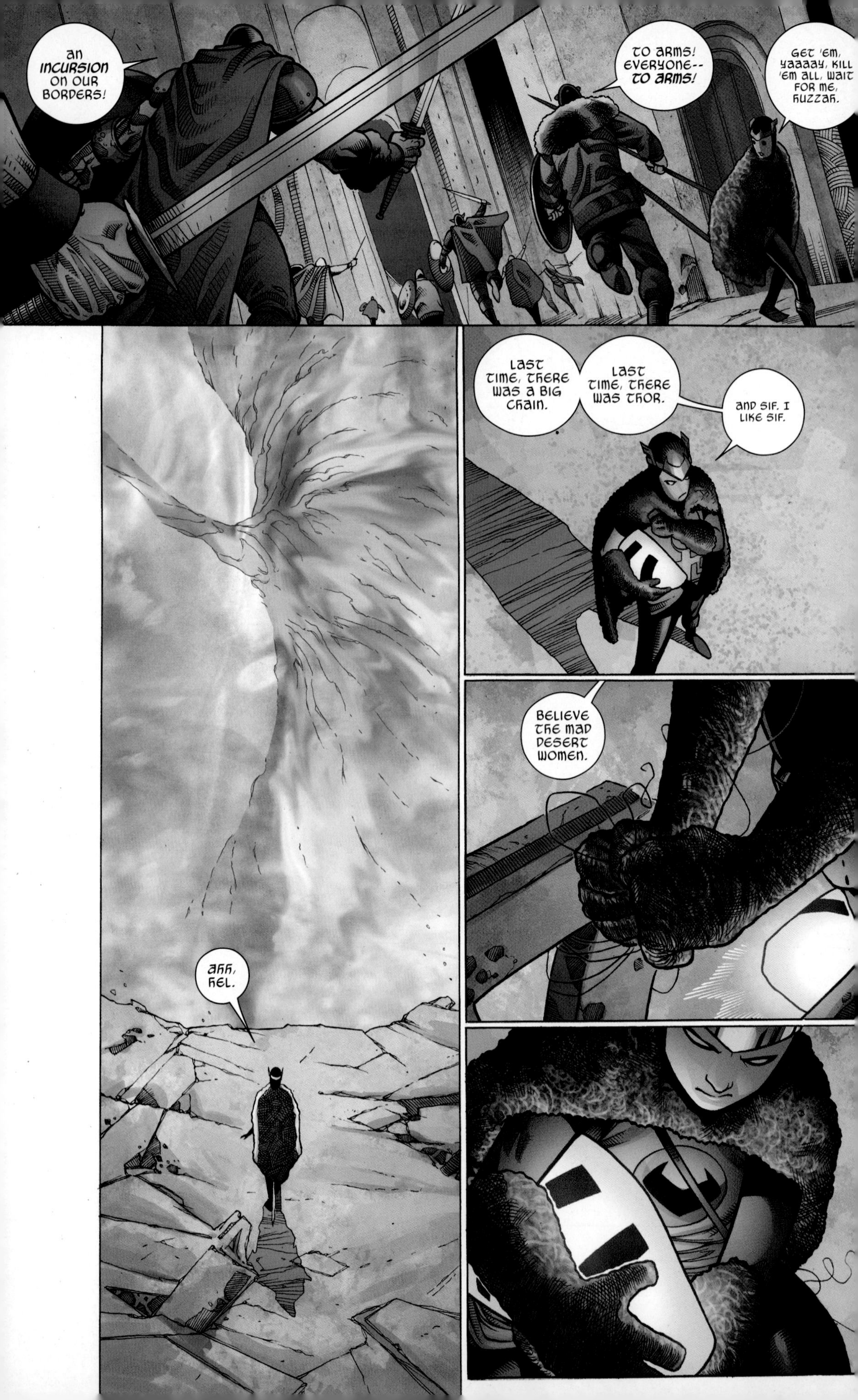

AN INCURSION ON OUR BORDERS!
TO ARMS! EVERYONE-- TO ARMS!
GET 'EM, YAAAAY, KILL 'EM ALL, WAIT FOR ME, HUZZAH.
AHH, HEL.
LAST TIME, THERE WAS A BIG CHAIN.
LAST TIME, THERE WAS THOR.
AND SIF. I LIKE SIF.
BELIEVE THE MAD DESERT WOMEN.

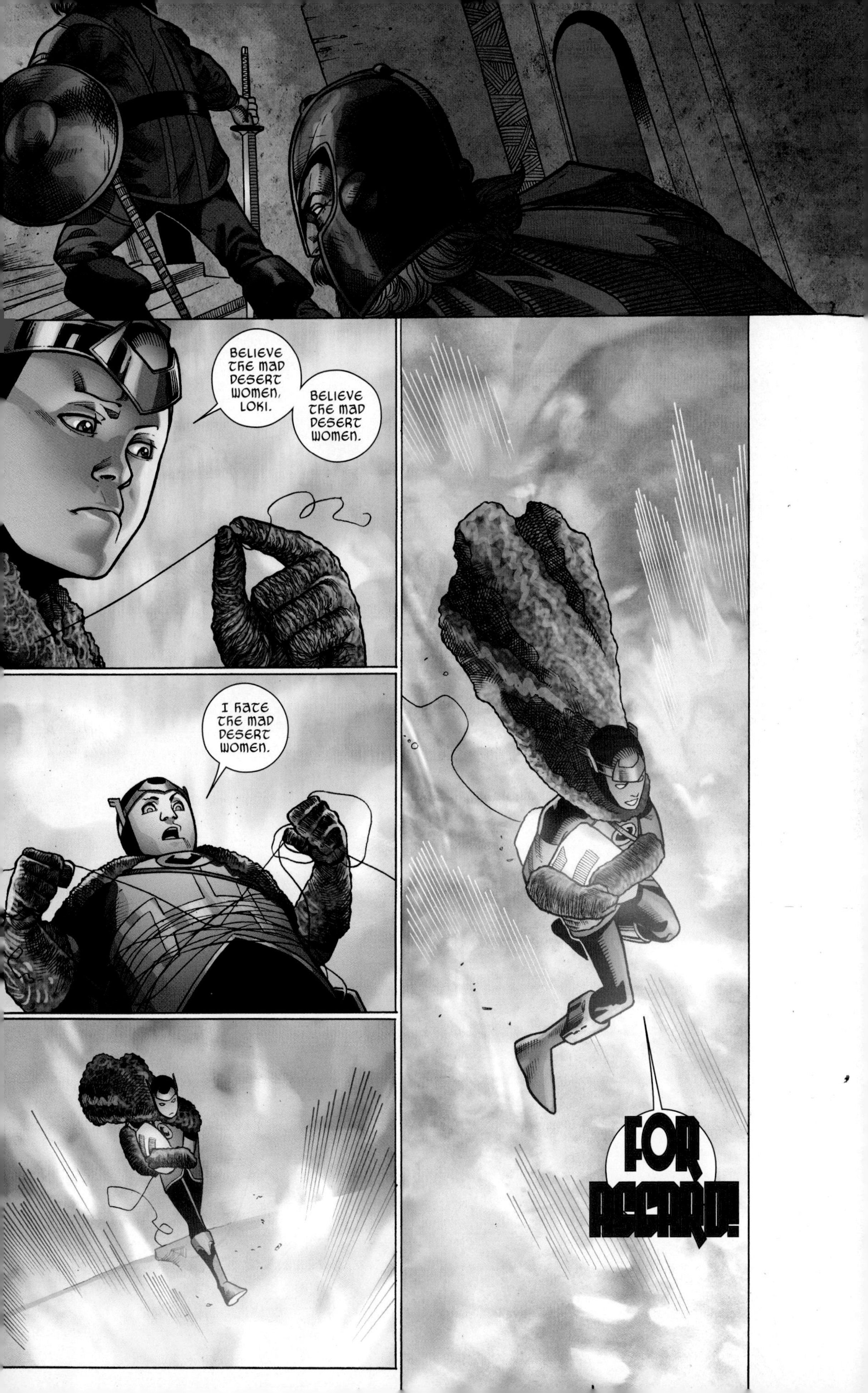
BELIEVE THE MAD DESERT WOMEN, LOKI.
BELIEVE THE MAD DESERT WOMEN.
I HATE THE MAD DESERT WOMEN.
FOR ASGARD!

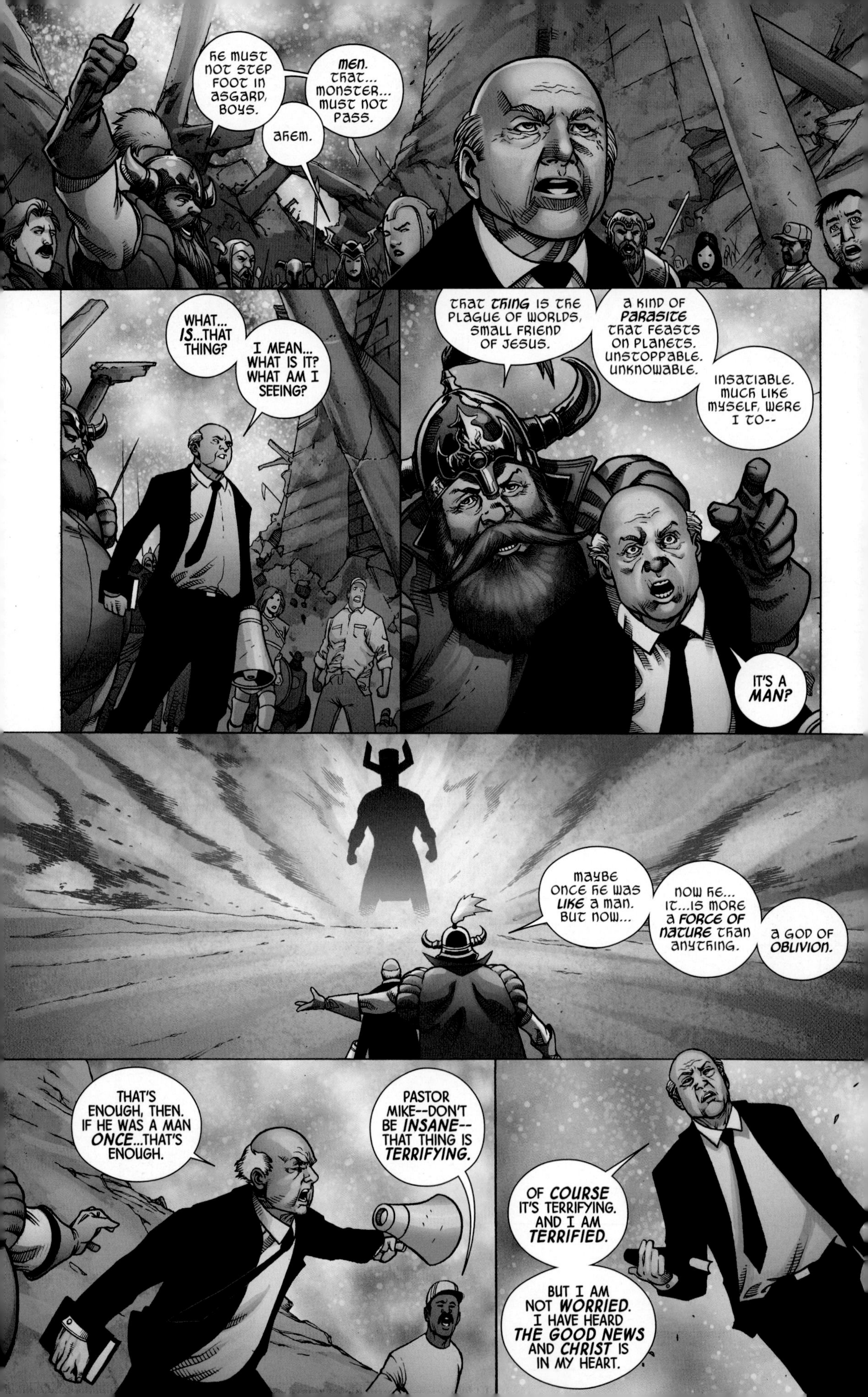
HE MUST NOT STEP FOOT IN ASGARD, BOYS.
AHEM.
MEN. THAT... MONSTER... MUST NOT PASS.
WHAT... IS...THAT THING?
I MEAN... WHAT IS IT? WHAT AM I SEEING?
THAT THING IS THE PLAGUE OF WORLDS, SMALL FRIEND OF JESUS.
A KIND OF PARASITE THAT FEASTS ON PLANETS. UNSTOPPABLE. UNKNOWABLE.
INSATIABLE. MUCH LIKE MYSELF, WERE I TO--
IT'S A MAN?
MAYBE ONCE HE WAS LIKE A MAN. BUT NOW...
NOW HE... IT...IS MORE A FORCE OF NATURE THAN ANYTHING.
A GOD OF OBLIVION.
THAT'S ENOUGH, THEN. IF HE WAS A MAN ONCE...THAT'S ENOUGH.
PASTOR MIKE--DON'T BE INSANE--THAT THING IS TERRIFYING.
OF COURSE IT'S TERRIFYING. AND I AM TERRIFIED.
BUT I AM NOT WORRIED. I HAVE HEARD THE GOOD NEWS AND CHRIST IS IN MY HEART.

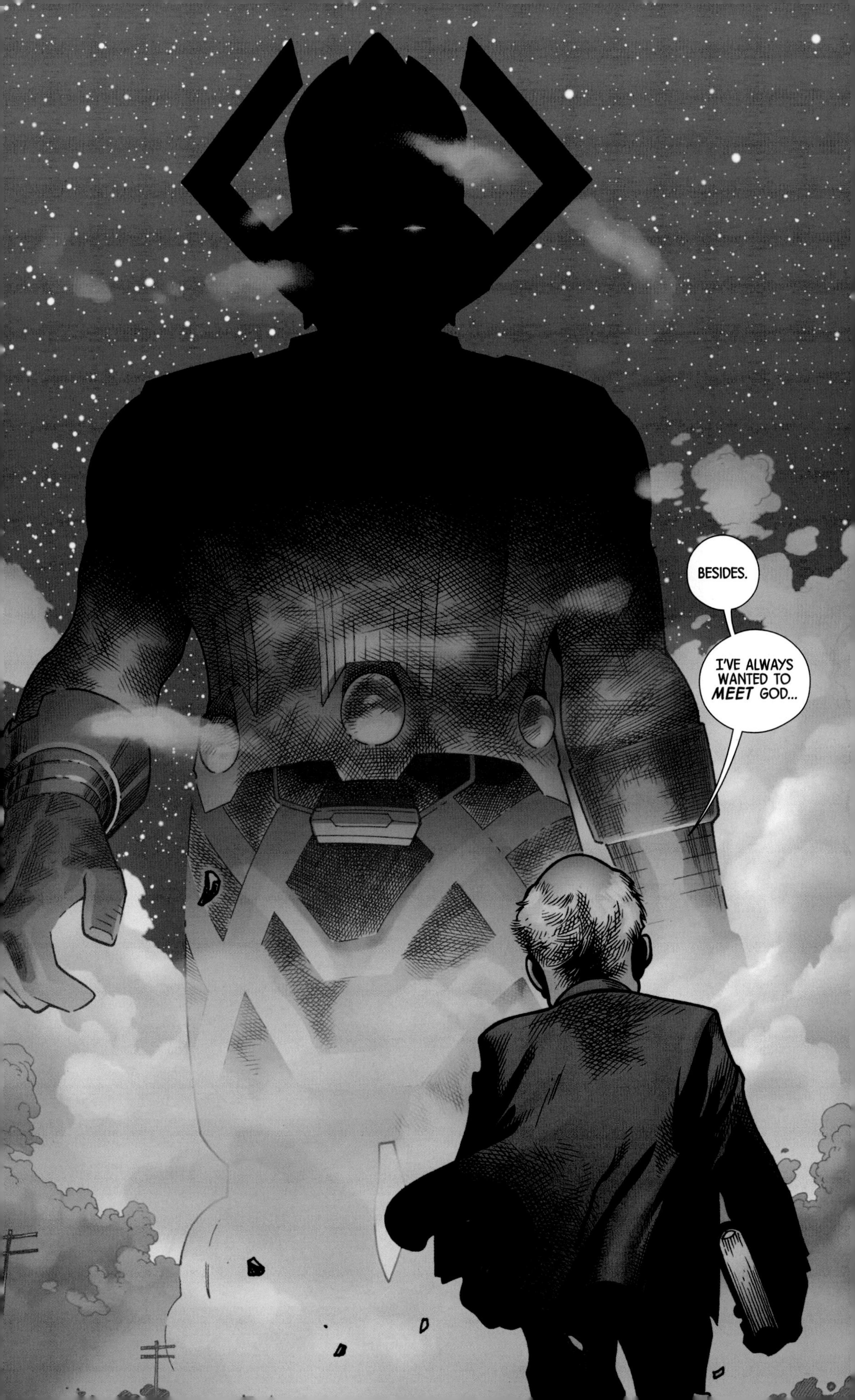
BESIDES.
I'VE ALWAYS WANTED TO MEET GOD...

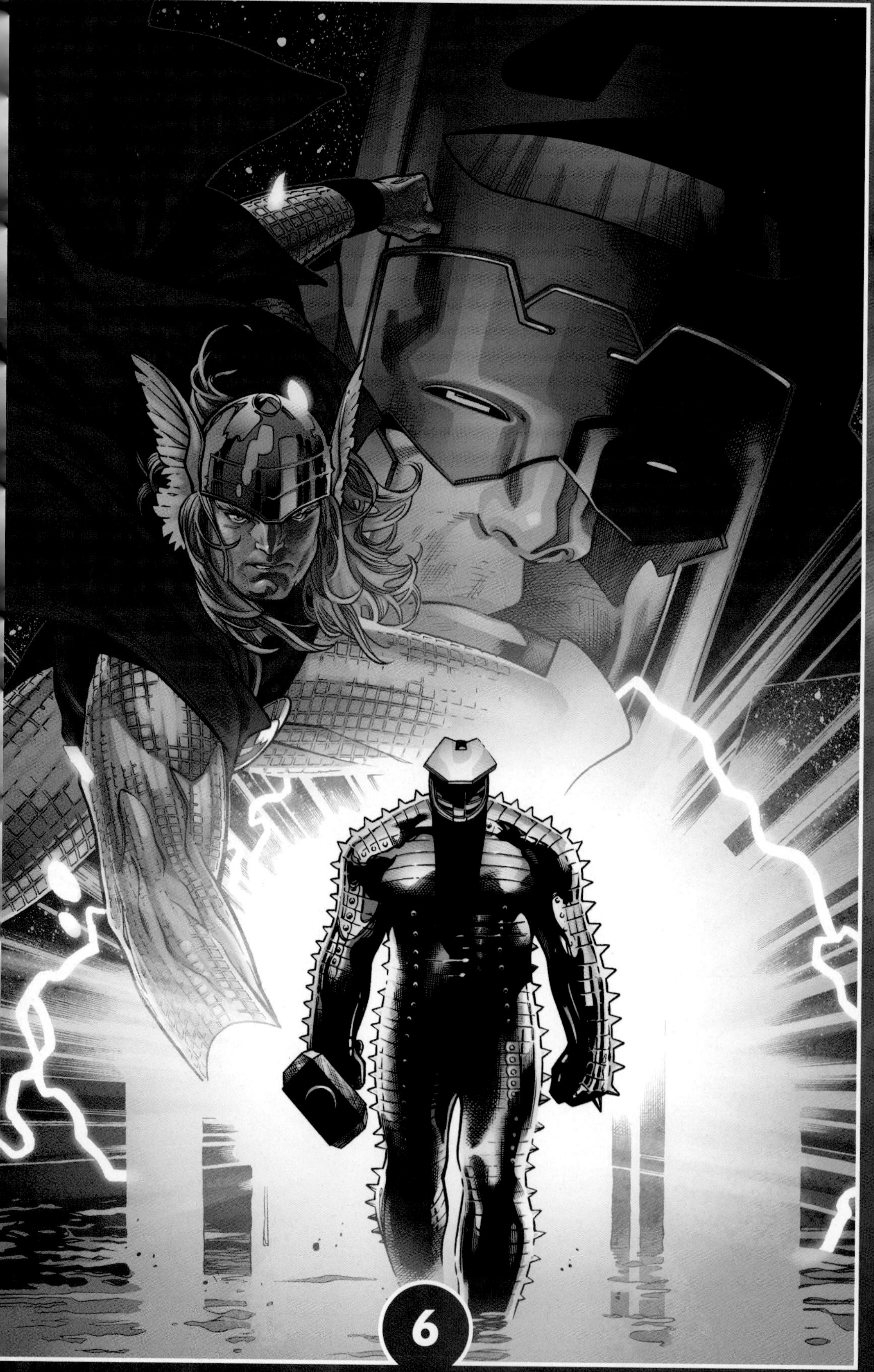
6

THE GALACTUS SEED 6: THE PROPOSITION

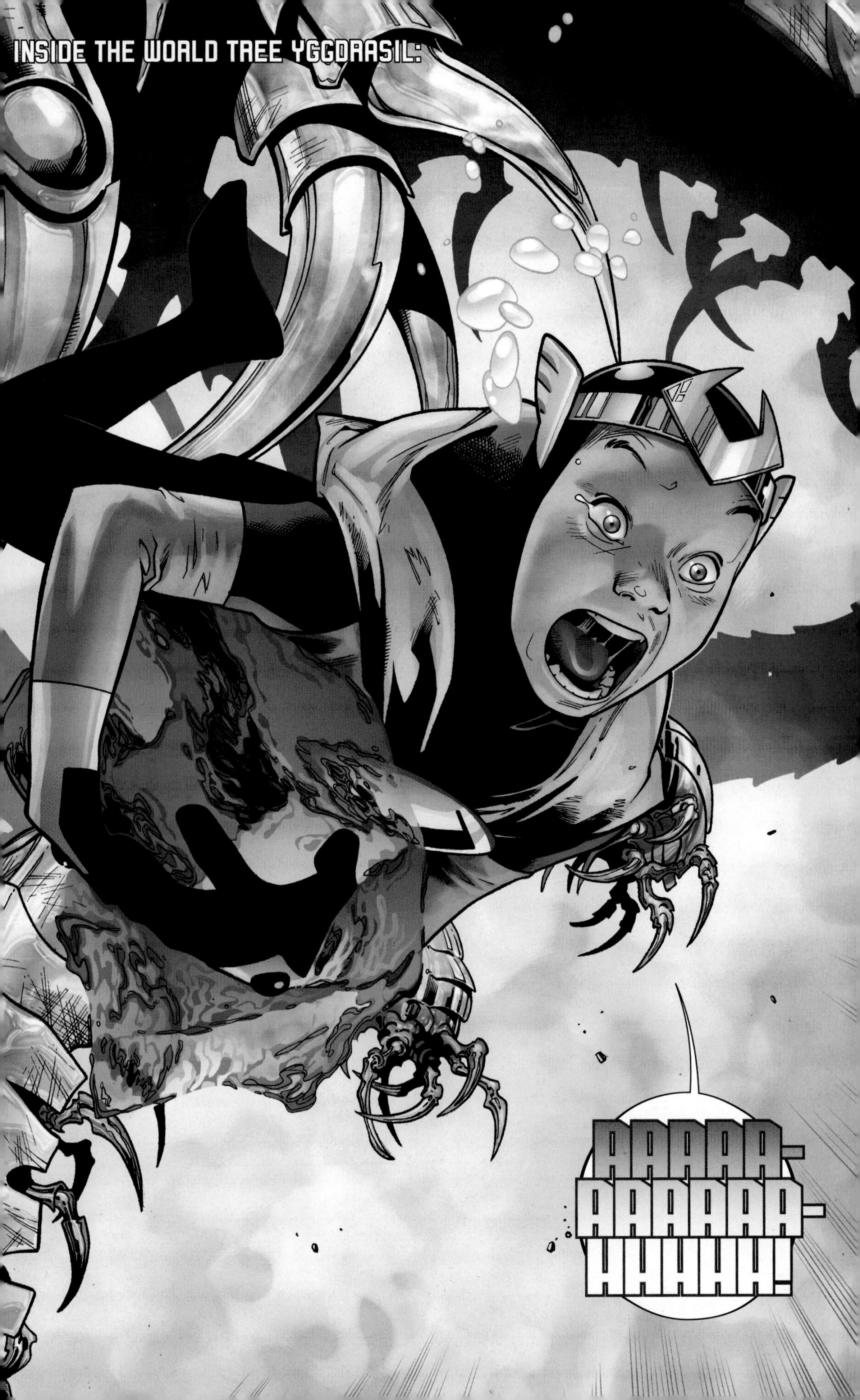
INSIDE THE WORLD TREE YGGDRASIL:
AAAAA-AAAAAA-HHHHH!

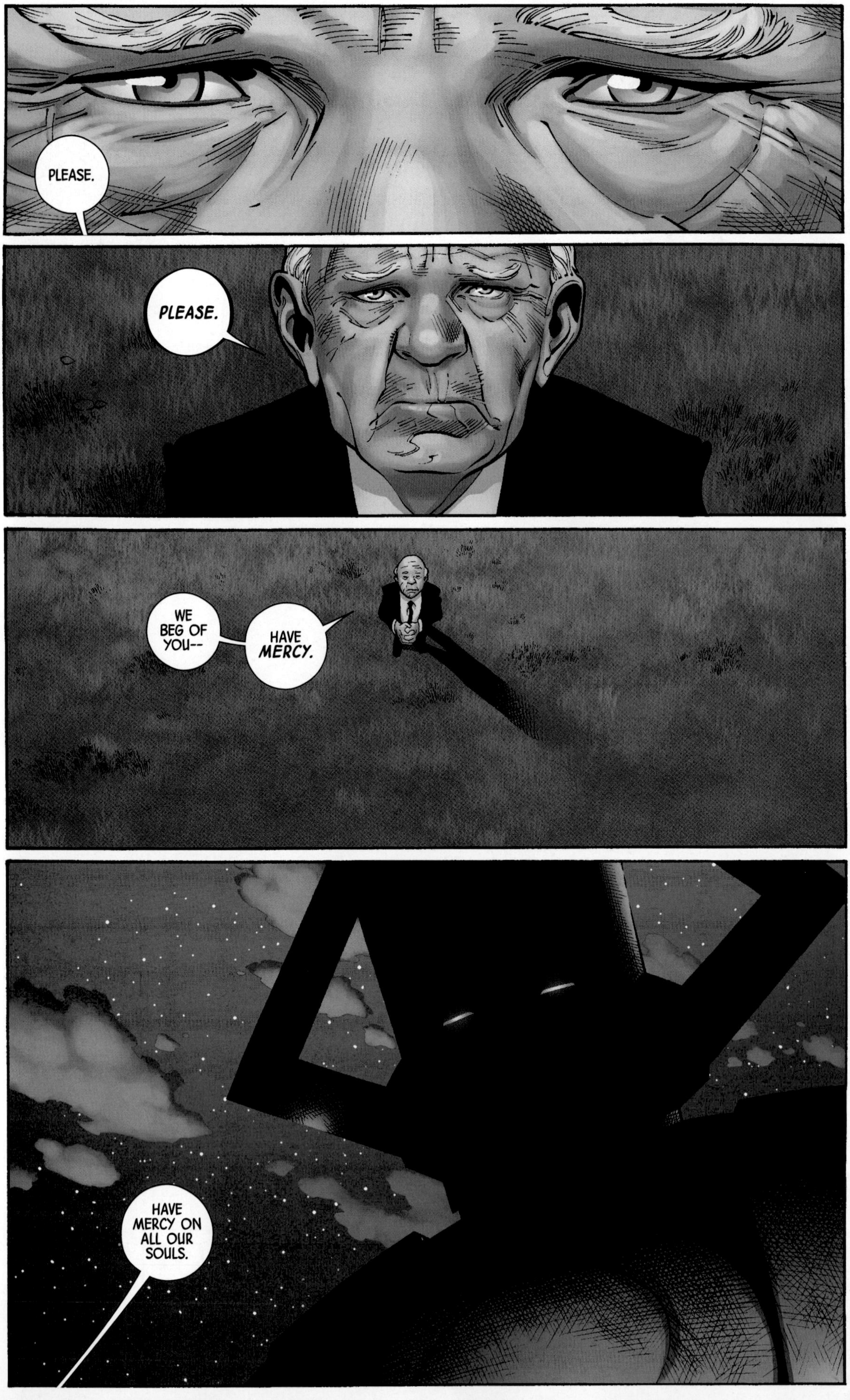
PLEASE.
PLEASE.
WE BEG OF YOU--
HAVE *MERCY.*
HAVE MERCY ON ALL OUR SOULS.

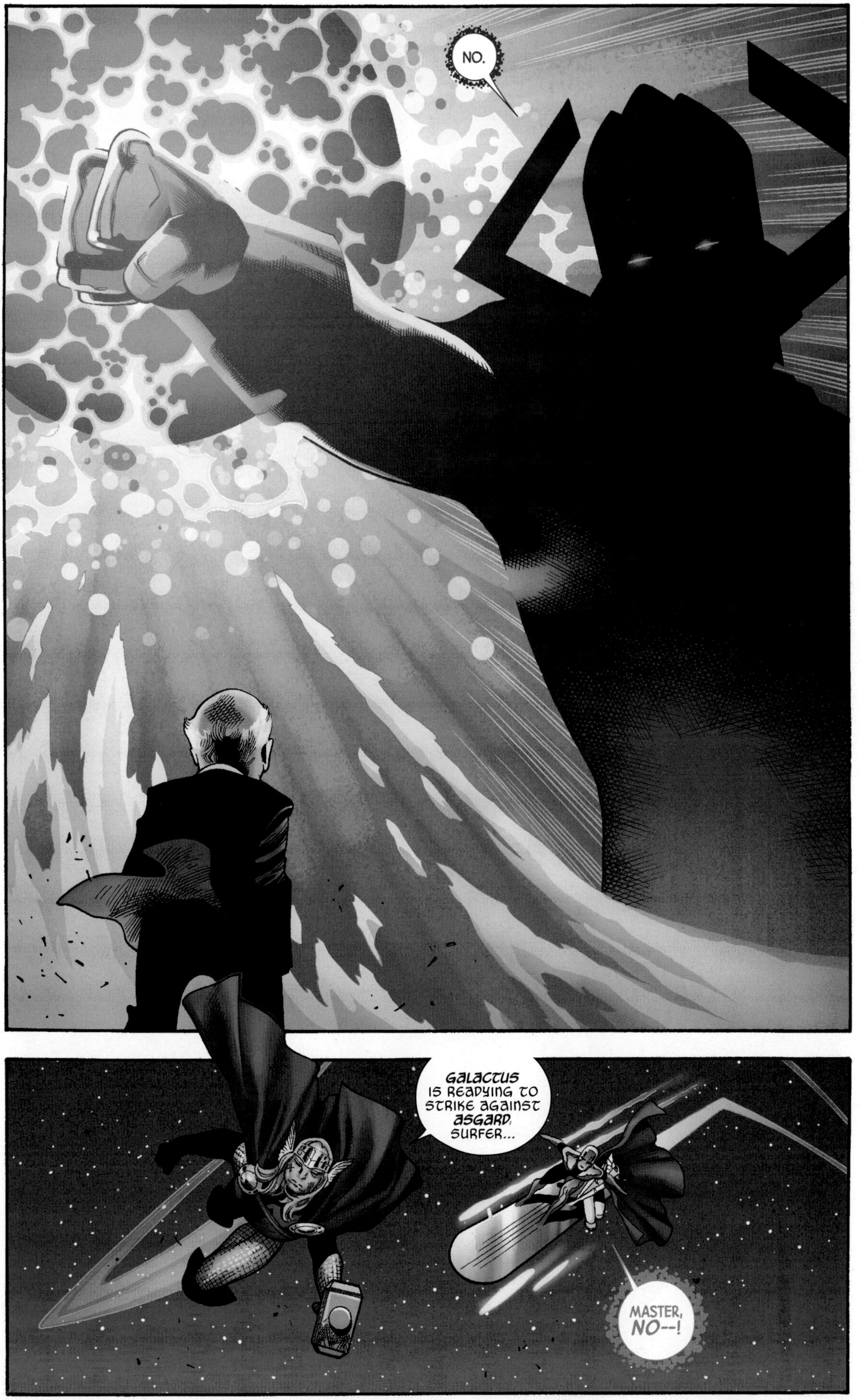
NO.
GALACTUS IS READYING TO STRIKE AGAINST ASGARD, SURFER...
MASTER, NO--!

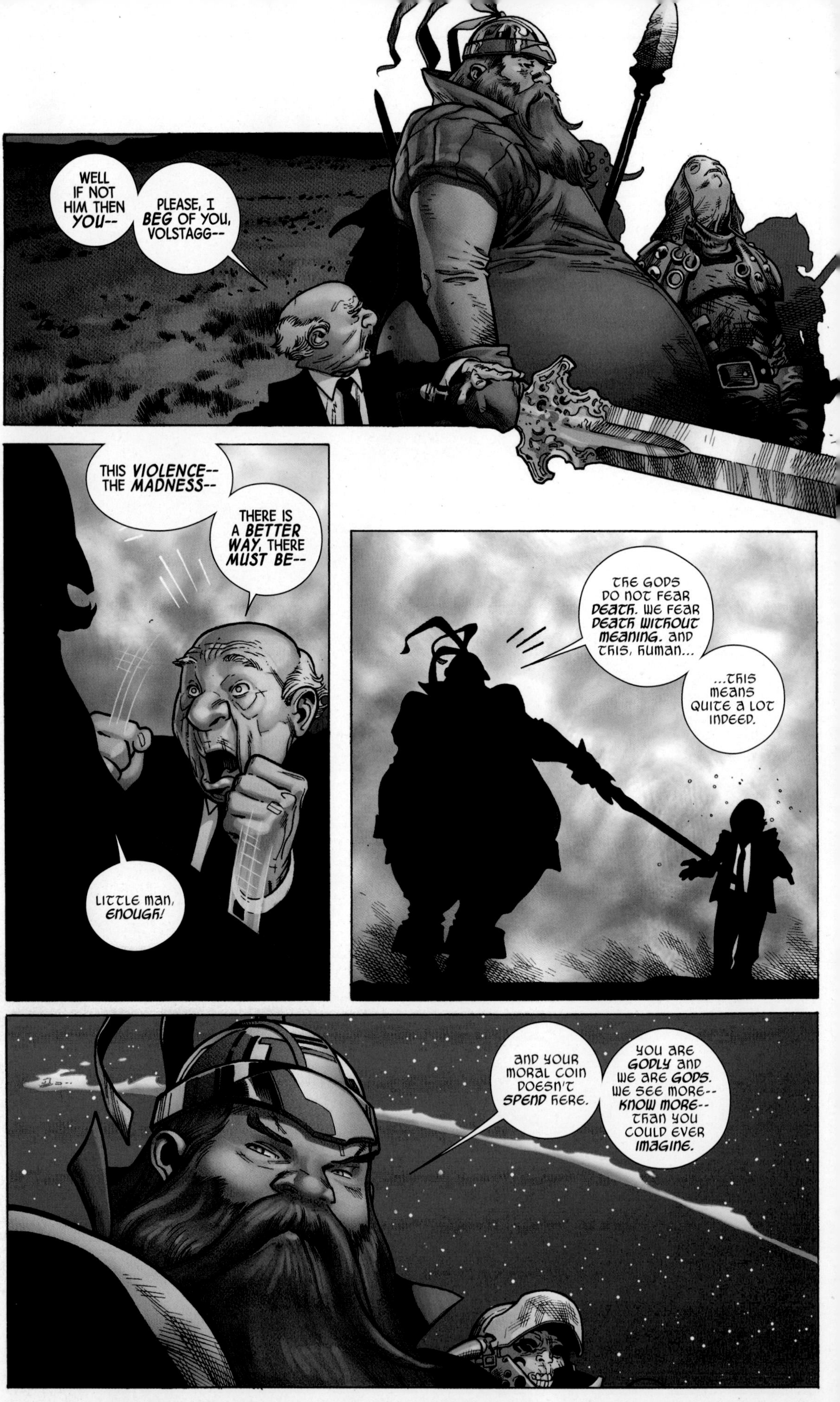
WELL IF NOT HIM THEN YOU--
PLEASE, I BEG OF YOU, VOLSTAGG--
THIS VIOLENCE-- THE MADNESS--
THERE IS A BETTER WAY, THERE MUST BE--
LITTLE MAN, ENOUGH!
THE GODS DO NOT FEAR DEATH. WE FEAR DEATH WITHOUT MEANING. AND THIS, HUMAN...
...THIS MEANS QUITE A LOT INDEED.
YOU ARE GODLY AND WE ARE GODS. WE SEE MORE-- KNOW MORE-- THAN YOU COULD EVER IMAGINE.
AND YOUR MORAL COIN DOESN'T SPEND HERE.

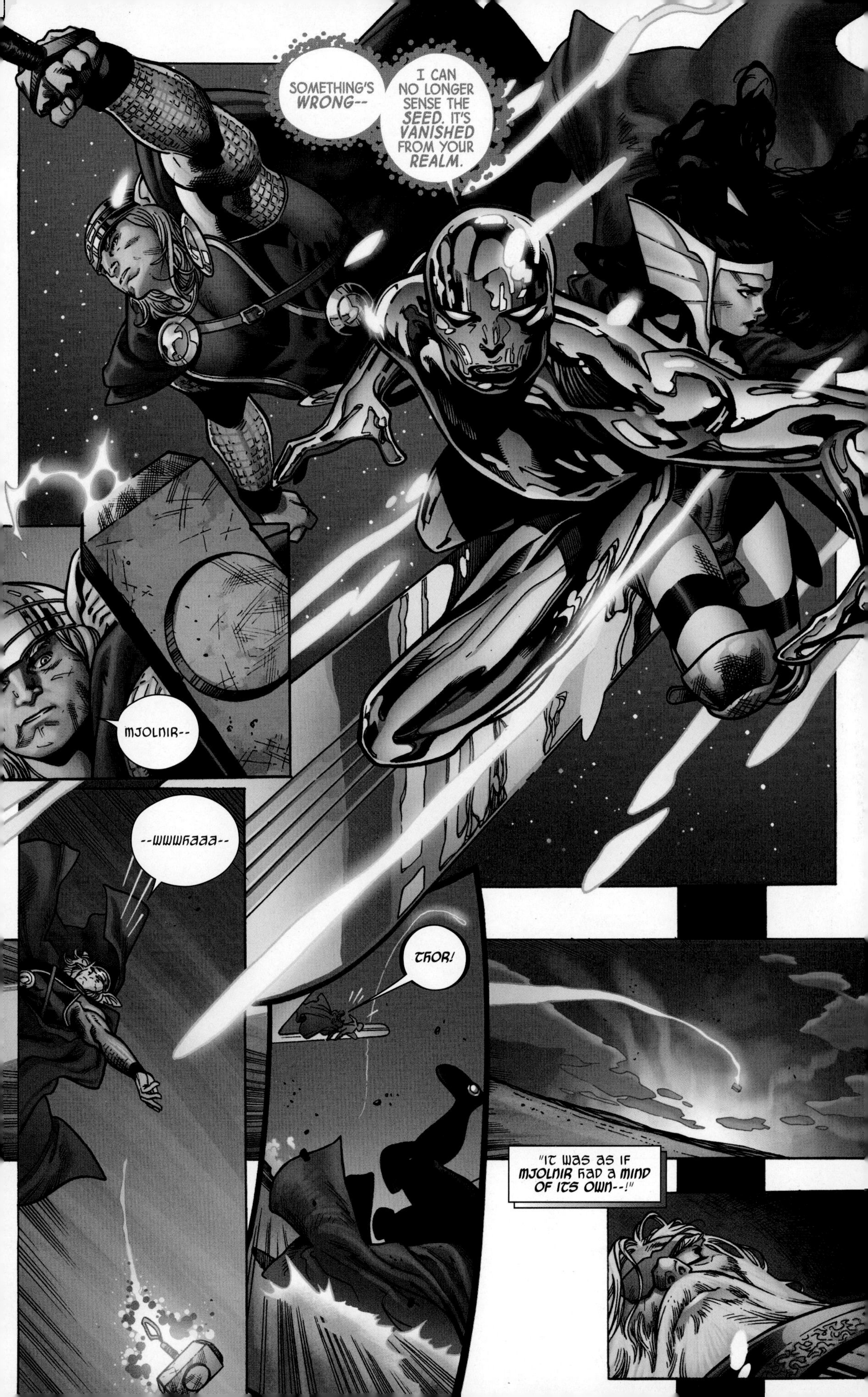
SOMETHING'S WRONG--
I CAN NO LONGER SENSE THE SEED. IT'S VANISHED FROM YOUR REALM.
MJOLNIR--
--WWWHAAA--
THOR!
"IT WAS AS IF MJOLNIR HAD A MIND OF ITS OWN--!"

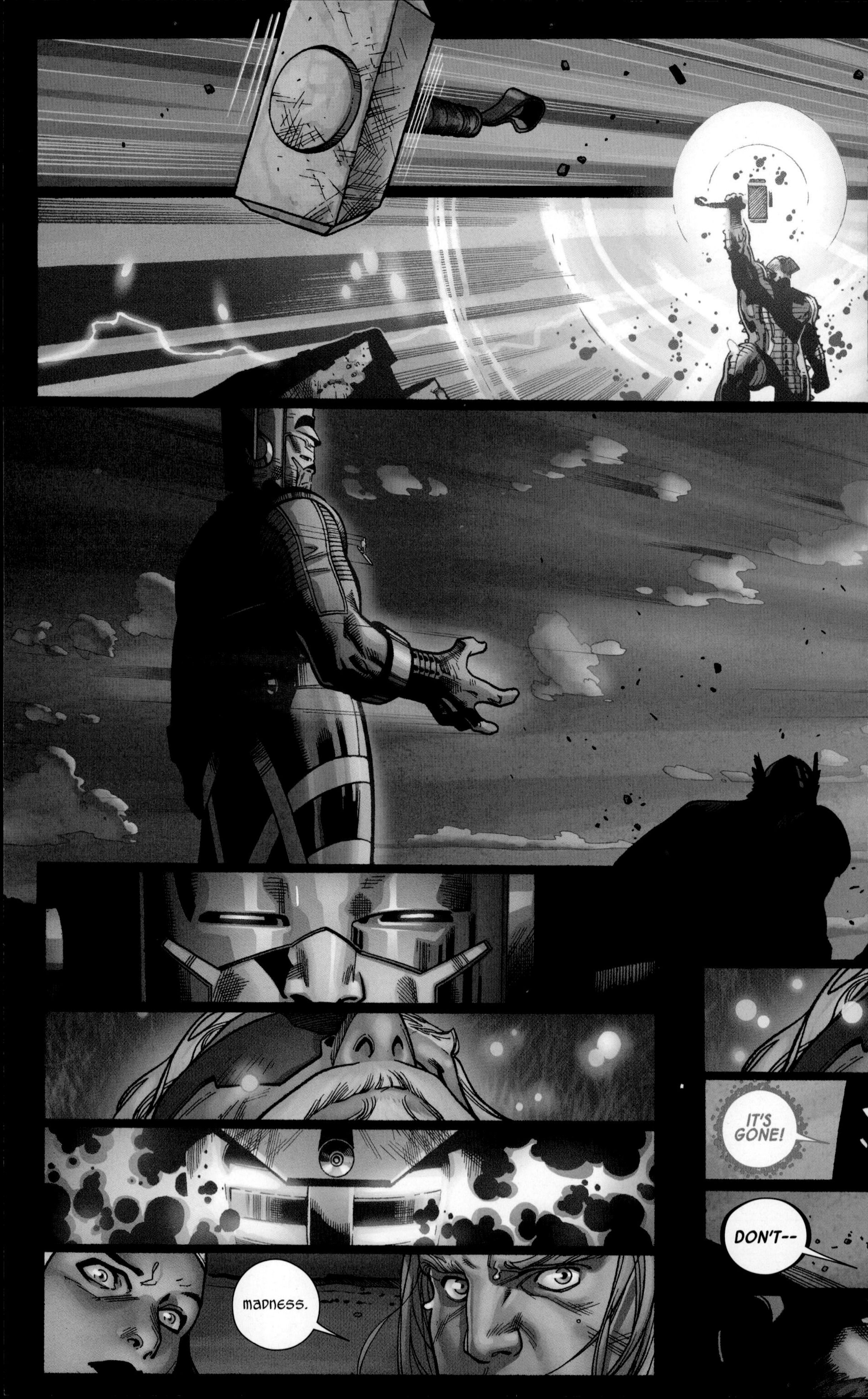
IT'S GONE!
DON'T--
MADNESS.

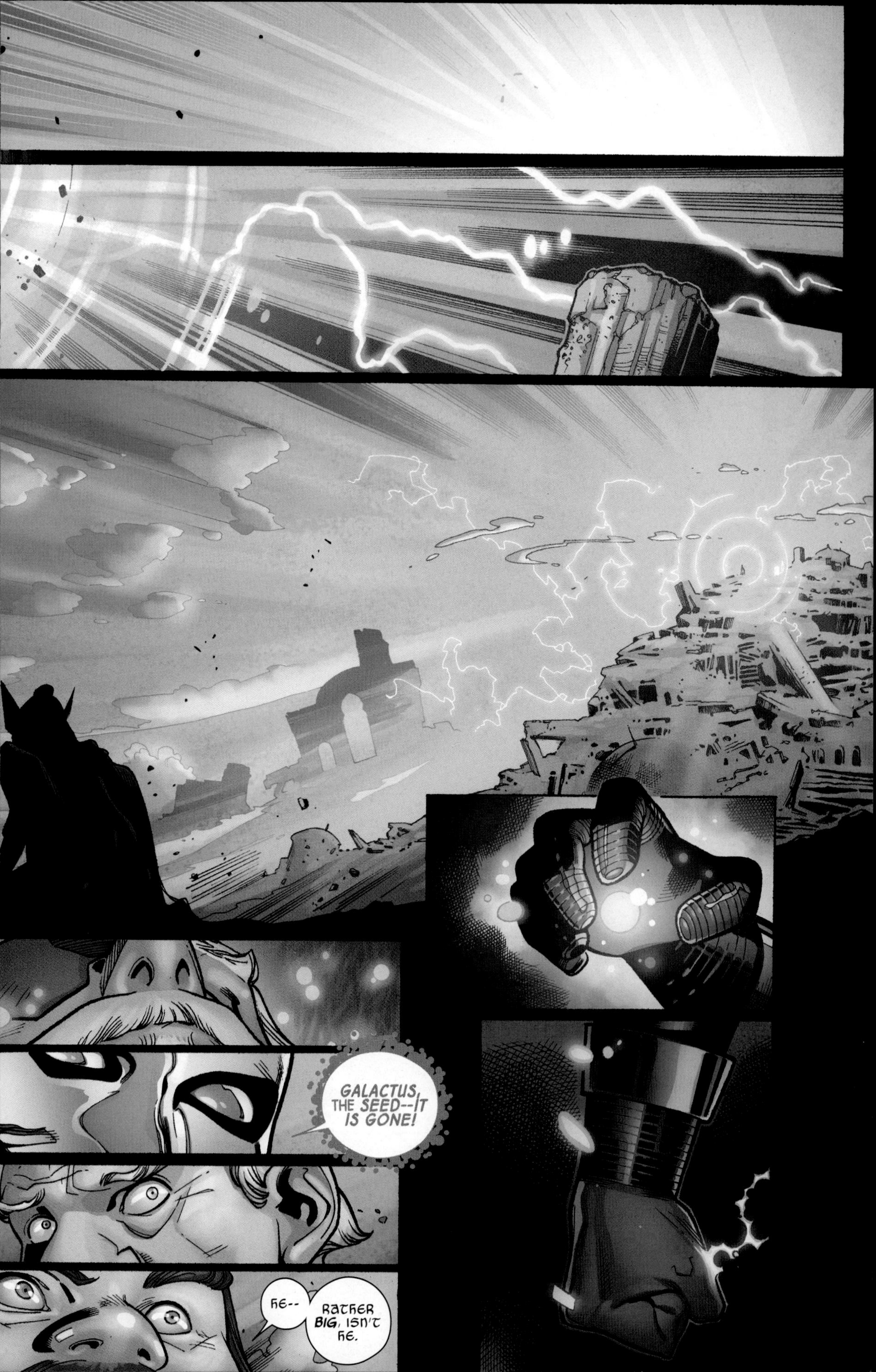
GALACTUS, THE SEED--IT IS GONE!
HE--
RATHER BIG, ISN'T HE.

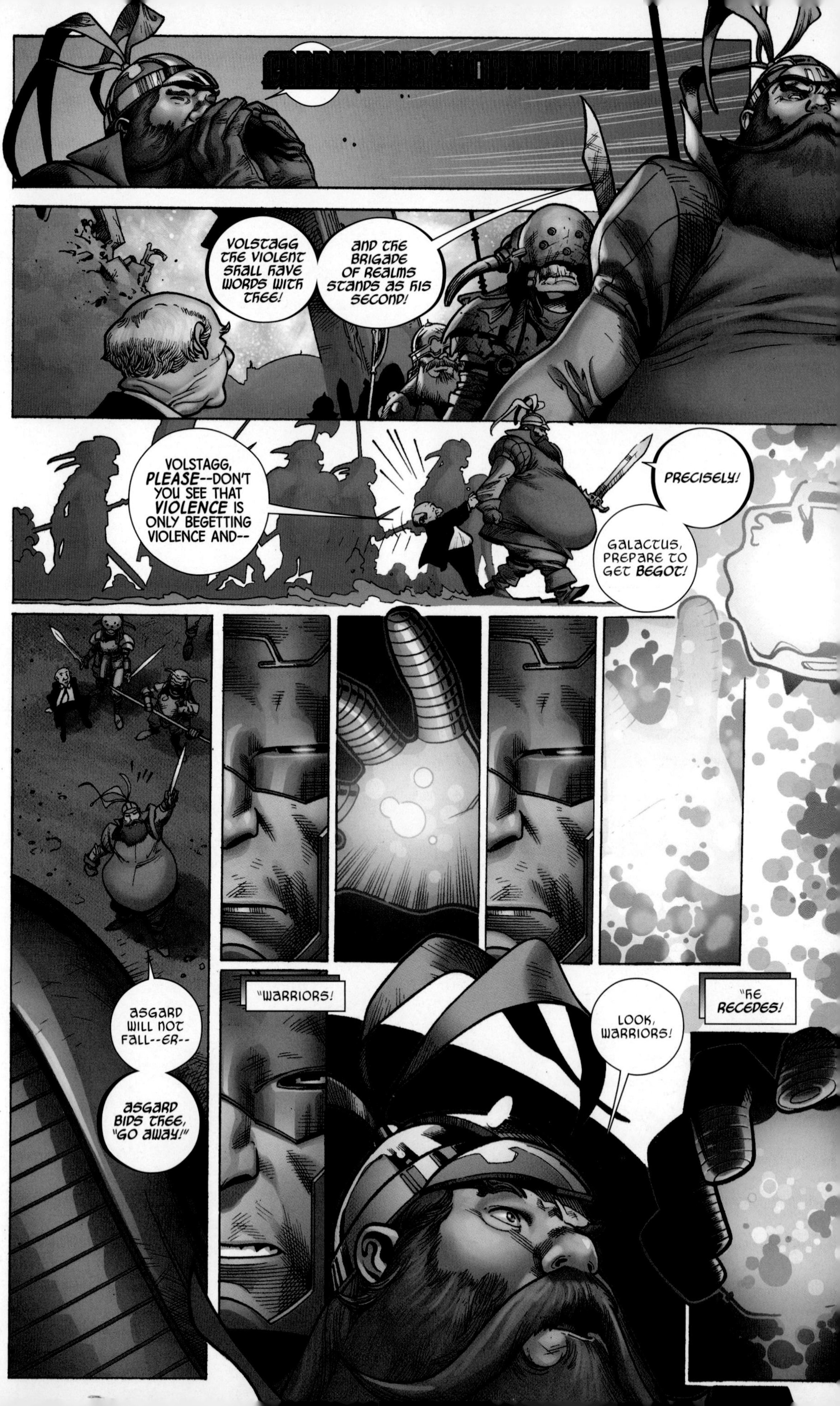
VOLSTAGG THE VIOLENT SHALL HAVE WORDS WITH THEE!
AND THE BRIGADE OF REALMS STANDS AS HIS SECOND!
VOLSTAGG, PLEASE--DON'T YOU SEE THAT VIOLENCE IS ONLY BEGETTING VIOLENCE AND--
PRECISELY!
GALACTUS, PREPARE TO GET BEGOT!
ASGARD WILL NOT FALL--ER--
ASGARD BIDS THEE, "GO AWAY!"
"WARRIORS!
LOOK, WARRIORS!
"HE RECEDES!

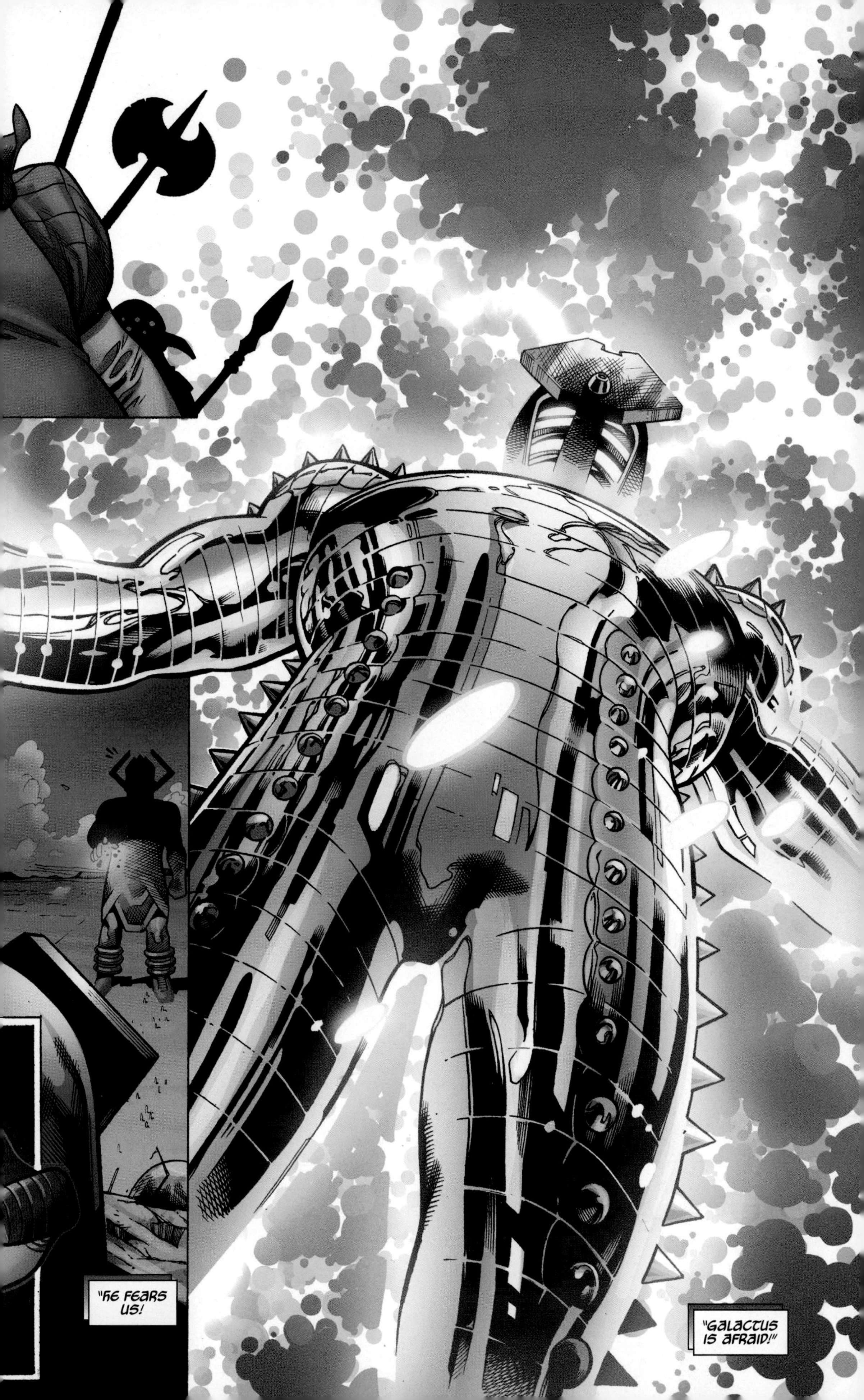
"HE FEARS US!
"GALACTUS IS AFRAID!"

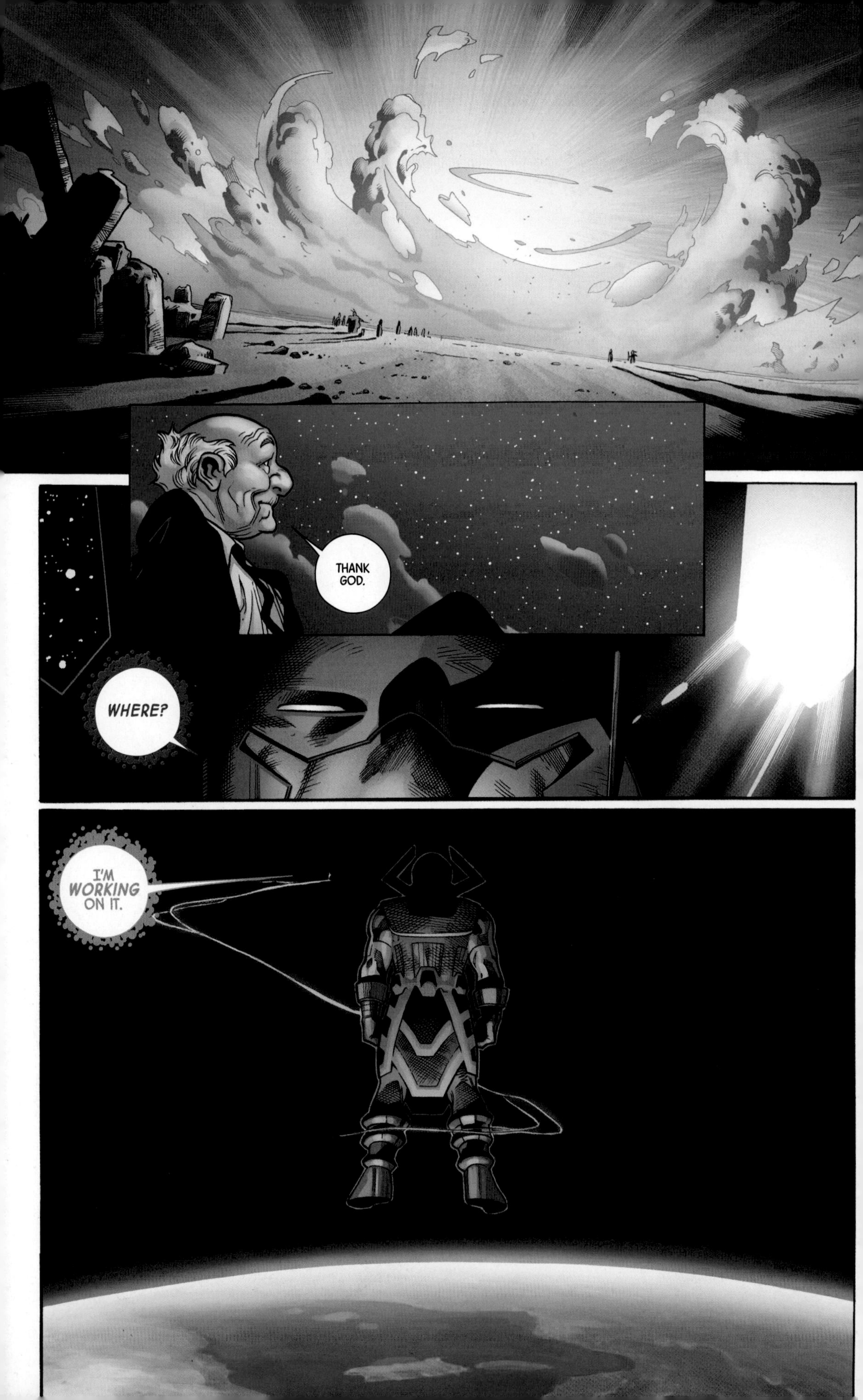
THANK GOD.
WHERE?
I'M WORKING ON IT.

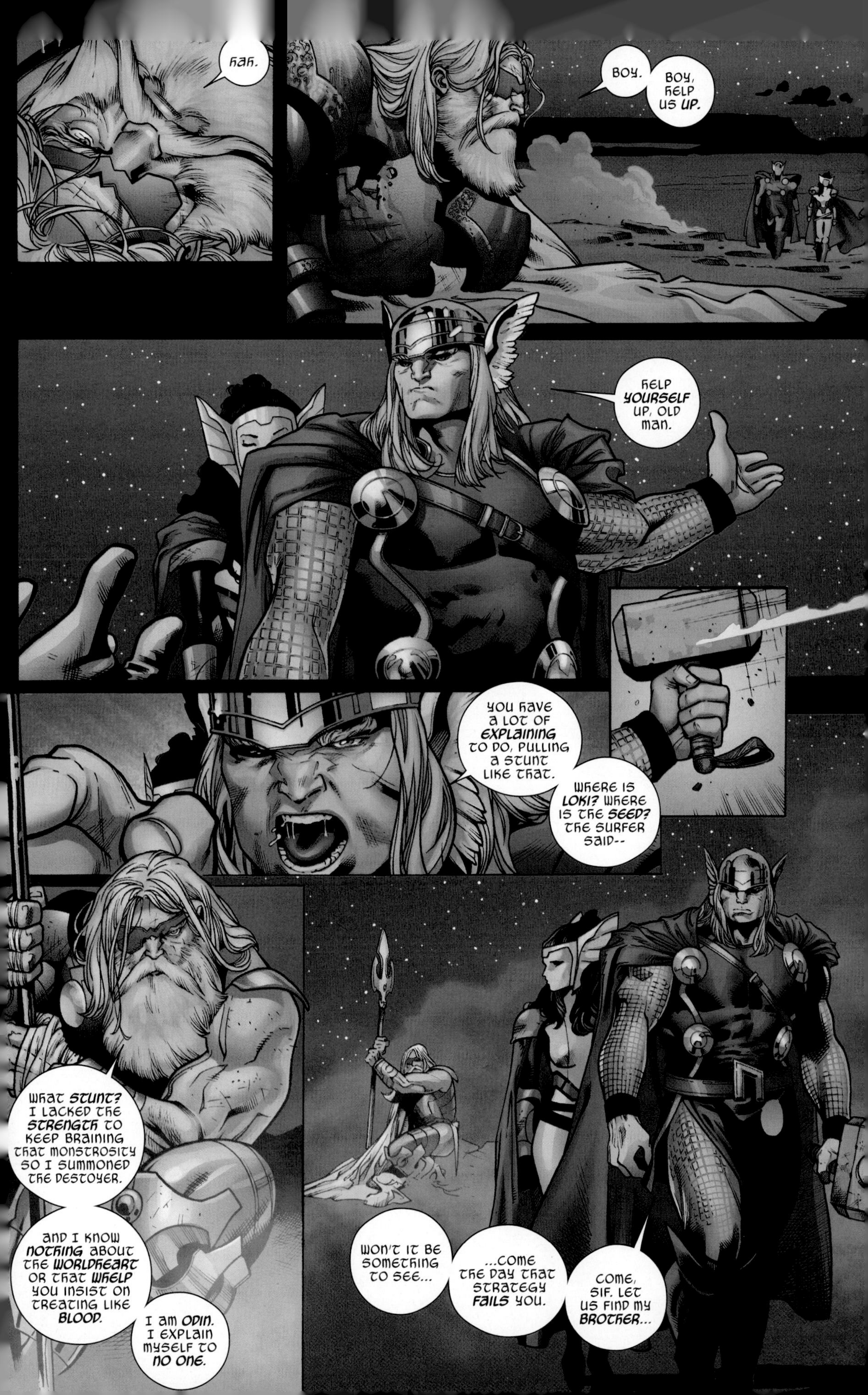
HAH.
BOY.
BOY, HELP US UP.
HELP YOURSELF UP, OLD MAN.
YOU HAVE A LOT OF EXPLAINING TO DO, PULLING A STUNT LIKE THAT.
WHERE IS LOKI? WHERE IS THE SEED? THE SURFER SAID--
WHAT STUNT? I LACKED THE STRENGTH TO KEEP BRAINING THAT MONSTROSITY SO I SUMMONED THE DESTOYER.
AND I KNOW NOTHING ABOUT THE WORLDHEART OR THAT WHELP YOU INSIST ON TREATING LIKE BLOOD.
I AM ODIN. I EXPLAIN MYSELF TO NO ONE.
WON'T IT BE SOMETHING TO SEE...
...COME THE DAY THAT STRATEGY FAILS YOU.
COME, SIF. LET US FIND MY BROTHER...

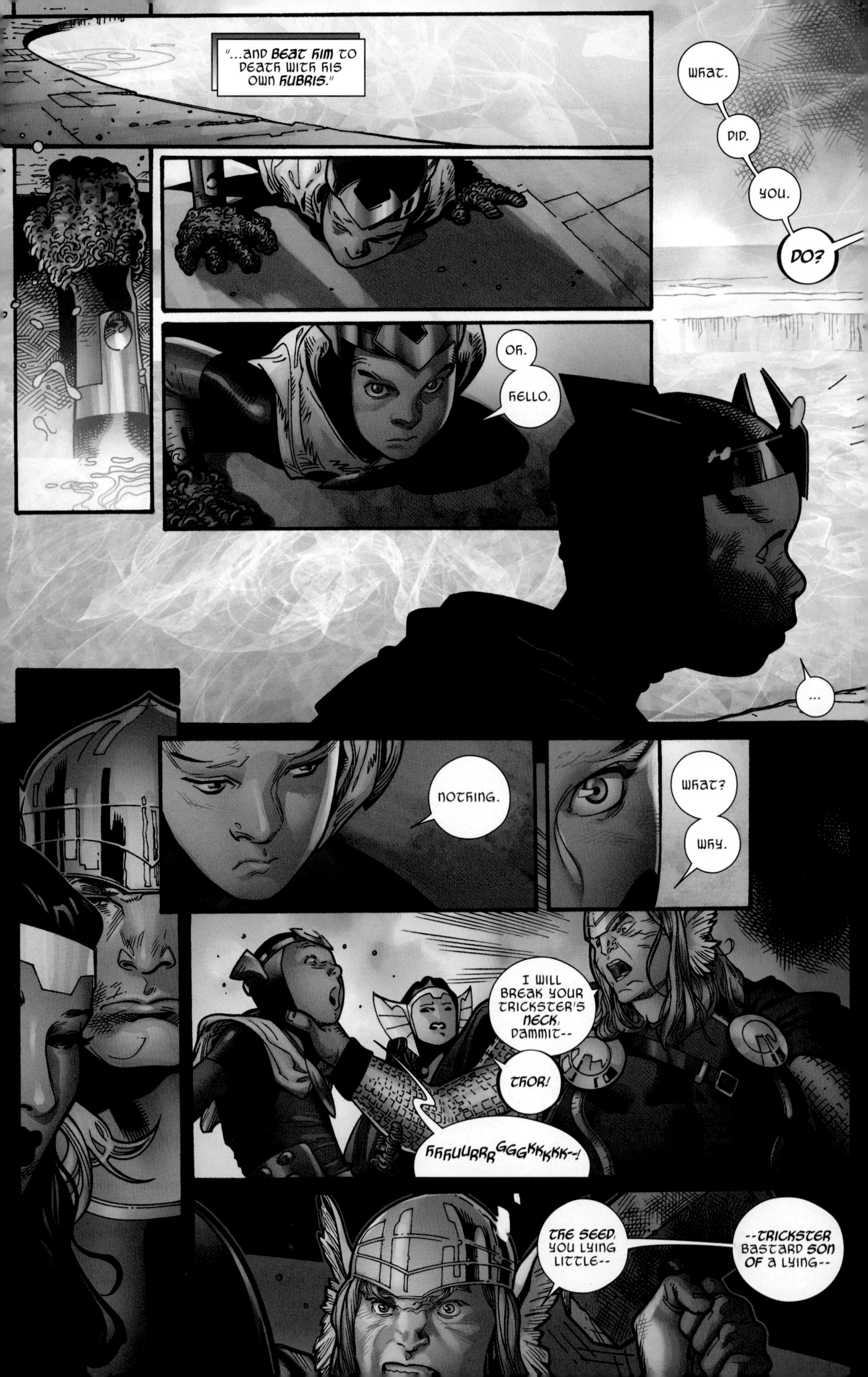
"...AND BEAT HIM TO DEATH WITH HIS OWN HUBRIS."
WHAT.
DID.
YOU.
DO?
OH.
HELLO.
...
NOTHING.
WHAT?
WHY.
I WILL BREAK YOUR TRICKSTER'S NECK, DAMMIT--
THOR!
HHHUURRRGGGKKKKK--!
THE SEED, YOU LYING LITTLE--
--TRICKSTER BASTARD SON OF A LYING--

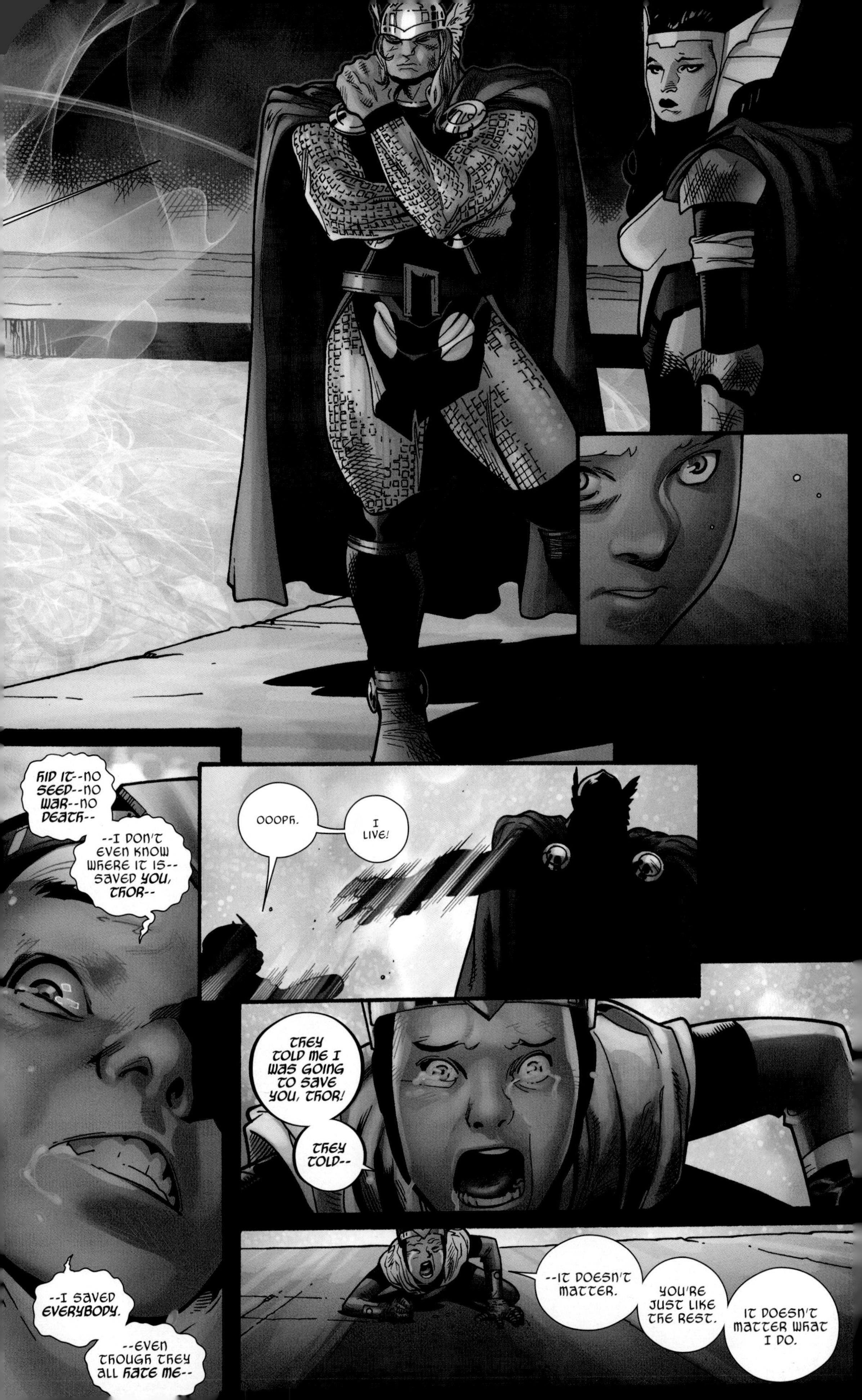
HID IT--NO SEED--NO WAR--NO DEATH--
--I DON'T EVEN KNOW WHERE IT IS--SAVED YOU, THOR--
OOOPH.
I LIVE!
THEY TOLD ME I WAS GOING TO SAVE YOU, THOR!
THEY TOLD--
--I SAVED EVERYBODY.
--EVEN THOUGH THEY ALL HATE ME--
--IT DOESN'T MATTER.
YOU'RE JUST LIKE THE REST.
IT DOESN'T MATTER WHAT I DO.

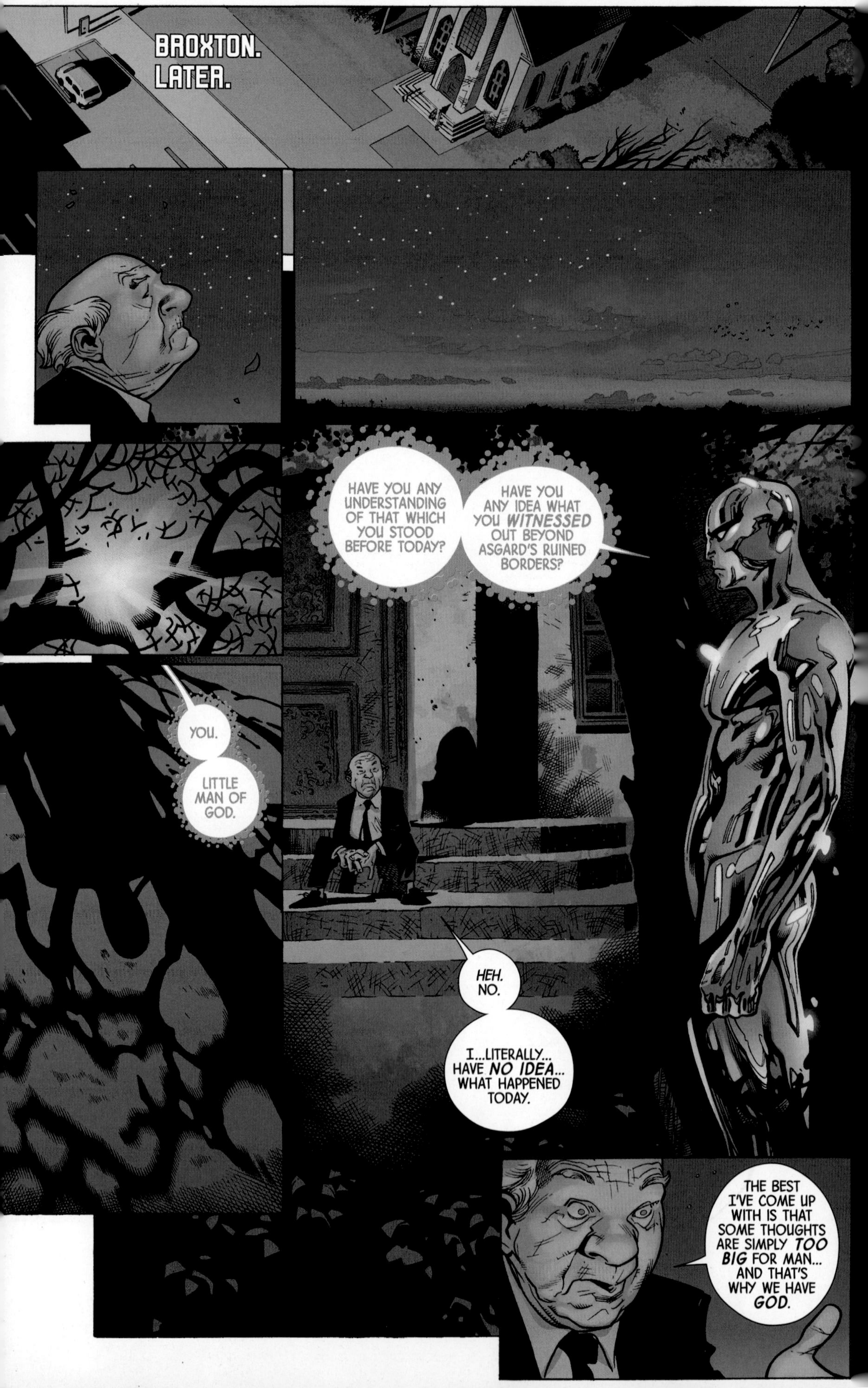

BROXTON.
LATER.
HAVE YOU ANY UNDERSTANDING OF THAT WHICH YOU STOOD BEFORE TODAY?
HAVE YOU ANY IDEA WHAT YOU WITNESSED OUT BEYOND ASGARD'S RUINED BORDERS?
YOU.
LITTLE MAN OF GOD.
HEH. NO.
I...LITERALLY... HAVE NO IDEA... WHAT HAPPENED TODAY.
THE BEST I'VE COME UP WITH IS THAT SOME THOUGHTS ARE SIMPLY TOO BIG FOR MAN... AND THAT'S WHY WE HAVE GOD.

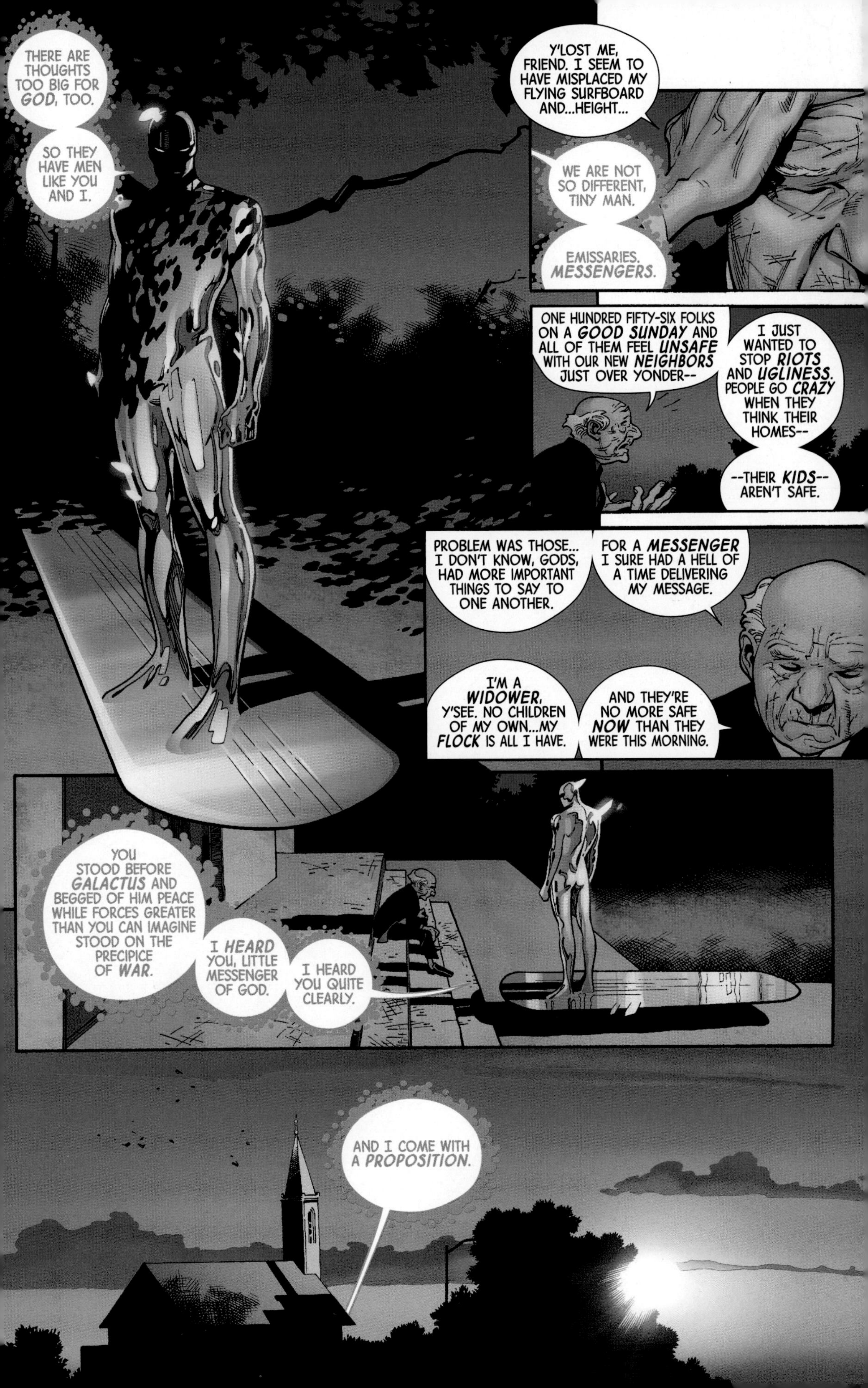

THERE ARE THOUGHTS TOO BIG FOR GOD, TOO.
SO THEY HAVE MEN LIKE YOU AND I.
Y'LOST ME, FRIEND. I SEEM TO HAVE MISPLACED MY FLYING SURFBOARD AND...HEIGHT...
WE ARE NOT SO DIFFERENT, TINY MAN.
EMISSARIES. MESSENGERS.
ONE HUNDRED FIFTY-SIX FOLKS ON A GOOD SUNDAY AND ALL OF THEM FEEL UNSAFE WITH OUR NEW NEIGHBORS JUST OVER YONDER--
I JUST WANTED TO STOP RIOTS AND UGLINESS. PEOPLE GO CRAZY WHEN THEY THINK THEIR HOMES--
--THEIR KIDS-- AREN'T SAFE.
PROBLEM WAS THOSE... I DON'T KNOW, GODS, HAD MORE IMPORTANT THINGS TO SAY TO ONE ANOTHER.
FOR A MESSENGER I SURE HAD A HELL OF A TIME DELIVERING MY MESSAGE.
I'M A WIDOWER, Y'SEE. NO CHILDREN OF MY OWN...MY FLOCK IS ALL I HAVE.
AND THEY'RE NO MORE SAFE NOW THAN THEY WERE THIS MORNING.
YOU STOOD BEFORE GALACTUS AND BEGGED OF HIM PEACE WHILE FORCES GREATER THAN YOU CAN IMAGINE STOOD ON THE PRECIPICE OF WAR.
I HEARD YOU, LITTLE MESSENGER OF GOD.
I HEARD YOU QUITE CLEARLY.
AND I COME WITH A PROPOSITION.

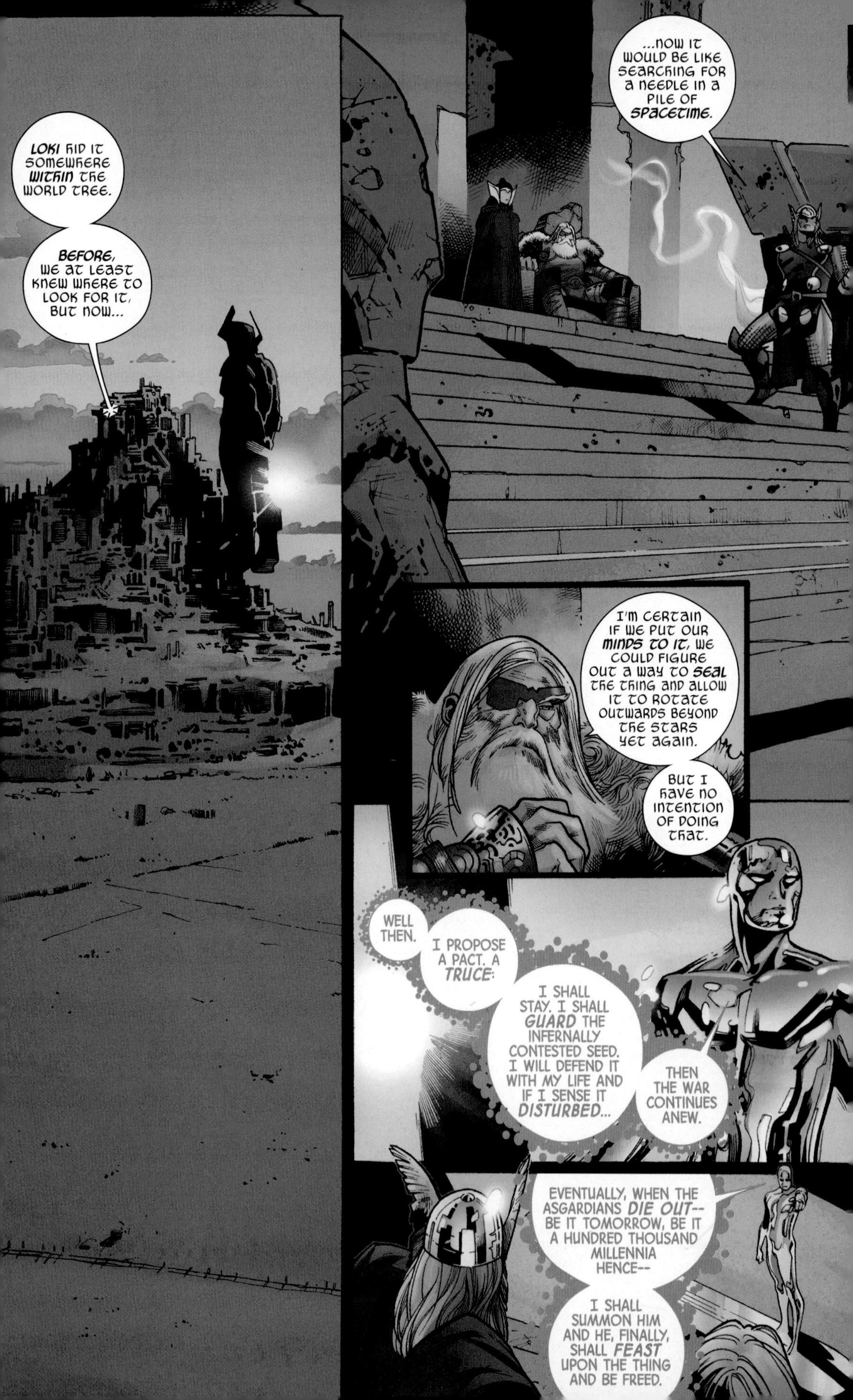
LOKI HID IT SOMEWHERE WITHIN THE WORLD TREE.
BEFORE, WE AT LEAST KNEW WHERE TO LOOK FOR IT, BUT NOW...
...NOW IT WOULD BE LIKE SEARCHING FOR A NEEDLE IN A PILE OF SPACETIME.
I'M CERTAIN IF WE PUT OUR MINDS TO IT, WE COULD FIGURE OUT A WAY TO SEAL THE THING AND ALLOW IT TO ROTATE OUTWARDS BEYOND THE STARS YET AGAIN.
BUT I HAVE NO INTENTION OF DOING THAT.
WELL THEN.
I PROPOSE A PACT. A TRUCE:
I SHALL STAY. I SHALL GUARD THE INFERNALLY CONTESTED SEED. I WILL DEFEND IT WITH MY LIFE AND IF I SENSE IT DISTURBED...
THEN THE WAR CONTINUES ANEW.
EVENTUALLY, WHEN THE ASGARDIANS DIE OUT-- BE IT TOMORROW, BE IT A HUNDRED THOUSAND MILLENNIA HENCE--
I SHALL SUMMON HIM AND HE, FINALLY, SHALL FEAST UPON THE THING AND BE FREED.

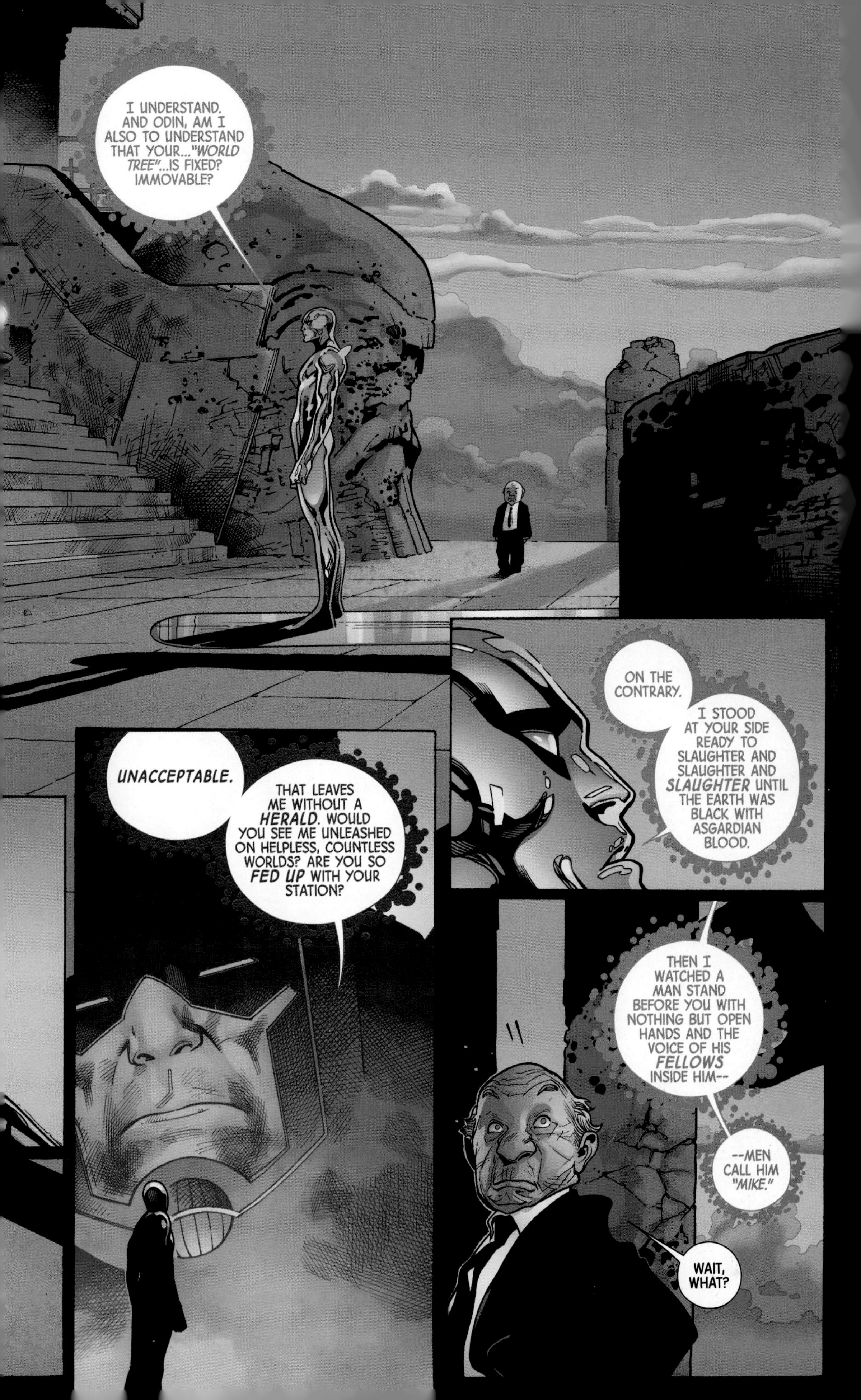
I UNDERSTAND. AND ODIN, AM I ALSO TO UNDERSTAND THAT YOUR..."WORLD TREE"...IS FIXED? IMMOVABLE?
UNACCEPTABLE.
THAT LEAVES ME WITHOUT A HERALD. WOULD YOU SEE ME UNLEASHED ON HELPLESS, COUNTLESS WORLDS? ARE YOU SO FED UP WITH YOUR STATION?
ON THE CONTRARY.
I STOOD AT YOUR SIDE READY TO SLAUGHTER AND SLAUGHTER AND SLAUGHTER UNTIL THE EARTH WAS BLACK WITH ASGARDIAN BLOOD.
THEN I WATCHED A MAN STAND BEFORE YOU WITH NOTHING BUT OPEN HANDS AND THE VOICE OF HIS FELLOWS INSIDE HIM--
--MEN CALL HIM "MIKE."
WAIT, WHAT?

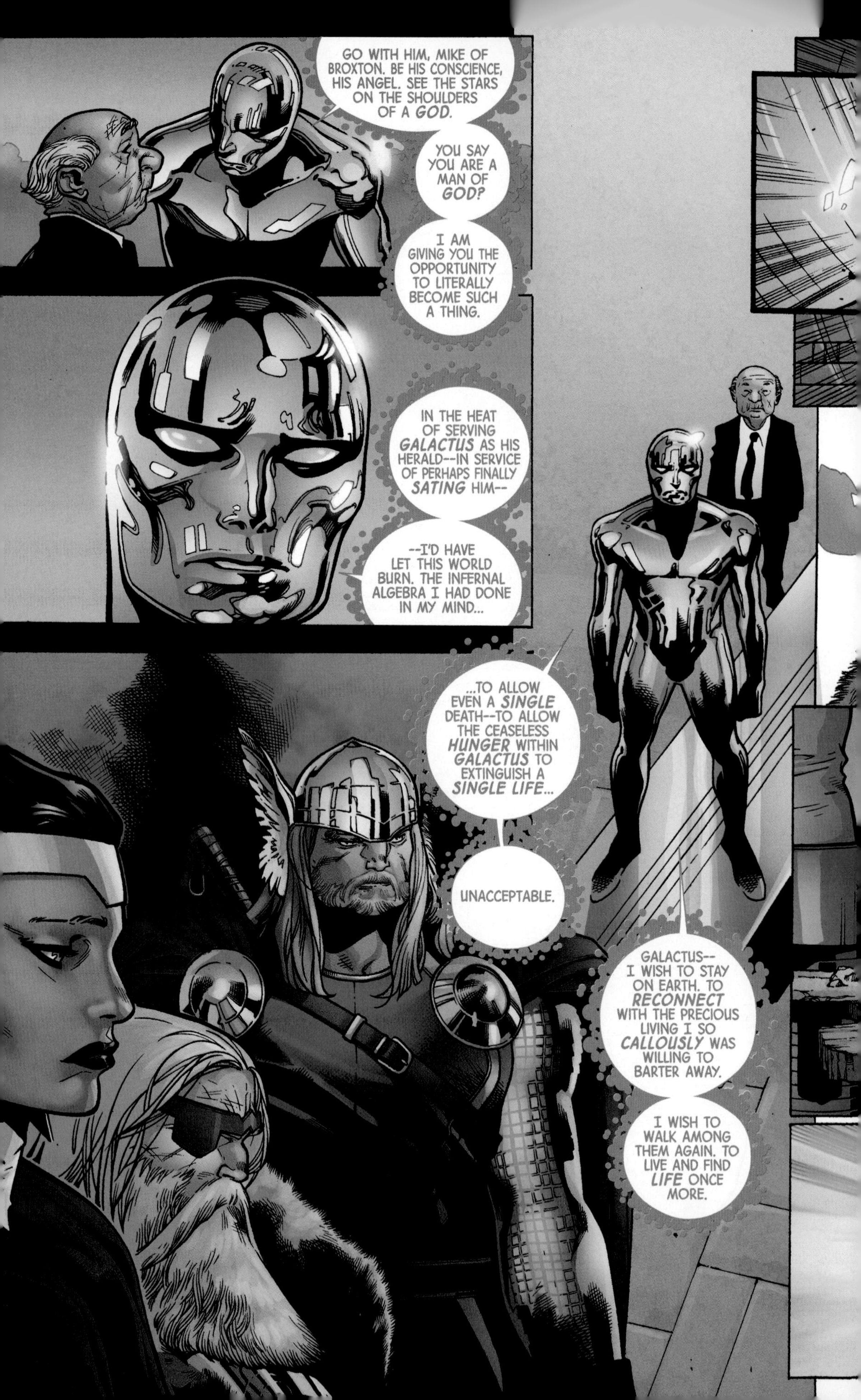
GO WITH HIM, MIKE OF BROXTON. BE HIS CONSCIENCE, HIS ANGEL. SEE THE STARS ON THE SHOULDERS OF A GOD.
YOU SAY YOU ARE A MAN OF GOD?
I AM GIVING YOU THE OPPORTUNITY TO LITERALLY BECOME SUCH A THING.
IN THE HEAT OF SERVING GALACTUS AS HIS HERALD--IN SERVICE OF PERHAPS FINALLY SATING HIM--
--I'D HAVE LET THIS WORLD BURN. THE INFERNAL ALGEBRA I HAD DONE IN MY MIND...
...TO ALLOW EVEN A SINGLE DEATH--TO ALLOW THE CEASELESS HUNGER WITHIN GALACTUS TO EXTINGUISH A SINGLE LIFE...
UNACCEPTABLE.
GALACTUS-- I WISH TO STAY ON EARTH. TO RECONNECT WITH THE PRECIOUS LIVING I SO CALLOUSLY WAS WILLING TO BARTER AWAY.
I WISH TO WALK AMONG THEM AGAIN. TO LIVE AND FIND LIFE ONCE MORE.

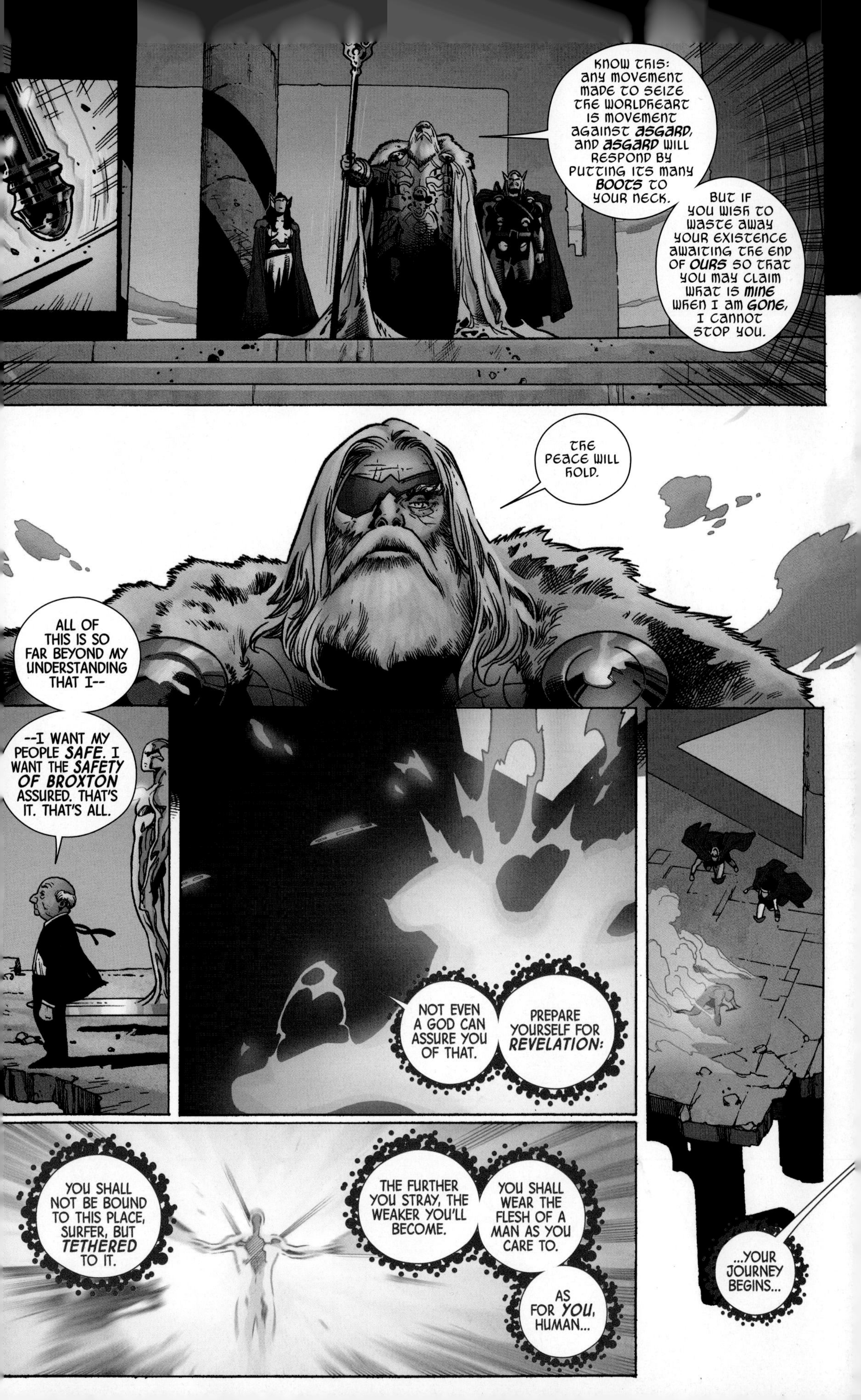
KNOW THIS: ANY MOVEMENT MADE TO SEIZE THE WORLDHEART IS MOVEMENT AGAINST ASGARD, AND ASGARD WILL RESPOND BY PUTTING ITS MANY BOOTS TO YOUR NECK.
BUT IF YOU WISH TO WASTE AWAY YOUR EXISTENCE AWAITING THE END OF OURS SO THAT YOU MAY CLAIM WHAT IS MINE WHEN I AM GONE, I CANNOT STOP YOU.
THE PEACE WILL HOLD.
ALL OF THIS IS SO FAR BEYOND MY UNDERSTANDING THAT I--
--I WANT MY PEOPLE SAFE. I WANT THE SAFETY OF BROXTON ASSURED. THAT'S IT. THAT'S ALL.
NOT EVEN A GOD CAN ASSURE YOU OF THAT.
PREPARE YOURSELF FOR REVELATION:
YOU SHALL NOT BE BOUND TO THIS PLACE, SURFER, BUT TETHERED TO IT.
THE FURTHER YOU STRAY, THE WEAKER YOU'LL BECOME.
YOU SHALL WEAR THE FLESH OF A MAN AS YOU CARE TO.
AS FOR YOU, HUMAN...
...YOUR JOURNEY BEGINS...

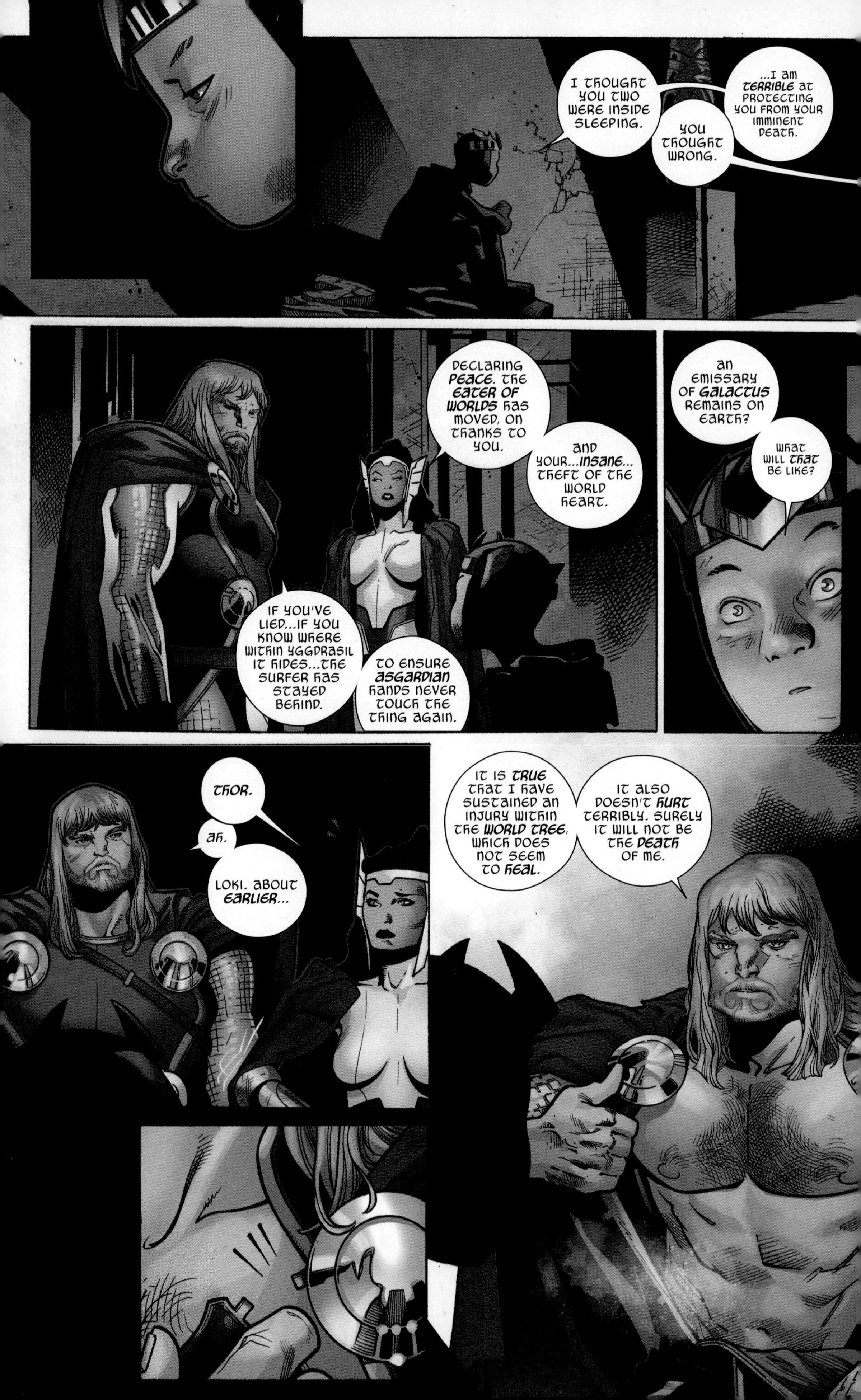

I THOUGHT YOU TWO WERE INSIDE SLEEPING.
YOU THOUGHT WRONG.
...I AM TERRIBLE AT PROTECTING YOU FROM YOUR IMMINENT DEATH.
DECLARING PEACE. THE EATER OF WORLDS HAS MOVED, ON THANKS TO YOU.
AND YOUR...INSANE... THEFT OF THE WORLD HEART.
IF YOU'VE LIED...IF YOU KNOW WHERE WITHIN YGGDRASIL IT HIDES...THE SURFER HAS STAYED BEHIND.
TO ENSURE ASGARDIAN HANDS NEVER TOUCH THE THING AGAIN.
AN EMISSARY OF GALACTUS REMAINS ON EARTH?
WHAT WILL THAT BE LIKE?
THOR.
AH.
LOKI. ABOUT EARLIER...
IT IS TRUE THAT I HAVE SUSTAINED AN INJURY WITHIN THE WORLD TREE, WHICH DOES NOT SEEM TO HEAL.
IT ALSO DOESN'T HURT TERRIBLY. SURELY IT WILL NOT BE THE DEATH OF ME.

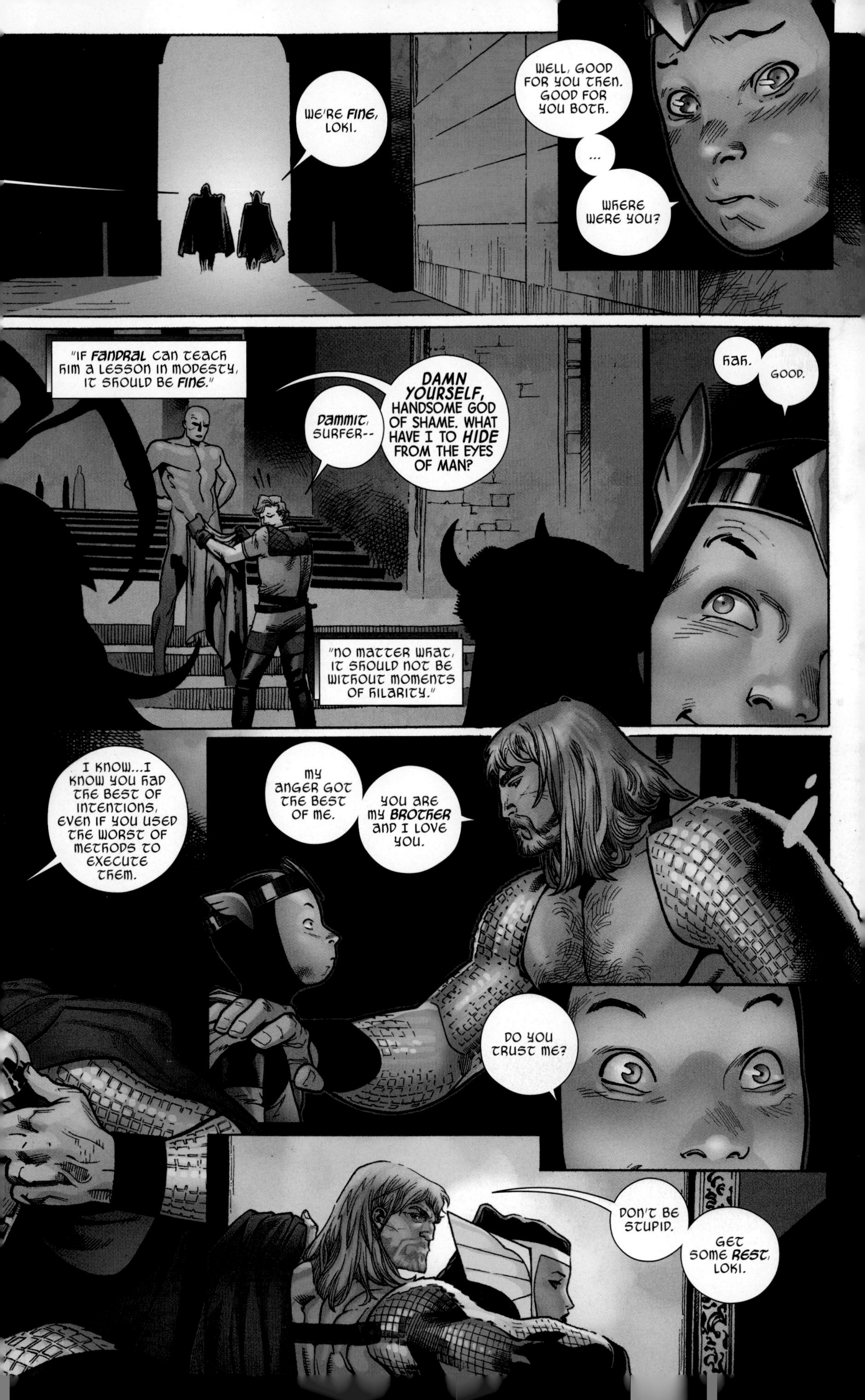
WE'RE FINE, LOKI.
WELL, GOOD FOR YOU THEN. GOOD FOR YOU BOTH.
...
WHERE WERE YOU?
"IF FANDRAL CAN TEACH HIM A LESSON IN MODESTY, IT SHOULD BE FINE."
DAMMIT, SURFER--
DAMN YOURSELF, HANDSOME GOD OF SHAME. WHAT HAVE I TO HIDE FROM THE EYES OF MAN?
"NO MATTER WHAT, IT SHOULD NOT BE WITHOUT MOMENTS OF HILARITY."
HAH.
GOOD.
I KNOW...I KNOW YOU HAD THE BEST OF INTENTIONS, EVEN IF YOU USED THE WORST OF METHODS TO EXECUTE THEM.
MY ANGER GOT THE BEST OF ME.
YOU ARE MY BROTHER AND I LOVE YOU.
DO YOU TRUST ME?
DON'T BE STUPID.
GET SOME REST, LOKI.

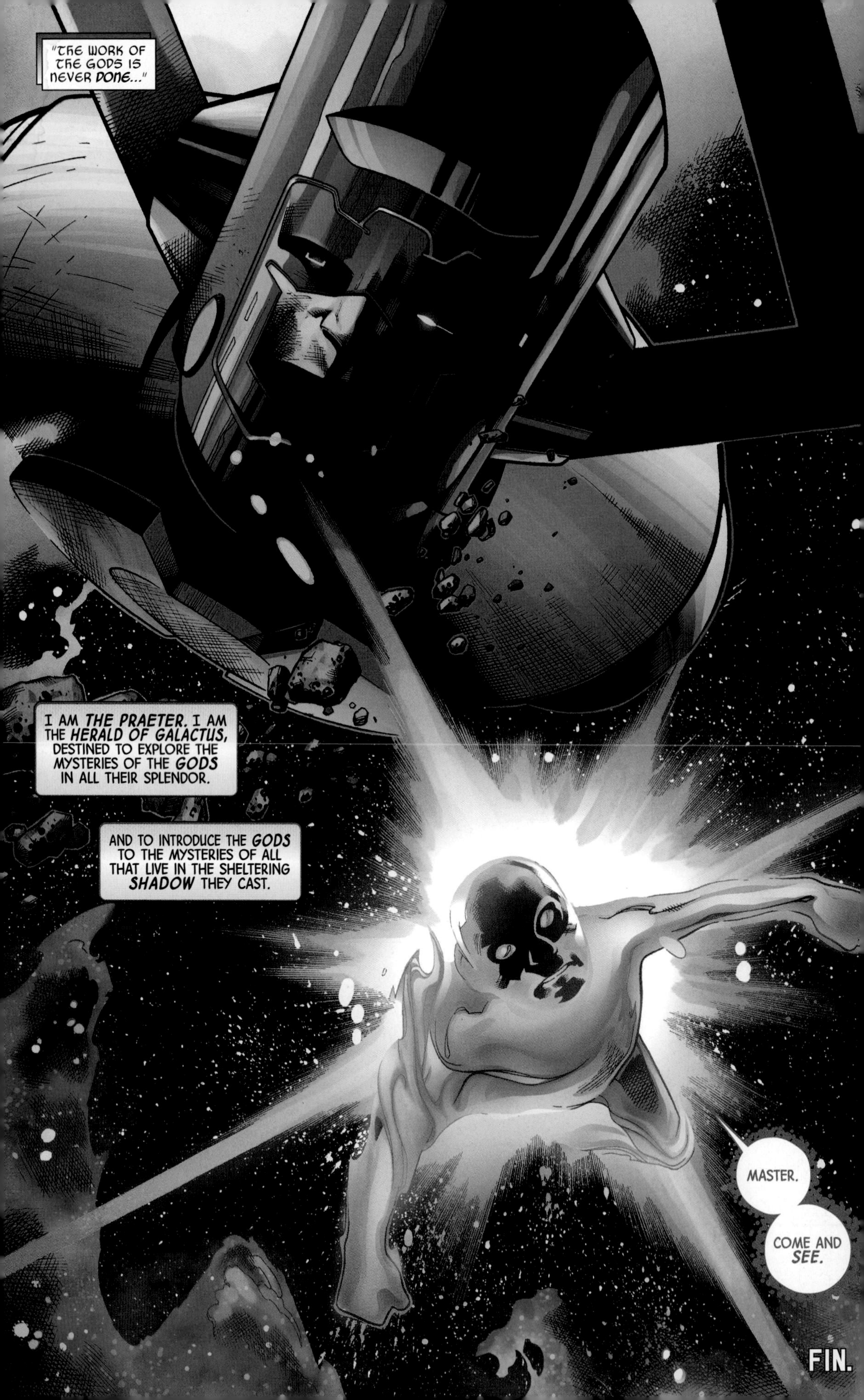
"THE WORK OF THE GODS IS NEVER DONE..."
I AM THE PRAETER. I AM THE HERALD OF GALACTUS, DESTINED TO EXPLORE THE MYSTERIES OF THE GODS IN ALL THEIR SPLENDOR.
AND TO INTRODUCE THE GODS TO THE MYSTERIES OF ALL THAT LIVE IN THE SHELTERING SHADOW THEY CAST.
MASTER.
COME AND SEE.
FIN.

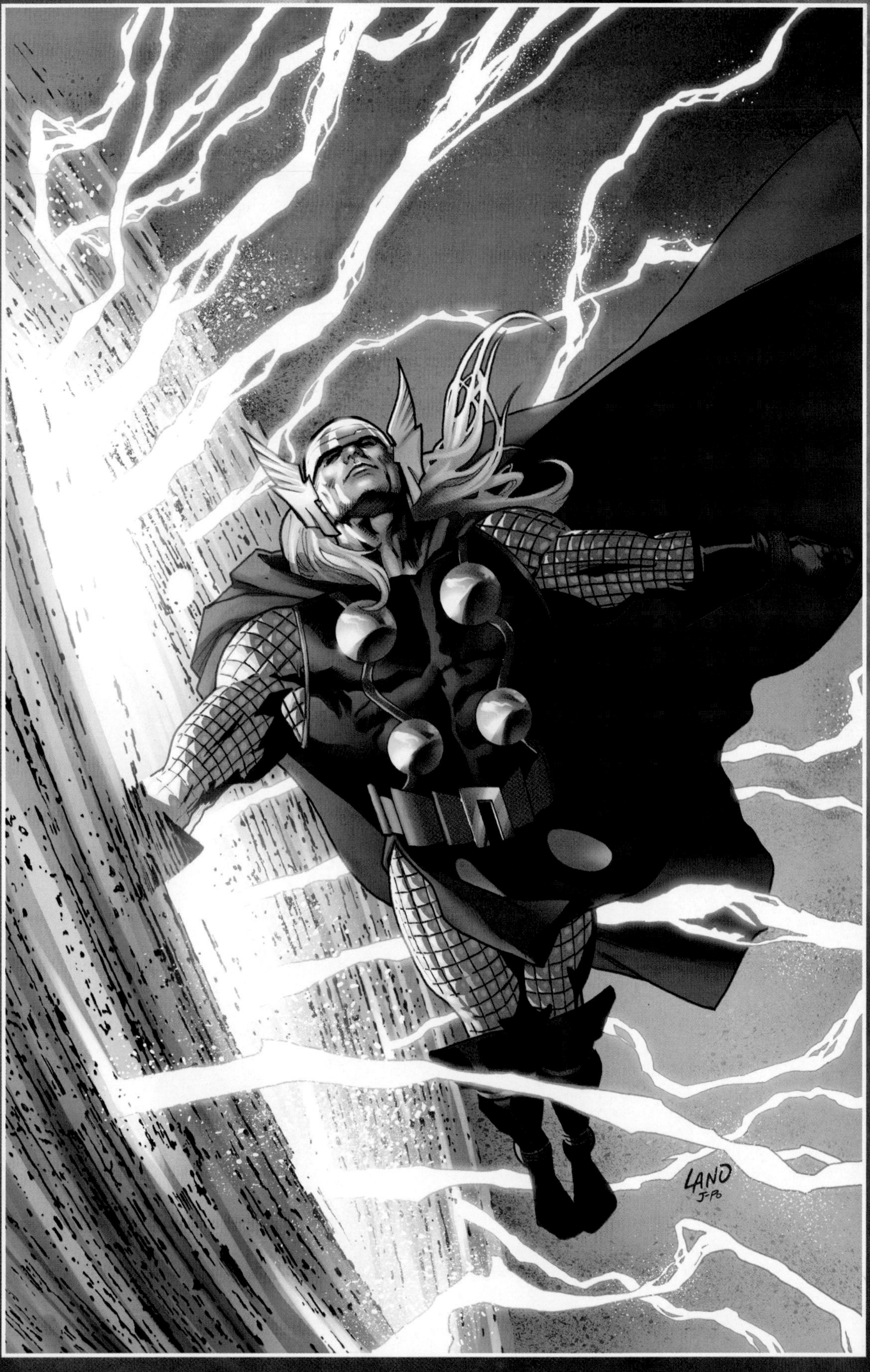
LAND
J-Po

#5 VARIANT BY GREG LAND & JUSTIN PONSOR

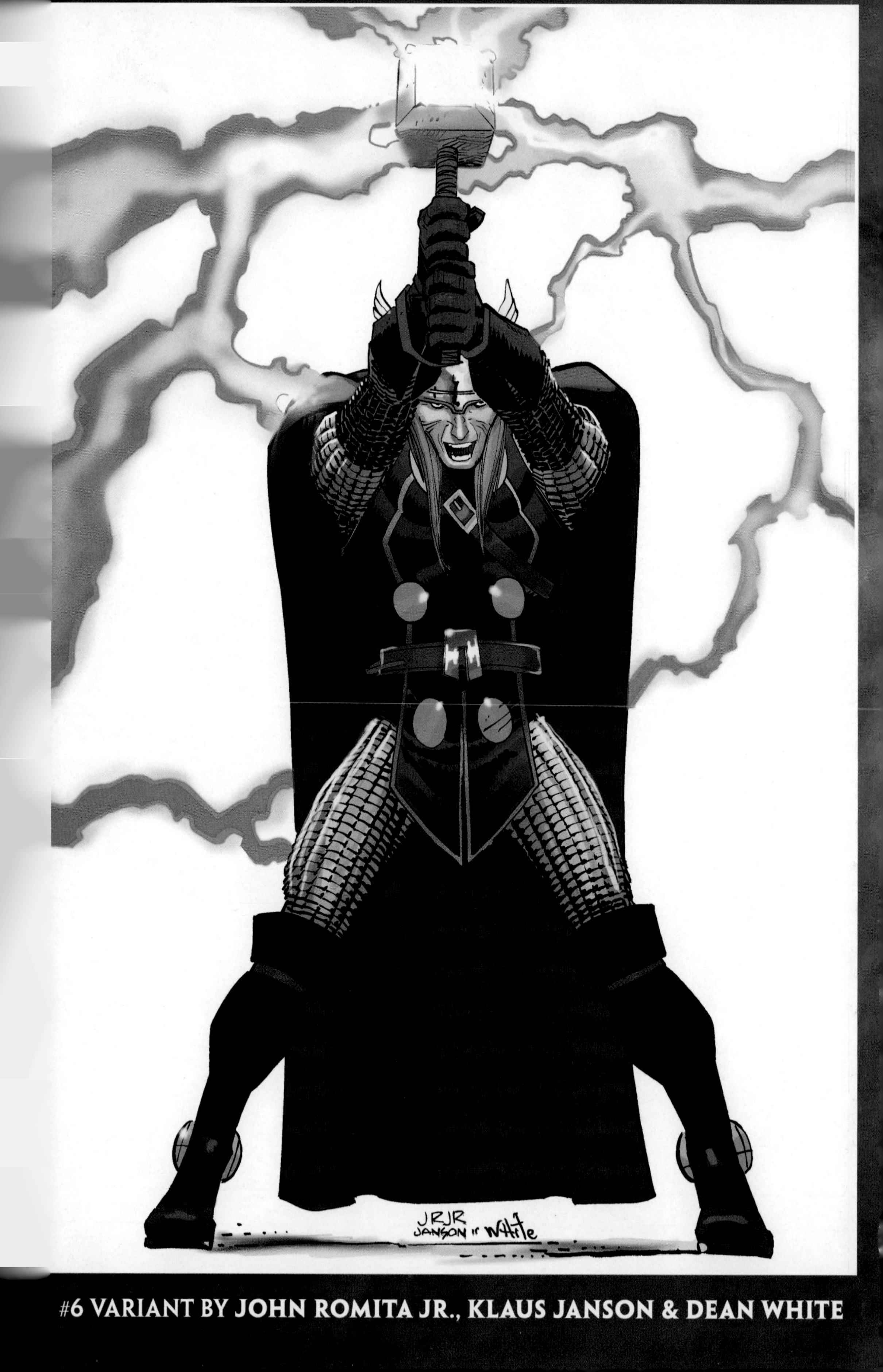
JRJR
JANSON jr White

#6 VARIANT BY JOHN ROMITA JR., KLAUS JANSON & DEAN WHITE